THE LOGIC OF RELATIVISM

Mark Ressler

INCREASINGLY SKEPTICAL PUBLICATIONS

©2013 by Mark Ressler.

All rights reserved.

ISBN 978-1-940551-00-5 (HB)
ISBN 978-1-940551-20-3 (PB)
ISBN 978-1-940551-40-1 (PDF)

Contents

Acknowledgements   7

Preface   9
    Plato's *Theaetetus* 151d–179d 9

1 Introduction   15

2 Preliminary Investigations   25
    2.1 The Structure of Relativism 26
    2.2 Relativism and Indexicality 28
    2.3 Relativism and Pluralism 33
    2.4 Relativism and Conventionalism 36
    2.5 Relativism and Reductionism 39
    2.6 Relativism and Relativity 45
    2.7 Relativism and Contextualism 51

3 Definition of Relativism   59
    3.1 Proposed Definition 61
    3.2 Protagoras 67
    3.3 Nelson Goodman 77
    3.4 Gilbert Harman 81
    3.5 Joseph Margolis 86
    3.6 Max Kölbel 92
    3.7 Jean-François Lyotard 94

4 Formal Requirements for Relativity   101
    4.1 Relativizing Domain 102
    4.2 Range of Relativized Sub-Theories 108
    4.3 Indexing 116
    4.4 Modeling Conceptual Relativism 121

5 Thesis of Objective Equity — 125
- 5.1 Various Conceptions of Objectivity 128
- 5.2 Richard Rorty 138
- 5.3 Objectivity in History 143
- 5.4 Objective Equity in Relativism 148

6 Thesis of Incommensurability — 157
- 6.1 Ancient Greek Mathematics 158
- 6.2 Benjamin Whorf 160
- 6.3 Thomas Kuhn 165
- 6.4 Paul Feyerabend 172
- 6.5 Value Incommensurability 178
- 6.6 Incommensurability in Relativism 180

7 Proposed Logics of Relative Systems — 189
- 7.1 Steven D. Hales' System RL 191
- 7.2 Complications 201
- 7.3 RL1: Simple Relativity Semantics 215
- 7.4 RL2: Multiple Relativities 219
- 7.5 RL3: Relativized Accessibility Relations 223
- 7.6 RL4: Both Complications 226
- 7.7 RL5: Non-Normal Relativity 229

8 Relativism and Self-Refutation — 233
- 8.1 Nature of Self-Refutation 234
- 8.2 Varieties of Self-Refutation in Relativism 245
- 8.3 Self-Refutation and the Relative Systems 249
- 8.4 Language, Pragmatics, and Incoherence 264

9 Conclusion — 277

References — 281

List of Figures

2.1 Haack's Identikit for Relativism 26

7.1 Sample RL1 System 216
7.2 Sample RL2 System 221
7.3 Sample RL3 System from the perspective of m_1 224
7.4 Sample RL3 System from the perspective of m_2 224
7.5 Sample RL4 System from the perspective of p_1 228
7.6 Sample RL4 System from the perspective of p_2 228
7.7 Sample RL5 System 231

8.1 Model for Theorem 1 250
8.2 Failure of For-x objection for true sentences in RL1+F 254
8.3 Model for Theorem 10 260

Acknowledgements

Graham Priest served as advisor for the dissertation on which this book is based. His guidance has influenced this book in ways too numerous to make explicit.

Hartry Field and Max Kölbel served as the remainder of my dissertation committee and provided helpful and challenging comments.

I also owe a debt to Protagoras for bequeathing such a troublesome subject for analysis. Had he been clearer about what he meant by his relativistic doctrine, perhaps I would have had to find something else to write about.

Substantial portions of chapters 8 and 9 were previously published as "Thoroughly Relativistic Perspectives" in *Notre Dame Journal of Formal Logic*, Volume 53(1) (2012), pp. 89–112. This material is reprinted here with the permission of the editors.

Preface

Plato's *Theaetetus* 151d–179d

The earliest surviving discussion of relativism occurs in Plato's dialogue *Theaetetus*, and many of the important elements for understanding relativism are present within this dialogue. The discussion is primarily between Socrates, the young Theaetetus, and Theaetetus' teacher Theodorus, and the topic that Socrates introduces in the dialogue is the nature of knowledge. On being asked by Socrates what knowledge is, Theaetetus begins by listing kinds of knowledge, whereupon Socrates makes his usual complaint that he did not ask about the kinds or the objects of knowledge, but what knowledge itself is. After Socrates spends some time developing the metaphor of midwifery as a description of the method he employs, Theaetetus offer his first proposal for the nature of knowledge.

Theaetetus suggests that knowledge is perception, upon which Socrates immediately equates that definition with the doctrine of Protagoras that man is the measure of all things (151d–152a).[1] Furthermore, Socrates continues to link that doctrine with the notion of the Heraclitean flux according to which everything is in the process of becoming, which he suggests might be a secret doctrine that Protagoras taught only to his disciples (152c–e). Socrates proceeds to elaborate these doctrines at some length to flush out their consequences (153a–160e) before turning to evaluate them. Yet rather than continuing the discussion directly with Theaetetus, Socrates attempts to draw Theodorus into the debate (160e–162c), perhaps realizing from the beginning that if he is going to

---

[1] Citations here are standard Stephanus numbers. Quotations are from John McDowell's translation in (Plato, 1973).

refute Protagoras, he will need someone to speak authoritatively on Protagoras' behalf, which the young Theaetetus cannot do. As it happens, Theodorus was a friend of Protagoras. Unfortunately, Theodorus declines to enter the discussion at this point.

Failing his attempt to enlist Theodorus into the debate, Socrates continues the discussion with Theaetetus by suggesting an objection against Protagoras on the basis of seeing or hearing an unknown language: does perception of that language count as knowledge? Theaetetus readily counters by making a distinction, namely that in one sense such perception counts as knowledge, but in another sense not (162c–163c). Theaetetus' response here is apparent so effective that there seems to be nothing more to be said about the matter, so Socrates proceeds to another objection based on memory: if someone who knows something preserves his knowledge through memory, then it seems that that person can have knowledge even without perception, namely through memory. Theaetetus recognizes this as a problem and promptly concedes the defeat of his proposed definition of knowledge as perception (163c–164c).

Socrates must have been disappointed that Theaetetus gave up so soon, and in particular, perhaps, that Theaetetus did not address the problem of memory with a distinction in the same way that he addressed the problem of an unknown language. In any case, recognizing that Theaetetus' concession does not constitute Protagoras' defeat, Socrates launches into a defense on Protagoras' behalf himself (164c–168c), in which Socrates ultimately makes the kind of distinction for Protagoras that he perhaps had hoped Theaetetus would eventually make, though not specifically with regard to the objection on the basis of memory. Curiously, though, Socrates shifts to a different issue altogether, away from memory, and offers a defense on behalf of Protagoras concerning the question of whether everyone is equally wise, which appears to be denied on the basis of Protagoras' doctrine. In his defense, Socrates has Protagoras claim that a wise person is "anyone who can effect a change in one of us, to whom bad things appear and are, and make good things both appear and be for him" (166d). So the distinction that Socrates makes is that while man is the measure in perceptual matters, some people are better in effecting changes in the perceptions of others for their own improvement, and this ability is what wisdom consists in. "Thus it is true, both that some people are wiser than others, and that no one judges what's false" (167d).

Yet this distinction would be a dangerous admission for Protagoras himself to make, since people likewise judge whether someone is wise or not (170a–b), so a distinction between judgments and abilities will ultimately undermine the equality of judgment inherent in claim that man is the measure of all things. Since the distinction is one that Socrates himself introduces, he realizes that he must have a more authoritative spokesman for Protagoras, one who can provide testimony concerning what Protagoras actually did or at least would say. Consequently, he finally persuades Theodorus to enter into the conversation on Protagoras' behalf (168d-169d).

Now Socrates states his aim of getting Protagoras himself to make the admissions that had just been made on his behalf, according to Protagoras' own words (169d-e).[2] In this context (169d–171d), Socrates introduces two arguments designed to show that Protagoras' doctrine entails that "no one person ever believes of another that he's stupid and makes false judgments" (170c), which Theodorus acknowledges as an incredible contention for a follower of Protagoras to make. The first argument is that if most people disagree with Protagoras about his doctrine, then "it's more the case that it isn't true than that it is: more in the proportion by which those to whom it doesn't seem to be outnumber those to whom it does" (171a). The second argument demonstrates that Protagoras himself must acknowledge the truth of other people's judgments that his doctrine is false. These arguments have come to be recognized as Socrates' self-refutation arguments against Protagorean relativism. Even if there are flaws in these arguments, as subsequent commentators have claimed, due perhaps to a shift in the qualification of truth from true-for-someone to true absolutely, I think it likely that Socrates considered these arguments primarily as provocations to Theodorus on Protagoras' behalf to show that these arguments are indeed flawed and thereby to show

---

[2] Mi-Kyoung Lee understands the reference to Protagoras' own words at (169e) to indicate that the restatement of the measure doctrine at (170a3–4) is a direct quotation from Protagoras (M.-K. Lee, 2005, p. 12). On the contrary, I think the words that Socrates is seeking from Protagoras come later (178e), not as a direct quotation from Protagoras' written work in the form of a statement of his doctrine, but direct testimony from Theodorus concerning what Protagoras actually claimed about his abilities.

that Protagoras himself considers his own judgments concerning the validity of these arguments to be superior to Socrates' judgments, thereby undermining Protagoras' own doctrine.³ If Protagoras could successfully argue that Socrates' self-refutation arguments are flawed, then Socrates' judgments are not as good as Protagoras' judgments. If that is so, then man is not the measure of all things. Something else would measure each man's judgments, namely knowledge. Unfortunately, Theodorus does not rise to the occasion on Protagoras' behalf, but simply accepts the results of the self-refutation argument. In fact, Theodorus seems to be more easily led by debating points than even Theaetetus had been (162d), so Socrates invokes the image of Protagoras rising from the ground to "convict [Socrates] of talking a great deal of nonsense" (171c). Yet perhaps even if Protagoras himself had been present, he might not have taken the bait that Socrates had offered, but may have slipped through the net that I am suggesting Socrates had spread to catch him, since Protagoras was acknowledged to be a skillful dialectician.⁴

What follows is an unusual digression concerning how ridiculous philosophers appear in courts of law (172b–177c). After discussing the interpretive confusion over this digression, Myles Burnyeat offers a fairly sympathetic interpretation: "The discussion of what knowledge is is interrupted so that we may be jolted into reflecting for a moment that the question what knowledge is is important because there are certain things it is important to know" (Burnyeat, 1990, p. 36). Be that as it may, I think that what Socrates himself calls a digression (177b) is not really a digression at all, but precisely part of Socrates' strategy for extracting an ad-

---

³ Luca Castagnoli compares this situation with the kind of provocation found in the *Euthydemus* (Castagnoli, 2004, pp. 23–24, 2007, pp. 21–25). I think a comparable situation also occurs in the *Republic* at the end of Socrates' argument with Thrasymachus in Book 1, during the strange discussion concerning non-competition, whereby Socrates seems to have a hidden strategy to elicit certain behavior from his interlocutor. If I am right about this strategy in the *Republic*, Thrasymachus does not take the bait that Socrates seems to be offering, likely accounting for Socrates' manifest disappointment at the end of Book 1.

⁴ And perhaps this is a significant part of Socrates' imagery of Protagoras appearing from the ground only from the neck up, then running away, namely that he does not expose himself completely to arguments, and slips away before bearing their full force. It may not be the case that "he is not prepared to stay and defend it in discussion" (Burnyeat, 1976b, p. 191), but that his defense within the argument is simply a particularly skillful one, enabling him to escape objections.

mission from Protagoras through Theodorus that some judgments are better than others. First, it establishes that philosophers like Socrates are not competent in courtrooms, which will be significant for the later testimony that Theodorus will offer on Protagoras' behalf (178e). Second, the context of the discussion makes it easier for Theodorus to remember the particular piece of testimony that Socrates surely knew that Theodorus could provide. I do not think it is a piece of idle talk when Plato has Theodorus say, "I don't at all mind listening to this kind of thing [namely, the digression], Socrates: it's easier for me to follow at my age" (177c). If I am right, Socrates demonstrates great cunning in presenting a pleasant piece of discussion that prepares Theodorus for the next and final stage of the argument against Protagoras.

The discussion following the digression is fairly brisk and direct (177c–179d). Socrates raises the question of future judgments, ultimately to raise the issue of whether Protagoras would be a better judge of what will be effective in a speech made in the courtroom than an ordinary person, let alone a philosopher, as the digression made clear. Here, properly prepared, Theodorus readily provides the testimony that Socrates needs: "Yes, Socrates, that was certainly a point on which he used to give firm assurances that he was better than anyone one else" (179e). So according to Theodorus' testimony, Protagoras himself held that some judgments are better than others, namely his own judgments, at least on one subject. Socrates has already established in the so-called digression that his own judgments in courts of law are not to be trusted. This provides precisely the kind of refutation that Socrates was looking for, namely an admission on Protagoras' behalf that at least on one matter some judgments are better than others. Once this admission is extracted from Theodorus, the discussion of Protagorean relativism is quickly brought to a close, and Socrates moves on to discuss the doctrine of the flux. It is true that Theodorus still seems to be more impressed with the clever self-refutation arguments offered before the digression (179b), but Socrates makes very clear that his aim is directed not so much against the coherence of the doctrine itself, but rather specifically to "show that not every judgment of every person is true" (179c), that not every judgment is objectively equal, so to speak.

Therefore, it seems that what Socrates considers to be decisive against Protagorean relativism is not the self-refutation arguments that traditionally attract the greatest attention in this dialogue, but something quite different. The key aspect of the Protagorean doctrine on which Socrates' ultimate refutation relies is not any formal requirement for global relativity, but rather the notion of the equality of judgments that is inherent in Protagoras' relativisitic doctrine.

Chapter 1

Introduction

Suppose that several parties disagree with regard to the truth of some statement, and that their disagreement cannot be reconciled. Consider three different responses to this situation: skepticism, anti-realism, and relativism.[1]

According to skepticism, since the disagreement in question is irreconcilable, there is no way to know the truth of the matter, and therefore all parties should suspend any assent to the statement.

According to anti-realism, the irreconcilable disagreement suggests that there is no fact of the matter, and therefore there is nothing in the statement that strictly even requires assent by any party.

According to relativism, however, the irreconcilable disagreement suggests that each party may be correct, but only for that party, and therefore assent should be granted only relatively.

These three responses embody different attitudes toward the problem of irreconcilable disagreement. Skepticism takes a negative attitude toward the epistemology of the situation. Anti-realism takes a negative attitude toward the metaphysics. Relativism by contrast takes a somewhat mixed attitude toward both the epistemology and the metaphysics, thereby enabling assent with regard to the disputed statement, but only a qualified assent. Yet it is important to recognize that these descriptions are little more than cartoon characterizations of the three different responses, each of which is considerably more complex than the simplistic presenta-

---

[1] These three responses are not exhaustive. I discuss just these three here because they sometimes get conflated.

tions offered here.

This study is about relativism, and its major aim is to replace any cartoon characterization with a rigorous analysis of what relativism is, how it functions, and what needs to be demonstrated in order to support any claim of relativism with regard to some subject matter.

Alasdair MacIntyre writes:

> ...relativism, like skepticism, is one of those doctrines that have by now been refuted a number of times too often. Nothing is perhaps a surer sign that a doctrine embodies some not to be neglected truth than that in the course of the history of philosophy it should have been refuted again and again. Genuinely refutable doctrines only need to be refuted once. (MacIntyre, 1985, p. 5)

It is in this spirit that I undertake this study of relativism. I have been suspicious of arguments purporting to show that relativism is self-refuting ever since I first read the argument against the relativistic doctrine of Protagoras in Plato's *Theaetetus*. It seemed to me that in those self-refutation arguments Plato simply misconstrued what was claimed by relativism and what was required by the position, and subsequent attempts to show that relativism is self-defeating seemed to me likewise based upon a misunderstanding of relativism and its specific requirements.

Yet herein precisely lies the problem. Protagoras himself does not seem to have delineated very clearly what relativism is and what it requires. Instead, he has left behind only an enigmatic aphorism: "a man is the measure of all things: of those which are, that they are, and of those which are not, that they are not" (Plato, 1973, p. 16, 152a). Nor is it clear that anyone else has subsequently articulated the nature of relativism adequately, leading Joseph Margolis to complain that relativism and its companion doctrine pluralism "are poorly analyzed in their own right" (Margolis, 2006, p. 239).[2]

What is at issue, then, is the question whether relativism is indeed a self-refuting doctrine, or whether it embodies some impor-

---

[2] And there are reasons to doubt that Margolis himself has provided an adequate analysis, as will be discussed in section 3.5.

tant truth as MacIntyre suggests, or at the very least, whether it represents a viable philosophical doctrine. Insofar as self-refutation seems to be mainly a formal phenomenon, indicated by certain structural features of a particular doctrine, this issue requires an investigation of the structure of relativism and how it functions according to that structure. What is needed then is an explication of the logic of relativism, or more generally, the logic of relative systems.[3]

The literature on relativism is enormous and continues to grow at an increasingly rapid pace, due in part to a recent resurgence of interest in semantic contextualism and relativism.[4] One approach to a study of relativism would be to trace this prior literature in order to identify the key arguments surrounding the question of the self-refutation of relativism, then to evaluate those arguments and to supplement them with clever new arguments. However, since the volume of literature is so great, and the lines of criticism and defense are so complex to trace through, it is not clear to me that this approach would serve to clarify the issue at hand, but may merely add yet more commentary to complicate or even to obfuscate the issue. I therefore propose to make a fresh start on the issue.

Such a fresh start might take different forms. For example, I might start by evaluating the grounds for adopting relativism.[5] By contrast, I intend to ignore the grounds for adopting relativism altogether, in order to focus more directly on the nature and logic of relativism. I propose to treat relativism essentially as an abductive hypothesis that might be contemplated with regard to some domain of discourse and to investigate the nature of that hypothesis

---

[3] According to a distinction I make between relativity and relativism in section 2.6.

[4] See, for instance, the articles in the anthologies *Contextualism in Philosophy* (Preyer & Peter, 2005) and *Relative Truth* (García-Carpintero & Kölbel, 2008).

[5] This is an approach claimed to be adopted in (Phillips, 2007). However, the structure of that book suggests that its approach is primarily directed toward an investigation of various instances of relativism in Wittgenstein, Winch, and Rorty, rather than a comprehensive or even directed study of the general grounds for adopting relativism. Such a comprehensive and detailed study would be invaluable, I think, as would a comprehensive history of relativism in the manner of Richard Popkin's history of modern skepticism (Popkin, 2003). Brief historical overviews are given in (Baghramian, 2004) and (Mosteller, 2008), but each overview includes discussions of relativists not covered by the other, and of course neither overview is presented in any great detail.

in itself, independently of any grounds for claiming that the hypothesis would represent a best explanation within that domain.

Alternatively, I might make a fresh start by investigating the various possible forms of metaphysics or epistemology that might underlie a claim of relativism. By contrast, I intend largely to ignore substantive metaphysical or epistemological accounts of relativism, since these substantive accounts tend to result in distinctly different forms of relativism, such as ontological relativism, conceptual relativism, or moral relativism. Insofar as there is something by virtue of which each of these forms of relativism can properly be called 'relativism', there should be some account of relativism in general, and it is this generic relativism that is my concern in this study.

I propose to treat relativism in general as a structural phenomenon, a generic form that individual theories might adopt in various domains of discourse to yield specific forms of relativism on the basis of substantive epistemological or metaphysical claims. Since the aim of this study is to formulate the structure and logic of relativism in order to evaluate the charges of self-refutation, treating relativism in general as a fundamentally structural phenomenon would be particularly convenient.

Yet it is by no means obvious that relativism is indeed a structural phenomenon, so this proposal will need to be evaluated ultimately by the overall success of the study, namely by the extent to which the results of this study help to clarify the nature of relativism in all of its specific forms. If the characterization of relativism that emerges from this study advances the debate over relativism by providing a useful framework according to which the claims of relativism and other instances of relativity can be investigated and evaluated, then to that extent the proposal concerning the essentially structural nature of relativism will seem to be vindicated. If however this study only adds to the confusion surrounding relativism and associated doctrines, then perhaps the proposal is not fruitful after all.

Besides the guiding proposal concerning relativism as a structural phenomenon, this study proceeds on the basis of a few presuppositions that will simply be treated as assumptions, which I make explicit here as follows.

First, this study will assume that relativized theories can be formalized. So, for example, in a case of moral relativism according to cultures, it is assumed that the terms in each culture's moral theory can be disambiguated sufficiently in order that the theory could be expressed as a formal system.

Second, once these terms are disambiguated, it is assumed that there is some means by which terms can be correlated between relativized theories. So if a term such as 'good' appears in two different relativized theories, either the term has the same meaning in each of those theories, or further disambiguation needs to occur to yield distinct terms that can be correlated between relativized theories. This assumption may be a contentious one, since various arguments concerning relativism rest upon the question of whether such correlation can properly occur in the first place. Yet the assumption here is merely that there is some general procedure for correlating terms, even if in fact the procedure fails to make any correlation in any actual circumstance. Section 4.4 discusses how the failure of this assumed procedure can be managed with regard to the formalization of relativized theories into an overall relative system.

Third, it is assumed that a formal account can be given of the two relativity terms 'relative' and 'absolute'. These two terms are critical to the language of relativism and therefore to its logic. If no formal account can be given of them, then there would appear to be no basis for formulating the logic of relativism at all. However, even if there are doubts concerning the possibility of a single uniform formal treatment of these relativity terms, this does not preclude the possibility of any formal account of them, since a formal account might be given that can tolerate differing conceptions of the terms, as will be discussed in sections 7.7 and 8.3. Yet this possibility is bound together with the very question of whether relativism is a self-refuting doctrine, so this claim would ultimately need to be justified by the results of this study. Still, in order for the study to proceed to a point at which the charge of self-refutation can be evaluated, this assumption needs to be made, at least provisionally.

One potential objection to these assumptions and to other assumptions that might not be explicitly mentioned here is that such assumptions run the risk of relativization of this very study of relativism. If different assumptions are made, then perhaps quite different conclusions about relativism will be reached, even concerning the nature of relativism itself. The consequence would be that the account of relativism itself might only be able to be given relatively to certain assumptions, which appears to risk incoherence.

However, I would argue that if global relativism is indeed a coherent doctrine, then the alleged relativism of the account of relativism should be able to be incorporated coherently within an account of relativism. So if the results of this study show that global relativism is not self-refuting, then any relativism directed against the assumptions of this study will not obviously form an objection to the assumptions. Further, if relativism in general is self-refuting, then so will be the charge of relativism with regard to this account of relativism. Since this study aims to evaluate the charge of self-refutation against relativism, the results of the study will demonstrate either that the potential objection is not an objection at all or that the objection itself is self-refuting. What I would suggest at this point is that even if there is some potential relativity with regard to this study and its assumptions, that instance of relativity must therefore be understood from some perspective, and the assumptions outlined here simply articulate the perspective from which I propose to understand relativism, even if that relativism applies reflexively to this very study. There may be other perspectives from which relativism might be evaluated, but they do not represent the perspective adopted in this study.

Charles Sanders Peirce considered himself a plodder, proceeding by slow and sure steps rather than brilliant leaps (Brent, 1998, p. 43), and I have endeavored to proceed in a similar manner. This will be a slow, plodding investigation designed to carve out a strong foundation for further investigations.

In its initial stages, this study relies heavily on the language of seeming and appearance, namely that relativism appears to be this way or that way. My general argument is not that because relativism seems to be a certain way to me that it is that way, at least for me, as some have interpreted Protagoras' relativistic doctrine. Rather, my approach is to articulate the appearances that need to be explained by an adequate account of relativism. A consideration of these appearances leads me to suggest certain concrete proposals for understanding relativism, and these proposals are presented as candidates for best explanations of relativism.[6] This

---

[6] Though of course the assertion of a best explanation of the nature of relativism does not in any way suggest that relativism is the best explanation of any

study offers further considerations or arguments for why these proposals should be accepted as best explanations, but ultimately the success of the proposals will rest on their overall fruitfulness in understanding relativism in all of its forms. This seems to be the best way to make a fresh start on a topic with a very long history.

Many books on relativism are undertaken with a particular agenda in mind, typically either to denounce relativism or to defend it from such attacks. By contrast, I am not concerned with the question of whether relativism is true or not. Rather, my reasons for undertaking this study of relativism are primarily methodological in nature, namely in order to support future methodological inquiries in which relativism plays a role. Consequently, the question of the coherence of relativism in general is important to these future inquiries, since it seems that if relativism is fundamentally incoherent, then so will be any methodological arguments that rely on relativism in some way.

Most books on relativism offer a very brief description of relativism in general followed by extensive discussions of specific relativistic claims found in the philosophical literature. In this study, I propose to do the opposite. Throughout the study, I frequently discuss key pieces of the literature on relativism to canvass alternative ways to understand some issue or to provide concrete applications of the proposals of this study, but typically I do not engage critically with the specific arguments in those pieces, since the major concerns of those pieces often do not accord well with the general approach I have taken in this study. It is my intention, certainly, that the results of this study will enable better critical engagement with the entire range of concerns in the literature on relativism. However, in order to establish a better foundation for such critical engagement, it will be necessary to maintain focus on the approach I have outlined for this study and not to be distracted by extensive critical evaluation of specific arguments for or against relativism of various forms.

Once I have offered specific proposals for understanding relativism, I proceed to formulate the logic of relativism in order to apply that logic to the question of whether relativism is self-refuting. My strategy in formulating this logic is to consider the widest range of possibilities for including increasingly more complex relativistic

---

domain of discourse, such as morals or knowledge.

features into the logic. It seems to me that it would not be sufficient to formulate just one logical system of relativism and then to argue on that basis whether relativism is indeed self-refuting. The proposed logic may too weak. It may either lack the resources to demonstrate the strength and coherence of relativism, or it may omit precisely those troublesome features that enable a demonstration that relativism is self-refuting. Consequently, this study formulates not one but five logical systems for relativism.[7] It is my intention that these systems cover all possibilities for relativization that might be included within a formal system, but there may indeed be possibilities that I have not considered. Still, I think that these five systems are sufficient to evaluate the question of whether relativism is self-refuting.

This study unfolds in three major stages: (1) determine the nature of relativism, (2) formulate the logic of relativism, and (3) evaluate the charge of self-refutation based on the logic of relativism. The majority of this study is devoted to the first stage, since if the nature of relativism is poorly understood, the subsequent results would be dubious.

Chapter 2 provides a series of preliminary investigations toward the formulation of a definition of relativism in general, and proceeds by using a method of contrast to determine how relativism differs from other notions that seem structurally similar, such as indexicality, pluralism, conventionalism, reductionism, relativity, and contextualism. Chapter 3 proposes a definition of relativism, and applies that definition to specific relativistic accounts, such as Protagoras' "man is the measure" doctrine.

The proposed definition of relativism yields three substantive theses that must be demonstrated in order to support a claim of relativism, namely the formal requirements for relativity, the thesis of objective equity, and the thesis of incommensurability. Chapters 4 through 6 investigate each of these theses in greater detail to identify what requirements must be demonstrated to support each thesis.

---

[7] Three other systems are noted, but not formulated explicitly, since they merely combine the features of the first five systems. Furthermore, each system is extended to include an additional operator needed to evaluate a certain pattern of self-refutation argument against relativism. So a total of sixteen formal systems could be identified in this study, but only five plus their extensions are formulated and discussed.

Chapter 7 formulates and discusses five proposed logical systems that might represent the logic of relativism. Chapter 8 investigates the idea of self-refutation in general and develops a conception of self-refutation appropriate to a formal analysis of relativism. The question of self-refutation is then evaluated with regard to each of the five proposed relative systems.

The conclusion to this study summarized in chapter 9 is that there is indeed a formal logical system according to which relativism is not self-refuting, at least with regard to a formal analysis of self-refutation. This system is based on a non-normal modal logic, and there are good reasons to think that this kind of non-normal system embodies precisely what is required by a claim of global relativism that would apply reflexively even to its own logic.

This study takes relativism seriously, particularly with regard to its perspectival nature. I suggest that this kind of seriousness is necessary for understanding relativism equally for what it is and for what it is not. Whether relativism holds true anywhere is a separate question that I do not pursue in this study, but this question must be answered based on a prior adequate understanding of what relativism is, and I hope that this study succeeds in expanding that understanding.

Chapter 2

Preliminary Investigations

Formulating the logic of relativism requires a proper understanding of the nature of relativism. However, there is no clear consensus even on the definition of relativism. For example, while some writers attempt to offer a general definition (Mosteller, 2008, p. 3), others seem to despair of finding such a definition, given the multiplicity of kinds of relativism, thereby offering only a means for classifying those varieties of relativism (Harré & Krausz, 1996). Admittedly, there are numerous kinds of relativism, ranging from cultural relativism, to moral relativism, to epistemic relativism, without any apparent limit to the range of phenomenon that might be considered to be relative to some factor. Yet it is tempting to think that there must be something common to these kinds of relativism according to which they all merit the term 'relativism'.

This chapter attempts to substantiate that temptation by laying the groundwork for a general definition of relativism. Rather than investigating each of the kinds of relativism in order to identify what is common to each of these kinds, I proceed by a method of contrast. There are a number of other doctrines or notions that seem relevantly similar to relativism, such as indexicality, pluralism, conventionalism, reductionism, relativity, and contextualism. By investigating the apparent differences between these notions and relativism, I hope to identify a number of distinguishing features that will be common to all forms of relativism.

Of course these other notions themselves may be subject to the same lack of consensus that seems to affect relativism, such that a comparison of these notions might appear only to result in

x is relative to y

(1) meaning
(2) reference
(3) truth
(4) metaphysical commitment
(5) ontology
(6) reality
(7) epistemic values
(8) moral values
(9) aesthetic values
.
.
.

(a) language
(b) conceptual scheme
(c) theory
(d) scientific paradigm
(e) version, depiction, description
(f) culture
(g) community
(h) individual
.
.
.

Figure 2.1: Haack's Identikit for Relativism

compounding confusion upon confusion. Yet I think that a comparison of apparent differences can serve to clarify both the notion of relativism and the notion to which it is compared. Consequently, in describing the differences between pluralism and relativism, for example, I intend not only to work toward an understanding of relativism, but also to propose an understanding of pluralism that makes clear how I see the relation between the two notions. As noted in the introduction, the definition of relativism that I will present later in section 3.1 should be considered as a proposal for clarifying the discussion of relativism. The articulation of the differences between relativism and other notions in this chapter, as well as the associated understanding of those other notions, should likewise be considered as proposals that will ultimately be judged according to their fruitfulness in further discussions of relativism.

2.1 The Structure of Relativism

Consider the chart in Figure 2.1, closely adapted from one by Susan Haack.

Haack claims, "'Relativism' refers, not to a single thesis, but to a whole family. Each resembles the others in claiming that something is relative to something else; each differs from the others in what it claims is relative to what" (1996, p. 297). The chart is presented by Haack as an "identikit" for classifying varieties of relativism.

I propose the following terminology to aid in discussing the nature and logic of relativism throughout this study. The first column in Haack's table indicates what sorts of things can be relative. In relativism, there will be differing theories of these things according to some item in the second column. I will call separate theories about some topic in the first column *relativized sub-theories*, and the set of all such relativized sub-theories on a particular topic the *range of relativized sub-theories* for that topic. I refer to them as sub-theories, since in relativism there will be a single overall relativistic theory encompassing all relativized sub-theories, each of which will be a part of the total relativistic theory. So for example a single theory of moral values will form one relativized sub-theory within a range of relativized sub-theories including all theories of moral values that get relativized to something, such as cultures. I will call the set formed by some item in the second column a *relativizing domain*. So if moral values are relativized to cultures, then the set of cultures would form a relativizing domain.

What I find significant about Haack's identikit is that it identifies something quite definite in the resemblance between members of the family of relativistic theses, namely the structure of the various theses. This structure is expressed in the general formula "x is relative to y" where x is the topic of a range of relativized sub-theories, and y is a relativizing domain. This common structure leads me to hypothesize that relativism in general is ultimately a structural phenomenon, and that a general definition of relativism can be formulated in terms of the features required to maintain this structure. For instance, there must be some relation between the relativized sub-theories and the relativizing domain, a relation that I will call *indexing*. These structural features indicate that there will be certain *formal requirements for relativity*, which are needed to enable the claim that x is relative to y for some x and y.[1]

Yet it is not clear that these formal requirements for relativity

---

[1] Compare: "To generate forms of relativism, we shall say that a '*relativist thesis*' is a thesis to the effect that: For all X-judgments, some feature, F, of an X-judgement is relative to Y" (Preston, 1992, p. 57). Yet Preston goes no further in analyzing these relativist theses, which I think is a significant oversight, since other notions seem to share this formal characterization, as the remainder of this chapter will illustrate.

are sufficient to define relativism in general. The problem is that certain other notions likewise seem to share these formal requirements. For example, since there is a relation of indexing between the range of relativized sub-theories and the relativizing domain, there is a question how relativism differs from indexicality, which also seems significantly to require such an indexing relation. In the remainder of this chapter, I will investigate each of these structurally similar notions in turn, noting the ways in which they share certain features of relativism, and seeking to identify key differences between them and relativism in general. These differences will provide the basis for a proposal for a general definition offered in the next chapter.

One contrast with relativism that I will not explore in any great detail is the contrast with comparatives. It is common to use the adverb 'relatively' to express a certain amount of imprecision, as in the statement "It is relatively hot today". Here the exact degree of heat is not specified, but the judgment of hotness seems to be relative to some frame of reference, perhaps to the current temperature in Antarctica. Given that such frames of reference do seem to represent a relativizing domain, such judgments do indeed seem to represent a kind of relativity. However, I would briefly note that these judgments involve comparative terms such as 'hot', 'tall', 'bald', and so forth, which are the kind of terms that can be subject to concerns with vagueness. The reason that I will not explore the use of comparative is that it is not clear that all varieties of relativism require the use of such comparative terms, and that an exploration of comparatives is not as fruitful for understanding relativism as the other notions investigated below.

2.2 Relativism and Indexicality

Indexicality is a feature of certain linguistic structures by which at least part of their meaning varies according to the context in which they are used. Certain words known as demonstratives, such as 'this', 'that', 'here' and 'now', exhibit this feature since the object, place or time to which these words refer must be determined according to the context in which they are used and the circumstances within the contexts. For example, if I utter the sentence "Now is not the time to panic", the time to which 'now' refers is

2.2. RELATIVISM AND INDEXICALITY 29

the time that the sentence was uttered, though it may be indeterminate how far that time may extend before and after the utterance, so that it may be the case that a time to panic can begin very shortly after the utterance is completed. However, the phrase is idiomatic enough within its usual context of use that competent speakers of English understand that 'now' refers to the current situation in which the speaker and the audience find themselves, not merely the exact moment in time in which the term gets uttered. Likewise, the object to which the demonstrative 'that' refers in a sentence is determined either by the context of the conversation alone or by an act of ostension, such as pointing, within that context. For example, if I say "That is disgusting", it may be unclear to what I am referring unless I point at something within the general locale that I find disgusting or unless I utter the sentence immediately after someone else has said something that I find disgusting. Note that it is not critically the case in indexicality that these words simply have multiple disparate meanings, perhaps by virtue of an etymological accident, as with the various meanings of the word 'bat', such that the context serves to disambiguate the two meanings. Rather part of the meaning of these words includes this contextual variance, so if I do not understand the way demonstratives vary by context, I do not fully understand the use of these words.

Indexicality is a broader feature of language encompassing this contextual feature of demonstrative words, but also including the contextual variance of phrases and sentences containing demonstratives. As David Kaplan notes, it is not merely the reference or extension of these words, phrases and sentences that vary with context, but also the conceptual content or intension (Kaplan, 1978, p. 81), as for example in the sentence "Now is not the time to panic" considered earlier, according to which competent users of a language are able to understand the relevant range of time surrounding the point in time at which 'now' was uttered in terms of an overall situation. As in the case of demonstratives, so with indexicality in general, competent speakers of a language understand this contextual variance so that they can both use indexicals appropriately and interpret them when others use them.

Yet this sort of variance seems similar to what is expressed by the structure of relativism presented in the last section, since indexicality could be characterized by saying that the extension and intension of indexicals are relative to the contexts in which they are used. The question thus arises whether indexicality and relativism are the same thing, whether one is a species of the other, or whether there is some distinguishing factor to differentiate the two.

It might be thought that the notion of a context would be sufficient to distinguish indexicality from relativism, for example by suggesting that indexicality is a form of relativism in which the relativizing domain is a set of contexts. Yet I do not think that this approach is successful, since it seems that whatever can appear within a relativizing domain can also serve to define a context. If I am considering a case of cultural relativism in which my relativizing domain is a set of cultures, then I could just as easily speak of the varying contexts of each culture. If I am considering a case of subjectivism in which the relativizing domain is a set of individuals, then I could just as easily speak of the varying contexts of individual perspectives.

There are distinguishing factors between indexicality and relativism, I will argue, but to introduce these differences it will be convenient to review a specific theory of indexicals, such as the Kaplan-Perry account. While currently very influential, this theory may indeed be found to be deficient is some way. However, I would suggest that any adequate account of indexicals should be able to demonstrate a difference between indexicality and relativism, according to the terms of that account. I simply choose to investigate that difference in terms of the Kaplan-Perry account since I think it provides for a clearer exposition.[2]

Kaplan divides the Fregean notion of sense into two components, content and character, and claims that content varies by context (Kaplan, 1978, p. 83). "This content is what Carnap called an 'intension' and what, I believe, has been often referred to as a 'proposition'. So my theory is that different contexts for [an indexical sentence] produce not just different truth values, but different propositions" (p. 84). Character on the other hand is the rule that coordinates contents with contexts.

> I call that component of the sense of an expression which determines how the content is determined by the context, the 'character' of an expression. Just as

---

[2] I suggest a way that a Quinean account of indexicals might be able to make sense of this difference in footnote 4 at the end of this section.

> contents (or intensions) can be represented by functions from possible worlds to extensions, so characters can be represented by functions from contexts to contents. The character of 'I' would then be represented by the function (or rule, if you prefer) which assigns to each context that content which is represented by the constant function from possible worlds to the agent of the context. (p. 84)

Kaplan continues by claiming that competent speakers of a language containing indexicals must know the character of particular demonstratives and indexicals within that language (p. 84). Perry contributes to this theory of indexicals by extending this account to belief states to show how indexicals are ineliminable within an explanation of many actions and thus to claim that indexicals are essential in that sense (Perry, 1979).

Note that knowledge of the character of an indexical thereby enables a competent user of that indexical to apply it not only to situations where it has been applied before, but also in novel situations. Even a small child hearing someone say "I have pneumonia" may understand that the speaker is saying something about himself and not about the child, even if the child does not know what pneumonia is.

Consider now a distinction that Max Kölbel makes between indexical relativism and genuine relativism. In a case of indexical relativism, the relativism in question results precisely from the indexicality of key terms within statements. In the example Kölbel gives, the word 'good' might be treated as an indexical term according to an indexical form of moral relativism. Consequently, the content of such statements would vary by context according to indexical relativism. By contrast, such terms and statements are not indexical according to genuine relativism, and therefore the content would remain constant. What varies by context for the genuine relativist is not the content, but the truth-values assigned to the stable content of a statement (Kölbel, 2004, pp. 306–307). While I do not necessarily endorse Kölbel's distinction between two kinds of relativism itself, his distinction seems to suggest a distinction between indexicality and relativism according to the terms of the Kaplan-Perry account of indexicals. In a case of relativism the content for a statement seems stable across all contexts, whereas according to the Kaplan-Perry theory of indexicals, the content of indexicals and statements containing indexicals varies by context. This variability of content in indexicality seems to distinguish indexicality from relativism.

Furthermore, there does not seem to be anything corresponding to Kaplan's notion of character in relativism in general. Certainly in a case of what Kölbel calls indexical relativism, the indexicality that is part of that putative kind of relativism would involve the character of certain indexical terms. Yet consider a case of genuine relativism in Kölbel's sense, which is primarily the sense in which I would think of relativism in general. Here it is the assignment of truth-values that is important, not the understanding of the meaning and use of indexical terms and phrases. Whereas in a case of indexicality, knowledge of the character of indexical terms and phrases allows me to determine the content of those terms and phrases in novel contexts, in a case of genuine relativism, there does not seem to be any competence that could enable me to determine the truth or falsity of statements when the context relevantly changes. So for example, if morality is genuinely relative, then the truth of certain moral statements will vary by context. However, even if I know the truth of moral relativism under this assumption, there is no rule or competence that I can possess that will help me determine whether for example charity is good in a relevantly different moral context. Rather, it seems that I must determine the truth or falsity of that moral claim empirically. Further, even if I know the truth-values of certain moral statements in several different moral contexts, this will not help me determine the truth-values of those statements in a new moral context. The concept of character thus also seems to distinguish relativism from indexicality according to the terms of the Kaplan-Perry account.

Although both indexicality and relativism rely on indexing, there is a difference in the way in which indexing functions in each case. According to indexicality, the content of statement varies according to context, and there is a linguistic competence that provides access to that content given the context. According to relativity, however, the content of statements is stable across the relativizing domain, and the truth-values for those statements must be determined empirically, particularly in novel contexts. Therefore, once the content of the statements in an instance of indexicality has been identified, it should be possible to eliminate the indexing relation by disambiguating terms according to the various contexts in which they appear.[3] In an instance of relativism, however, once any disambiguation has occurred to provide a formalization of each statement according to the assumptions of this study outlined in the introduction above, the indexing relation remains part of the structure of the overall theory.[4]

2.3 Relativism and Pluralism

When used in an ontological context, pluralism refers to the position according to which there are multiple kinds of substances, as opposed to the doctrine of monism claiming only a single kind of substance, as found for example in the work of Spinoza. However, it is in a meta-theoretical context rather than an ontological one

---

[3] According to Perry, this elimination would thereby eliminate the explanation of actions with regard to certain statements, such as "I am making a mess" (Perry, 1979, p. 3), but such personal explanations do not seem to be part of the kinds of theories that are subject to relativistic treatment, so I will ignore such complications.

[4] Indeed, this strategy of disambiguation underlies a Quinean account of indexicals that seems to ignore any Fregean distinction between sense and reference, as well as any requirement for Kaplan's notion of character. For Quine, indexical statements are ambiguous with regard to what he calls eternal sentences, in which all indexical terms are resolved into their proper references. "Corresponding to 'It is raining' and 'You owe me ten dollars' we have the eternal sentence 'It rains in Boston, Mass. on July 15, 1968' and 'Bernard J. Ortcutt owes W. V. Quine ten dollars on July 15, 1968', where 'rains' and 'owes' are to be thought of now as tenseless" (Quine, 1986, p. 13). On this account, then, the difference between indexicality and relativism would be that in indexicality all statements can be resolved into eternal sentences with stable truth-values, whereas in relativism statements can only be resolved into eternal sentences whose truth-values vary according to certain contexts. The problem that arises on this account of indexicals for this study is that some contexts appear easily to resolve into eternal sentences, such as times and places, whereas certain other contexts would need to resist resolution into eternal sentences in order to preserve relativism, such as cultures. It may be that a distinction between the context of utterance and context of assessment would be able to resolve this problem (MacFarlane, 2003), allowing all contexts of utterance to be resolved into eternal sentences to eliminate indexicals, while contexts of evaluation are maintained to form relativizing domains. Since my purpose here is only to distinguish between relativism and indexicality, the assumption that relativized sub-theories can be disambiguated will serve to make this distinction, however that disambiguation may occur, and whichever supporting theory of indexicals according to which that disambiguation is based.

that pluralism is most relevant to the question of relativism. In this context, pluralism refers to a position according to which, for some given issue, there is more than one theory understood in some positive manner. For example, consider the following list of ways multiple theories may be understood, roughly ordered according to a descending degree of strength.

In pluralism, there are multiple theories that are:

1. True
2. Valid
3. Warranted
4. Plausible
5. Appropriate
6. Useful
7. Worthy of respect
8. Worthy of consideration
9. Such that it would be impolite to ridicule them in the presence of their adherents
10. Available

Depending on how one understands the notion of truth, items toward the top of the list may collapse into each other,[5] whereas the last item indicates the bare existence of multiple theories. It seems inappropriate to call this latter case pluralism, since it indicates a mere multiplicity of theories without taking a positive stance with regard to them. Consequently, it would seem better to use such terms as 'plurality' or 'diversity' to discuss such a situation. Item 9 is only a half-serious attempt to identify something minimally positive to say about a multiplicity of theories without merely acknowledging the diversity.

Pluralism involving items 6-9 represents a concern toward more practical than theoretical concerns and is the kind of pluralism most often invoked in discussions of multiculturalism, in which the metaphysical or epistemic status of differing theories or ways of life is less important than the practical necessity for diverse groups to live together. In those discussions, tolerance rather than

---

[5] Validity, for example, might be considered the same as either truth or warrant. However, it might be understood to be truth according to a given system, which might be considered weaker than unqualified truth and stronger than warrant.

2.3. RELATIVISM AND PLURALISM

truth seems to be the main concern, whereas this study is more concerned with truth.

To examine one philosophical discussion of pluralism as a means of illustrating these dimensions, consider Nicholas Rescher's characterizations of pluralism as "the epistemological doctrine of a variety of diverse positions, all viewed as being more or less appropriate and plausible" and "the doctrine that any substantial question admits of a variety of plausible but mutually conflicting responses" (Rescher, 1993, pp. 64f, 79). Here Rescher shies away from characterizing pluralism in terms of the truth of these multiple positions and seems to weaken the characterization still further in his later discussion of pluralism in terms of "seeing a range of alternative positions as deserving of our respect, consideration, and the like" (p. 100), which indicates a more practical than theoretical concern. However, this weaker characterization is perfectly appropriate to his central thesis, namely that "it is fallacious to insist on a quest for consensus on the grounds that dissensus and pluralism are rationally intolerable" (p. 125). Whereas Rescher may have a theoretical concern in determining what is and is not required for rationality, the pluralism he acknowledges seems oriented more toward the practice of rationality than toward rationality as such, since nowhere does Rescher even suggest that pluralism is required for rationality any more than consensus is required, but merely argues that the presence of plurality of plausible positions can be rationally tolerated. This contrast becomes clearer when Rescher claims the compatibility of pluralism with what he calls preferentialism, namely "seeing only one of [the alternative positions] as having a valid claim to our acceptance" (pp. 100–101), which relies on a notion, namely validity, closer to truth in the list given above than any of the notions by which Rescher characterizes pluralism. Thus I may understand only one position as being a valid theory while practically recognizing many other positions as being plausible, worthy of respect, or worthy of consideration.

For the purposes of this discussion, the kind of pluralism that will be important is one that takes alternative theories to be true, or at least something close to true, rather than merely plausible or worthy or respect. In this sense, it seems that relativism counts as a variety or species of pluralism, since relativism also asserts the truth of multiple, distinct theories. The difference seems to be that in relativism these distinct true theories are indexed to some relativizing domain such as cultures or conceptual schemes, whereas in pluralism in general no such indexing is required. Thus, for example, where in a relativistic system two theories might be true, one for one culture, the second for another culture, in a more general pluralistic system two theories might be true for anyone regardless of their culture or anything else that might be considered a relativizing factor. So relativism would seem to be a species of pluralism according to which the multiplicity of theories is indexed to some relativizing domain, as given by the formal requirements for relativity.[6]

2.4 Relativism and Conventionalism

Conventions seem to exhibit the same kind of variability as relativism does. If it is a convention to drive on the left side of the road in some societies and on the right side in other societies, then the question of which side of the road on which to drive would seem to be relative to the society in which one finds oneself. So the structural form of conventionalism seems similar if not identical to the structural form of relativism, in which there are multiple theories that vary according to some relativizing domain, in this case, the societies or groups that adopt particular conventions. Therefore, in conventionalism as in relativism, it seems, at least initially, that x is relative to y for some conventional x and some society y that adopts the convention.

Thus arises the question whether there is any significant difference between conventionalism and relativism. Indeed it would appear that some philosophers make no relevant distinction be-

---

[6] Compare: "In its most general form, pluralism is the idea that there can be more than one true story of the world; there can be incompatible, but equally acceptable, accounts of some subject matter. There are no absolute facts but a diversity of truths, all of which equally clamor for our attention" (Lynch, 1998, p. 1). Yet Lynch continues: "Metaphysical pluralism is pluralist because it implies that true propositions and facts are relative to conceptual schemes or worldviews..." (p. 3). Insofar as true propositions and facts are relative to something, this would seem to entail the sort of indexing by virtue of which a kind of pluralism would count as relativism. For my part, metaphysical pluralism as discussed by Lynch would be pluralist simply because it affirms the multiplicity of theories. If it also implies that something is relative to something else, then I suggest that what Lynch calls metaphysical pluralism would better be understood as metaphysical relativity or relativism.

2.4. RELATIVISM AND CONVENTIONALISM

tween the two. Perhaps the difference is merely that conventionalism represents one form of relativism. For example, in Neil Levy's discussion of moral relativism, the conventionality of patterns of activity learned by virtue of growing up in a particular society is proposed as the grounds for moral relativism. "If morality is merely conventional, then, it seems, moral relativism is true" (Levy, 2002, p. 44).

Yet suppose there is a difference between conventionalism and relativism, beyond a difference between species and genus. Where would such a difference lie, given the structural similarity between the two? Perhaps the difference would lie in the nature of the relativized theories, for example. Yemima Ben-Menahem contends, "...conventionalism does *not* purport to base truth on convention, but rather, seeks to forestall the conflation of truth and convention" (Ben-Menahem, 2006, p. 1). So perhaps the difference is that whereas sub-theories in relativism can properly claim to represent truths, albeit relativized truths, sub-theories in conventionalism fail to represent truths, but only indicate what to do given this failure of truth-aptness. If there is no ultimate fact of the matter concerning on which side of the road driving must occur, then any description of sides of the road on which to drive are not truths and therefore represent conventions.

However, I am not convinced that this supposed difference proves to be decisive. Even if there is no fact of the matter concerning the subject matter of conventions, once the conventions are established as such, there does seem to be some truths correlated with these conventions. Certainly there are truths concerning which groups adopt which conventions, but more importantly, there likewise seem to be truths about what to do when one finds oneself among those groups. If I am driving in Australia, for example, I had better drive on the left side of the road, or bad consequences will follow. These truths in conventionalism seem to be normative truths, but seem to be truths just the same. So perhaps this line of thinking, if successful, would only establish conventionalism to be a species of relativism, one whose relativized sub-theories are broadly normative in nature.

Nor does it seem promising to look for any differences with regard to the relativizing domain either. I might want to stipulate that the relativizing domain in conventionalism should not be a set of conventions itself, for example, that driving on a certain side of the road is relative to certain conventions, in which case what is relative to convention means nothing more than what is according to convention. However, I am not sure that this stipulation provides a sufficiently significant difference between conventionalism and relativism or that relativism might not contain comparable restrictions on the relativizing domain.[7]

If there is no difference within either the range of relativized sub-theories or the relativizing domains between conventionalism and relativism, it seems that the only place to find a difference would be in the relations between the relativized sub-theories and the relativizing domains. Here I think an important difference can be identified. In his study of conventions, David Lewis notes, "there is no such thing as the only possible convention. If R is our actual convention, R must have the alternative R', and R' must be such that it could have been our convention instead of R...' (Lewis, 2002, p. 70). This availability of alternatives is essential to conventionalism, but does not seem to be required by relativism. In fact, if such alternatives were available in an instance of relativism, it is not clear that that it would be appropriate to say that x is relative to y for some x and y. The relativity in question seems to represent a kind of non-arbitrary relation between the relativizing domain and the range of relativized sub-theories such that once an element in the relativizing domain is identified, the corresponding sub-theory is thereby determined.[8] If there were an alternative to the sub-theory that could likewise be indexed to the element in the relativizing domain, for example, if there were multiple sides of the street on which one could possibly drive within some society, then that would seem that the presence of such alternatives indicates that it is an instance of conventionalism. If driving on a particular side of the road were an instance of relativism, by hypothesis, then for any given society, there would be only one possible side of the street on which one could drive, which is absurd since streets do have two sides, so clearly it is an instance of conventionalism, not relativism.

Thus in conventionalism there would appear to be a certain amount of freedom concerning which theory could be adopted by

---

[7] As will be discussed in section 4.1 below.

[8] In terms of a set theoretical account of relations, the relation between the relativizing domain and the range of relativized sub-theories is a function, hence my use of the terms 'domain' and 'range'.

any element of the relativizing domain, whereas in relativism that freedom seems to be eliminated once an element in the relativizing domain is identified. This freedom suggests that conventionalism entails a choice between alternatives, whether an explicit or implicit choice, whereas relativism restricts such choice. If a choice of sub-theories can be made by elements of the relativizing domain, for example, if a given society has a choice between multiple courses of action, then it would appear to be a case of conventionalism. If however a choice of sub-theories can only be made by changing to a different element of the relativizing domain, for example, by changing to a different society, then it appears that there is a non-arbitrary relation between the sub-theories and the domain, which would indicate a case of relativism.

While conventionalism implies a measure of choice and freedom, it does not imply absolute freedom, since not every logical possibility may represent a practical possibility that can be chosen. So there may be constraints on freedom within conventionalism. Furthermore, this range of practical possibilities may change over time or even between groups.[9] This situation suggests that there may be an element of relativism possible within an account of conventionalism, if the range of conventional alternatives that might be selected differs according to groups. However, I think this hybrid case would still primarily be an instance of conventionality with regard to the subject of choice, insofar as there is freedom to choose between alternatives. Yet insofar as the range of alternatives may vary according to a non-arbitrary relation with regard to the group in question, the nature of that specific conventionality itself for the group would seem to represent an instance of relativism, thus preserving a distinction between the two notions.

2.5 Relativism and Reductionism

In any case of reduction, something gets smaller in some way. In the case of inter-theoretic reduction where one theory gets reduced to another, which is the sort of reduction that will concern me here, what gets smaller might be the number of types of entities

---

[9] In Lewis' account, the nature of conventions depends upon common knowledge of expectations. So both the range of expectations and knowledge of those expectations could vary (Lewis, 2002, p. 75).

that a theory postulates, the number of fundamental axioms in the theory's formulation, or perhaps the number of independent variables that characterize a given phenomenon. Such inter-theoretic reductions assert that one theory can be reduced down to another theory that is in some way simpler as a result of the reduction and that explains everything that the original theory explained. Implicit in most claims of reduction is the understanding that the reduction represents an improvement in the theoretical situation, namely that the reducing theory is to be preferred in some way over the reduced theory. Reductionism thus represents a claim within a given domain of discourse both that such a reduction succeeds and that such a reduction is desirable.

As an example of reduction, consider the case of a micro-reductive explanation, in which the behavior of entities in one theory is explained by the theory of the behavior of their parts. A standard example of a successful micro-reductive explanation is the reduction of the theory of molecules to the theory of atoms, whereby the properties of molecules such as water molecules are explained by the properties of the molecules' component atoms. In this case, since a large number of molecules with a wide variety of properties are explained by a comparatively small number of kinds of atoms with a small number of basic properties, the micro-reduction has clearly reduced certain features of molecular theory. Furthermore, the micro-reduction represents an advance not only insofar as it provides an explanation of molecular behavior already observed, but it also provides a framework in which new combinations of atoms may be postulated in order to synthesize new molecules with desirable properties. In this sense, the atomic theory is to be preferred over the molecular theory.[10]

This micro-reduction of molecular theory to atomic theory forms part of a broader, more contentious program of the Unity of Science in one sense of the phrase (Oppenheim & Putnam, 1956, pp. 3–8), since the success of the atomic micro-reduction seems to suggest that all branches of science might be unified by means of a series of reductions of one branch to another, down to the fundamental level of elementary particle physics. I will not review the debate over the contentious features of the Unity

---

[10] Though of course this argument does not establish that the atomic theory is to be preferred over the molecular theory in every sense.

2.5. RELATIVISM AND REDUCTIONISM

of Science program, since it does not directly contribute to the investigation of relativism. Nor will I review the various attempts to formalize the notion of reduction, since it is the general structure of reductionism, particularly within the Unity of Science program, that bears on the nature of relativism. Consider the list of reductive levels that Oppenheim and Putnam propose:

      6 Social groups
      5 (Multicellular) living things
      4 Cells
      3 Molecules
      2 Atoms
      1 Elementary particles (p. 9)

According to their model of the Unity of Science by means of micro-reduction, "a branch with the things of a given level as its universe of discourse will always be a potential micro-reducer of any branch with things of the next higher level (if there is one) as its universe of discourse" (p. 9). Though Oppenheim and Putnam themselves present their conception of the Unity of Science only as "working hypothesis", the position holding that these micro-reductions actually succeed and are desirable would count as an instance of reductionism with regard to science.

Leaving aside the proposed micro-reduction for the moment, this conception of the Unity of Science seems to meet the formal requirements for relativism, since there are a number of separate theories, each indexed to some member of a relativizing domain, in this case the set of reductive levels. Yet science is not typically characterized as a relativistic enterprise. Science is not understood to be relative to reductive levels.

One reason for resisting a relativistic characterization of science is that the various theories do not by themselves seem to concern the same things. Rather it is the proposed micro-reductions that make the links between the entities across the various theoretical levels to assert that the theory of what happens at a micro level is also a theory of what happens at the macro level. If the proposed relativized sub-theories are not about the same thing, then it seems that the formal requirements for relativism may not be met after all.[11] However, I think it would be a mistake to stop here and

---

[11] As will be discussed in section 4.2 below.

to accept this reason as the key difference between reductionism and relativism, since this reason affects only the formal structure of the branches of science prior to the proposed micro-reductions. As I shall attempt to show, the nature of reduction itself provides additional reasons for resisting a relativistic understanding of science as a whole, reasons which will be crucial in understanding the nature of relativism itself.

Kemeny and Oppenheim propose two "special features of reduction":

> Since it is to be progress in science, we must certainly require that the new theory should fulfill the role of the old one, i.e., that it can explain (or predict) all those facts that the old theory could handle. Secondly, we do not recognize the replacement of one theory by another as progress unless the new theory compares favorably with the old one in a feature that we can very roughly describe as its simplicity. (1956, p. 7).

I intend to show that these two features, understood more generically, suggest two non-formal requirements that distinguish reductionism from relativism.

First, if one theory reduces to another, there must be some path between the two theories, some justification for the claim of reduction. For example, an early account of reduction by J. H. Woodger proposes that there must be a translation from one theory to another by means of bridge laws in the form of bi-conditional statements linking terms of one theory to terms of the other (Woodger, 1952, pp. 271–272). Ernest Nagel's account of reduction similarly requires bridging postulates that link the terms of one theory with the terms of the other, with the related requirement that the laws of the reduced theory must be derivable from the laws of the reducing theory together with these postulates (E. Nagel, 1961, pp. 353–354). In the case of a micro-reduction, Robert Causey argues that bi-conditional statements linking two theories must be strengthened to identity statements, not only among the thing-predicates within the theories, but also among the attribute-predicates (Causey, 1972). Arguing that Woodger and Nagel's accounts of reduction were "too narrow in that they excluded most actual cases of reduction" (p. 17), Kemeny and Oppenheim replace

2.5. RELATIVISM AND REDUCTIONISM

the link between the two theories by means of bi-conditional statements with the requirement that "every observational statement implied by T_2 is also implied by T_1" (p. 15), as indicated in the first special feature of reduction quoted earlier. For his part, Quine minimally proposes merely that a proxy function be identified between the two theories, "a function whose values exhaust the old things ... as their arguments range over the new things" (Quine, 1964, p. 214). Regardless of the specifics, each of these accounts requires some path between the two theories in a reduction, whether that path is understood as a derivation, a translation, a demonstration of empirical equivalence, or whatever.

By contrast, in a case of relativism, no such path seems to be recognized. Relativized sub-theories are often said to be incommensurable. Whereas reduction seems keen to unite two theories, relativism seems concerned to keep its relativized sub-theories separate, since if relativized sub-theories can be derived from each other, for example, then their putative relativization becomes highly suspect, if not simply undermined. Rather than providing fundamentally different accounts of the same thing, commensurable accounts seem to provide different formulations of the same account, and this does not seem to be what is intended in an instance of relativism. In keeping with traditional usage in the literature on relativism, I will refer to this feature of relativism as the *thesis of incommensurability*. Yet I would caution at this point that the notion of incommensurability that will be operative in this study may not perfectly coincide with the conception of incommensurability that commonly appears within other accounts of relativism, as will be discussed in chapter 6. However this notion of incommensurability may ultimately be understood, reductionism must deny the thesis of incommensurability, since if theories are incommensurable, then there would seem to be no grounds for justifying that one theory could be reduced to another.

Second, as noted at the beginning of this section, a case of reduction is typically represented as an improvement in the theoretic situation. In their second special feature of reduction quoted above, Kemeny and Oppenheim acknowledge that a reduction must be counted as progress and claim that this progress is represented by an improvement in the simplicity of the reducing theory over the reduced theory. However this improvement is understood, in a case of reduction it seems that the reducing and reduced theories can be ordered by some relation, presumed to be an objective relation. It is not merely that certain scientists happen to prefer one reductive level to another according to their idiosyncratic tastes, but that there is some objective criterion to determine whether one theory is simpler than another and therefore better, if for example the relevant kind of improvement is considered to be an improvement in simplicity. Though such claims of objectivity in science can be challenged, such challenges are not important for my purposes, since it is the mere supposition of an objective ordering in reductionism that seems important in understanding the differences between reductionism and relativism, not the achievement of such an ordering.

By contrast, in a case of relativism, no such ordering is recognized. It is commonly asserted in relativism that there is no objective criterion by which to prefer one relativized sub-theory to another, that one theory is as good as the other. Whereas reductionism may posit a preferred state of objective simplicity to which theories should tend by means of a reduction, relativism seems to reject the possibility of ordering on any objective grounds. I will refer to this feature of relativism, rather infelicitously, as the *thesis of objective equity*, for reasons that will be discussed in chapter 5. Here again I would caution that the understanding of objectivity that is operative in the thesis of objective equity may not coincide with every conception of objectivity. Reductionism must reject the thesis of objective equity if it is to distinguish itself from a case of instrumentalism, according to which any theory is as good as any alternative theory so long as it predicts the same results. The point of an inter-theoretic reduction is to identify one theory as being objectively better than the other in some respect, whether in terms of simplicity, explanatory power, or some other factor.

Thus the investigation into reductionism seems to have identified two further requirements for relativism beyond the formal requirements for relativity: the thesis of incommensurability and the thesis of objective equity. These two requirements will feature significantly in the definition of relativism proposed in the next chapter.

2.6 Relativism and Relativity

Given the common etymology of their terms, it may be wondered whether there is any significant difference between relativity and relativism or whether these concepts are essentially the same and their terms simply interchangeable. It certainly seems that the term 'relativity' has fewer negative connotations than 'relativism', perhaps by the association of 'relativity' with Albert Einstein's illustrious theory, compared with the association of 'relativism' with less revered figures, so perhaps the difference in the use of the two terms is solely in their connotations. For example, Quine rarely uses the term 'relativism', preferring to name one of his doctrines 'Ontological Relativity' (Quine, 1969), rather than 'Ontological Relativism'. In one of the few articles in which he does use the term 'relativism', he writes, "Relativism of a higher order remains: relativity to one's language" (Quine, 1984), so it does not seem that Quine distinguishes between the two terms in any significant way.[12]

It may be that a detailed investigation of the use of 'relativity' and 'relativism' in scholarly literature would uncover some differential pattern of usage, but it seems equally likely to me that such an investigation would merely prove to be a tedious waste of time. After all, while there might be no difference in usage at all, it might also be the case that philosophers and others have been carelessly conflating the two concepts in their writings. It is not clear how to decide between these two possible cases in any particular instance of the use of these terms.

Yet I do think that a distinction between relativity and relativism can profitably be made. Michael Krausz makes a distinction as follows:

> *Relativism* holds that truth, or its cognates, is relative to a conceptual framework of some sort. It holds that once the meaning of 'truth' is univocally fixed *within a given framework*, it is uniquely assertable within that framework.... *Relativity*, on the other hand, holds that cultural entities are to be understood or make intelli-

---

[12] Likewise, a definition of relativism by Charles L. Stevenson relies solely on relative terms and thereby appears to make no distinction between relativity and relativism (Stevenson, 1962, pp. 28–29).

> gible in the cultural setting in which they appear. Insofar as intentional settings change over historical time, our understanding of them changes over time. But this does not mean that the multiplicity of frameworks, at any particular time, necessitates the systematic equivocation of truth. (Krausz, 1984, p. 397)

I confess that I do not entirely understand Krausz's distinction, which seems to depend upon a principled distinction among kinds of relativizing domains, whether they count as conceptual frameworks or as mere cultural settings. It seems to me that a distinction between relativity and relativism should account for the bad connotations linked to the term 'relativism' that do not seem to affect the term 'relativity', and indeed, Krausz's distinction appears to make relativity less objectionable than relativism. However, according to Krausz, Einstein's special theory of relativity would appear to count as a form of relativism, since it assigns truth-values to certain statement relative to a framework of inertial motion rather than to cultural setting. Yet the special theory of relativity seems to count as the most respectable and least objectionable kind of relativity, not a reviled form of relativism. Consequently, I will not adopt this distinction. Krausz does not provide reasons for accepting his distinction, so it would appear to be a stipulation, and I suspect that any such distinction must count as a stipulation at this point. The distinction I have in mind, though, will preserve the special theory of relativity as a form of relativity not relativism and will seek to account for objectionable features of relativism precisely by identifying features of the special theory of relativity that kinds of relativism might lack.

To help introduce this distinction, I will first review one attempt to make distinctions between various kinds of relativity. In their examination of certain claims of ancient skeptics, Julia Annas and Jonathan Barnes distinguish three varieties of relativity: epistemic relativity, ontological relativity, and semantic relativity. They characterize epistemic relativity as follows: "Fs are epistemically relative to Gs just in case Fs cannot be known unless Gs are known: good things, perhaps, are epistemically relative to bad things, inasmuch as you cannot recognize the good unless you can also recognize the bad" (Annas & Barnes, 1985, p. 132). Thus epistemic relativity represents a dependency relation between two things in which knowledge of one thing is dependent on knowledge of another.

On the other hand, ontological relativity "is a form of ontological or existential dependence. Fathers are relative to children in the sense that fathers exist only if children exist; right-hand things are relative to left-hand things in the sense that right-hand things exist only if left-hand things exist" (p. 135). While Annas and Barnes admit that these examples may not strictly hold up, the kind of relativity proposed seems clear enough. Expressed schematically, this variety of relativity holds that Fs are ontologically relative to Gs just in case Fs cannot exist unless Gs also exist. With regard to fathers and children, fathers cannot exist as fathers unless they have children. A man with no children is no father at all, though he may exist as a man. Note that this characterization of ontological relativity is distinctly different from Quine's doctrine of ontological relativity, according to which different formalizations of empirically adequate global theory will yield different sets of objects representing what exists, so that ontology itself is relative to the background language and structure of theories (Quine, 1969). Quine's doctrine does not assert an ontological dependence between objects, but a theoretic dependence of the existence of objects.

Lastly, according to semantic relativity, "Fs are semantically relative if sentences of the form 'x is F' are elliptical for sentences of the form 'x is F in relation to y' " (p. 139). As an example, Annas and Barnes suggest "darker things are semantically relative; for 'x is darker' is elliptical for, and so means, 'x is darker than y' " (p. 140). They continue to argue that these three forms of relativity are independent of each other in the sense that if something is epistemically relative to something else, it does not imply that it is ontologically relative to that thing, and likewise among all three forms of relativity (pp. 139–140).

All three varieties of relativity identified by Annas and Barnes express the relational character of something, whether of knowledge of certain things, of existence of certain things, or of the meaning of certain predicates. Indeed, etymology would suggest that relations should feature strongly in the characterization of relativity. However, the kinds of dependence relations that are important to epistemic and ontological relativity as described by Annas and Barnes do not seem to accord precisely with modern usage of the term 'relativity' in English. For example, some F might be relative to *G* according to modern usage even if *G* is known to exist while *F* might not be known or might not yet exist. However, according to the relations that Annas and Barnes describe, *F* would therefore not be epistemically or ontologically relative to *G*. Since the ancient skeptics expressed their notion of relativity by means of the common preposition πρός, meaning variously "near" or "towards" or "from before" according to the case of the prepositional object, perhaps the use of 'relativity' to translate what the skeptics had in mind is misleading in these cases. Perhaps some neologism such as 'relationality' would have been more precise.

Semantic relativity, on the other hand, seems better suited to modern usage of 'relativity'. If x is dark only in relation to y, according to the semantic relativity of the term 'dark', then once y is given, say within a conversational context, then the darkness of x is also given. Yet it should be noted that Peter Unger also articulates a different notion that he also calls semantic relativity. His version is characterized as follows:

> Suppose that there is no objectively right answer as to how a certain expression should be interpreted; no unique determinate meaning to be assigned. In such cases, if there really are any, we will have *semantic relativity*: One set of assumptions leads to one semantic interpretation, another set leads to another, and there is nothing to decide objectively in favor of either set. (Unger, 1984, p. 5)

Whereas Annas and Barnes' version of semantic relativity is a case of relativity within the semantics of a predicate, Unger's semantic relativity seems to be a case of relativity of the semantics itself, in that the semantics are relative to something else, namely a set of assumptions. Yet Unger's version also seems to involve a non-arbitrary indexing relation that I have suggested is part of the modern notion of relativism, since once the assumptions are fixed, the semantics are likewise fixed.

This characterization of relativity as a non-arbitrary relation between two things meets the formal requirements for relativity I indicated earlier, since in a case of relativity, the nature or valuation of one thing varies according to some relativizing domain,[13] thus

---

[13] Which is precisely why I called them the formal requirements for *relativity*

2.6. RELATIVISM AND RELATIVITY

seeming to confirm the suspicion that was raised at the start of this section, namely that relativity and relativism are the same thing. Both involve statements of the form "x is relative to y". However, in order to account for the negative connotations in the term 'relativism', I suggest that relativism represents a stronger claim than relativity in general, that relativism includes some further feature that may or may not be present in any instance of relativity, and therefore that relativism should be considered a species of relativity. It remains for me then to identify what additional feature relativism asserts over the formal requirements that seems to characterize more general claims of relativity.

Consider Einstein's special theory of relativity, in which intervals of space and time as well as the simultaneity of events are relative to an inertial framework. The question here is whether the special theory of relativity should count as relativism, and if it should not, what feature of relativism does it fail to exemplify. Einstein asks himself the following question about the relative inertial frameworks, which he presents in terms of a train and an embankment as different reference-bodies or frames of motion for purposes of explanation:

> Can we conceive of a relation between place and time of the individual events relative to both reference-bodies, such that every ray of light possesses the velocity of transmission c relative to the embankment and relative to the train? This question leads to a quite definite positive answer, and to a perfectly definite transformation law for the space-time magnitudes of an event when changing over from one body of reference to another. (Einstein, 1954, p. 31)

On the assumption that the velocity of light is constant in each frame of motion, there is a way to transform measurements of space and time in one frame of motion to measurements in another frame of motion, namely by means of the Lorentz transformations (pp. 32–33). Einstein speaks in this context of "remov[ing] the apparent disagreement between ... two fundamental results of experience" (p. 30). The disagreement then is not entirely radical so long as there is a transformation of measurements in one frame

---

rather than for *relativism*.

of reference into measurements in another frame. This transformation seems to be precisely a denial of what I have cautiously named the thesis of incommensurability in the earlier section on reductionism. The special theory of relativity provides a path from one frame of reference to another, just as reductionism provides a path from one theory to a different theory to which it reduces, as discussed in section 2.5. Unlike reductionism, though, which identifies a preferential ordering of theories, the special theory of relativity indicates no preference for one frame of reference over another; there is no absolute space and no frame of reference that enjoys a special status over any other. In a case of relativism, on the other hand, I have suggested earlier that the thesis of incommensurability holds. The difference between relativized sub-theories in an instance of relativism is not intended to be a merely apparent disagreement that can be dissolved by a transformational law or procedure. If ethical relativism is correct, for example, there is no way to translate the ethical requirements of one culture into the ethical requirements of another. This separateness of theories is precisely the point in positing relativism rather than seeking a common factor or translational rule between them. However, at least one form of relativity, namely the special theory of relativity, does provide such a translational rule.

Consequently, I suggest that the special theory of relativity should not be considered an instance of relativism, though it certainly counts as relativity, and that the difference lies in the denial of the thesis of incommensurability within the special theory of relativity by virtue of the Lorentz transformations. *Accordingly, I propose to understand relativity in general as any doctrine that meets the formal requirements for relativity, whereas relativism is an instance of relativity that also asserts the thesis of incommensurability.* I intend to adhere to this distinction of usage throughout this study, referring generally to relativity where the thesis of incommensurability may either be accepted or rejected, and referring specifically to relativism where this thesis is accepted. Likewise, I shall use the term 'relative' as an adjective correlated with relativity in general and 'relativistic' correlated specifically with relativism.[14]

---

[14] Unfortunately, I know of no neat pair of terms distinguishing a relativist adhering to relativity from a relativist adhering to a stronger relativism, and I would prefer not to coin a new term nor to resort to unhelpful subscripts such as 'relativist$_2$' whereby I would need to remember which kind of relativist

2.7 Relativism and Contextualism

Comparing relativism with contextualism is complicated by the wide variance in contextualist theories. Even restricting the consideration of contextualism to epistemology where it has had the greatest philosophical impact outside of semantics, there is considerable disagreement over what constitutes contextualism as opposed to relativism, besides the disagreement over the main issue concerning which contextualist theory best captures the way that knowledge claims work. Thus contextualism seems to be "just an umbrella term for a wide variety of theories. Their common starting point is the thesis that the truth values of knowledge ascriptions (or ascriptions of epistemic justification) are context-dependent" (Brendel & Jäger, 2004, p. 143). Thus according to contextualism the truth of any knowledge claim is relative to some context.

The differences between various contextualist theories begin to emerge as the details are worked out concerning exactly how the truth-values of knowledge claims are context-dependent. The main areas of current dispute are as follows:

- Whose context determines the variance in truth-values: the subject or the attributor; the agent making the claim or any evaluator of the claim?

- What provides the grounds for the contextual variance: indexicality within the knowledge claim or otherwise?

- What shifts in a change of context: the threshold of justification, epistemic standards, an alternative parameter, or otherwise?

- What governs a change of context: conversational or non-conversational features?

- How does the shift from a change of context behave: across a linear scale of epistemic standards or otherwise?[15]

---

was relativist$_1$ and which was relativist$_2$. I would furthermore plead with other philosophers to stop this abhorrent practice of numerical subscripting as well. It is neither helpful nor clever.

[15] See (Brendel & Jäger, 2004) for a brief overview of these contextualist controversies.

Note that not all combinations across these areas of dispute appear to be compatible. For example, if the relevant context in the evaluation of truth-values of a knowledge claim can shift on conversational grounds, by means of something said by one of the participants within a conversation concerning the knowledge claim, then this sort of contextualism does not seem to be a variety of subject contextualism, but rather must be understood as a form of attributor contextualism. Consider a case in which two people are discussing the knowledge of a third person who is not present. If the relevant context shifts according to conversational features, then the context of the subject of the knowledge claim, the third person, does not seem to play a role at all, since he is not part of the conversation. Instead, it is the attributor's context, namely the context of either of the two participants in the conversation, that determines the variance in truth-values of the knowledge claim in question.

As in the consideration of the difference between relativity and relativism, contextualism poses a difficulty for this study in that contextualism seems to be making exactly the same sort of claim that relativism makes. The difficulty lies in determining whether contextualists are merely using a different term to avoid the unpleasant connotations of relativism or whether there is a principled difference between the two doctrines. Given the similarity of claims, it seems that contextualism should certainly count as a variety of relativity, according to the usage I suggested in the last section, since it meets the formal conditions for relativity precisely by virtue of the contextual variance of truth-values for certain claims. So does contextualism count as a form of relativism as well, and if not, what distinguishes the two kinds of claims?

It might be thought that the use of contexts as a relativizing domain provides the key difference. So perhaps contextualism is relativity according to context, and relativism is relativity according to some non-context. However, as already noted in the discussion of indexicality, whatever forms a relativizing domain in a case of relativity, such as cultures or conceptual schemes, seems also to define a context. Therefore the notion of a context cannot properly be used to distinguish contextualism from relativism.

The mention of indexicality suggests another strategy, since as noted in the discussion of indexicality earlier, the content of a sentence varies by context in a case of indexicality, whereas in a case of relativism, the content remains the same but the assignment of truth-values varies. It might be thought that the same situation governs the difference between contextualism and relativism. Indeed, contextualism occasionally been characterized precisely in terms of a variance of content of a sentence: for example, "The contextualist claim about a given sentence is that it expresses different propositions as uttered in some different contexts" (Williamson, 2005, p. 93). The problem with this characterization is that the role of indexicality is disputed among contextualists, as noted above, and therefore there seems to be room for a contextualist to maintain that the content of a knowledge claim remains the same while other contextual features determine a variance in the truth-value of the claim. In fact, John MacFarlane claims that a conflation of context-sensitivity with indexicality has hampered the debate concerning contextualism, and he outlines a version of nonindexical contextualism distinct from what he calls relativism (MacFarlane, 2009).

MacFarlane's own way of distinguishing contextualism from relativism is to focus on which context governs the context-sensitivity, the context of use or the context of assessment. "Relativism about truth ... is the view that truth (of sentences or propositions) is relative not just to contexts of use but also to contexts of assessment" (MacFarlane, 2005, p. 305). Contextualism, on the other hand, makes truth relative to the context of use (p. 309). Andy Egan, John Hawthorne, and Brian Weatherson seem to endorse this distinction (Egan, Hawthorne, & Weatherson, 2005, p. 152). The problem, however, is that the question of which context governs context-sensitivity is a disputed issue within contextualism, as noted above, and some contextualists characterize contextualism in general in terms of the context of assessment. For example, "According to standard contextualist semantics, the ascriber calls the shots, so to speak: the standards of application for the verb 'know' are determined by the ascriber and not by the subject (unless the subject happens to be identical to the ascriber)" (Ludlow, 2005, p. 15). Thus it seems that what MacFarlane calls relativism is precisely what Peter Ludlow calls contextualism.[16] Perhaps this

---

[16] For a more detailed discussion of doubts concerning MacFarlane's distinction, see (Heck, 2006). The distinction between agent and appraiser contexts, which appears to align with MacFarlane's contexts of use and of assessment, is made in (Lyons, 1976), though Lyons does not use this distinction to characterize contextualism and relativism.

would suggest that relativism is a species of contextualism, just as I have suggested that relativism is a species of relativity, or perhaps the other way around. Yet it is not clear to me what motivates MacFarlane's characterization of relativism other than a need to distinguish between kinds of contextualism. Even if a useful distinction can be made in the way that MacFarlane does, why should relativism in general be understood according to this distinction outside of discussions of contextualism? MacFarlane does not seem to argue for his characterization of relativism, so perhaps it should count merely as a stipulative definition. It is not clear, for example, that relativism has been understood historically in the way that MacFarlane characterizes it. Perhaps Protagorean relativism would best be understood in terms of contexts of assessment, but moral relativism does not obviously meet MacFarlane's characterization.

Next consider the following account of relativism proposed by Jason Stanley. It is notable here that Stanley does not characterize relativism directly in contrast with contextualism, but contrasts each separately with his preferred position, interest-relative invariantism.

> The key idea behind any version of relativism is that there is a legitimate sense of 'proposition' according to which we may speak of the truth of propositions being relative to judges, or circumstances of assessment. More generally, on any version of relativism, there is a legitimate sense of 'proposition' according to which we may speak of propositions being true relative to certain 'non-standard' features of circumstances of evaluation — that is, features of circumstances of evaluations that go beyond possible worlds and times. Similarly, according to any version of relativism, there is a legitimate notion of propositional truth according to which it is relative to certain 'non-standard' features, such as a judge or a circumstance of assessment (whatever that may be). (Stanley, 2005, p. 137)

There seem to be two key elements of Stanley's account: (1) a legitimate sense of a proposition, and (2) non-standard features

2.7. RELATIVISM AND CONTEXTUALISM

of circumstances of evaluation. The first element seems to relate to the proposed distinction between indexicality and relativism in section 2.2, in that in a case of indexicality the content of a sentence varies by context whereas the content remains constant in a case of relativism. However, as noted above, the issue of indexicality is an area of dispute within contextualism, so it is not clear that reformulating this issue in terms of a legitimate sense of a proposition will help clarify the difference between relativism and contextualism.

The second element in Stanley's account seems to attempt to identify the key difference in the nature of the relativizing domain itself. Where this domain contains standard features, namely possible worlds and times, it seems that the relativity in question is a case of contextualism, but where the domain contains non-standard features such as a judge, then the relativity in question is a case of relativism. However, the role of the judge is one of the key areas of dispute within contextualism, namely whether the key context in evaluating a knowledge statement varies by the ascriber or by the agent. Nor is it clear what other circumstance of evaluation might be taken as a non-standard feature that could distinguish relativism from contextualism. As I noted earlier, it seems that anything in a relativizing domain can serve to define a context, and for that context to have any bearing on the evaluation of the knowledge claim, it would seem to have to relate either to the ascriber or to the agent or to both, which again brings this area of dispute within contextualism back into focus.

It seems unlikely that any factors in the areas of dispute noted at the beginning of this section will be useful in distinguishing contextualism from relativism, precisely because these factors form part of the dispute within contextualism and therefore because some philosopher evidently considers those factors to be key part of contextualism. Consequently, it seems that a distinguishing factor must be found outside these disputed areas. For example, perhaps it might be supposed that in a case of contextualism, the context can shift more easily than in a case of relativism. After all, if the relevant context for knowledge claims can shift merely by a skeptic suggesting deception by an evil demon, for example, then that sort of context shift can occur much more easily than by changing cultures or even by changing conceptual schemes. Perhaps there is something to this suggestion, but note that if this suggestion provides the key difference between contextualism and relativism, the difference seems to be a matter of degrees such that there may be vague boundaries in certain cases where it may not be clear whether it is a case of contextualism or relativism. It may be, however, that all of these problematic attempts to characterize the difference between contextualism and relativism result from an excessive focus on the issues surrounding contemporary contextualism,[17] while paying little attention to the wider history of relativism. Perhaps a distinction can be made based instead on structural features of the two notions, in accordance with the guiding proposal of this study.

I propose distinguishing contextualism from relativism according to the considerations offered in the previous section on relativity. There I identified relativity as a more general notion encompassing relativism, where relativism seems to be making a stronger claim than other forms of relativity. Likewise, I would claim that relativism is making a stronger claim than contextualism. For example, no one claims that in a case of contextual knowledge, the agents or attributors in different contexts inhabit different epistemic worlds, whatever these might be, as it might be claimed that moral agents in different cultures inhabit different moral worlds. Rather, epistemic agents or attributors inhabit the same world in which epistemic claims manifest themselves differently in different contexts, which is what makes it possible for a skeptic to confuse someone making an ordinary knowledge claim by appealing to an evil deceiving demon and thereby improperly changing the context, as the standard contextualist account would have it. Something shifts in the epistemic situation when the context changes, according to contextualism, but what shifts seems to be not quite as radical as a comparable shift according to relativism, else no one would be confused by the troublemaking skep-

---

[17] For example, since truth enters into knowledge claims twice, there is room for a double relativity with regard to knowledge, which the accounts considered do not seem to accommodate very well. Truth is certainly evaluated with regard to the knowledge claim itself, but truth is also evaluated with regard to the object of knowledge, the statement that is known or not known. Since both of these truth evaluations may be relative, perhaps relative to different factors, an account of relativity with regard to knowledge claims becomes correspondingly more complicated. A concern with relativism in general would need to take both possible relativizations of truth into account, as will be proposed later in sections 7.2.1 and 7.4.

2.7. RELATIVISM AND CONTEXTUALISM

tic. A more radical shift would leave an ordinary knower wondering what the skeptic was talking about or even flatly convinced that the skeptic was wrong or insane.

This line of consideration seems to capture my earlier suggestion that the difference between contextualism and relativism lies in the easier change of context in contextualism as compared with relativism. The problem I noted there was that this leaves the difference between the two doctrines merely as a matter of degree. If there is more to the difference than this, then the difference in strength between the claims of contextualism and relativism should lie in some determinate factor between the two.

I suggest that the same factor that differentiated relativism from other forms of relativity likewise differentiates relativism from contextualism. To be precise, *relativism is a variety of relativity that accepts the thesis of incommensurability whereas contextualism is a variety of relativity that denies it, where incommensurability involves the absence of some means for correlating the various relativized sub-theories.*[18] Consider the question of what shifts in a context change according to epistemic contextualism, whether the threshold of justification, epistemic standards, or alternative parameters (Schaffer, 2005). In the case of thresholds or standards, contextualist accounts hold that these thresholds or standards can be raised or lowered across some scale such that a skeptic can raise them to a level at which knowledge claims that once were considered true no longer are true. The ability to negotiate various knowledge claims across the variance of thresholds or standards is what constitutes understanding of the words like 'know' or 'knowledge'. Yet this ability to negotiate knowledge claims along a scale suggests that knowledge claims evaluated across the scale are somehow commensurable, that a common account can be provided such that raising standards or thresholds tends to make knowledge claims false at some point whereas lowering them tends to make them true at some point. If, on the other hand, it is some alternative parameter that is taken to shift upon a change of context, competent users of the word 'know' likewise understand how that shifting parameter gets applied to the knowledge claim and results in a difference in truth-values for the claim in different con-

---

[18] As in the prior discussions of reductionism and relativity, I leave the notion of incommensurability somewhat indeterminate at this point. Chapter 6 will be devoted to the task of clarifying this notion.

texts. Again, it would appear to be the very commensurability of knowledge claims under contextualism that accounts for the skeptic's ability to make an apparently plausible though allegedly fallacious argument, whereas the proper recognition of contextualism serves to disarm the skeptic's argument, at least according to the doctrine of epistemic contextualism.

As with my distinction between relativity and relativism, if the distinction I am drawing between contextualism and relativism here is not supported by actual usage, then I would offer it as a proposal for future usage, failing any other workable distinction between the two doctrines. Note, for example, that what Max Kölbel calls "indexical relativism" (Kölbel, 2004), insofar as it relies upon the indexicality of certain terms, would be considered contextualism not relativism under the distinction I am drawing here. Ultimately, though, the proposed distinction will be acceptable to the extent to which it helps clarify philosophical discussions beyond the bounds of this study, but within this study I will adhere to this distinction.

The distinctions drawn in this chapter were made primarily to provide the basis for a better understanding of relativism and its relation to structurally similar notions. These discussions suggest that relativism involves three major elements: (1) certain formal requirements for relativity, (2) the thesis of incommensurability, and (3) the thesis of objective equity. The next chapter will seek to combine the suggestions made in this chapter into a workable definition of relativism against which the logic of relativism could be formulated.

Chapter 3

Definition of Relativism

Several writers have commented on the difficulty of providing a general definition of relativism (Baghramian, 2004, p. 3; Kölbel, 2004, p. 298), while Joseph Margolis notes that relativism remains "poorly defined" (Margolis, 2006, p. 246). Max Kölbel identifies three reasons for this situation:

> First, the shere [sic] variety of claims that have been called 'relativist' makes it difficult to find a non-trivial core of theses that is shared by all relativists. Secondly, 'relativism' is sometimes used as a term of abuse. Those who use the term in this way might object to any definition of relativism that classifies as relativistic theses they regard as too reasonable-looking. Thirdly and relatedly, opponents of relativism frequently use unfavorable definitions of relativism as a starting point for their objections. The characterization of relativism that follows is therefore inevitably partly stipulative in character. (p. 298)

I think Kölbel's diagnosis is correct. Like Socrates in asking what justice or virtue is, what I am seeking is not an enumeration of particular kinds of relativism, but the meaning of relativism itself. So an analysis of moral relativism or conceptual relativism, for example, will only show how relativism gets applied in particular areas, not necessarily what relativism is in general. At the same time, it seems that a general definition of relativism should apply to every particular case of relativism. Yet this hope for a strict analysis of relativism into genus and species seems threatened by the wide diversity of kinds of relativism, which may in fact diverge too widely to be unified under a general definition.

However, while Kölbel in his second and third reasons identifies opponents of relativism as contributors to the confusion over the proper characterization of relativism in general, I would add a fourth reason that shares the blame with supporters of relativism. In attempting to formulate a workable version of relativism that overcomes the various objections to relativism that have been developed during its history, it may happen that supporters end up with a doctrine that is not really relativism at all. So while the aim originally may have been to save the doctrine of relativism, what is saved may mainly be the term 'relativism'. Of course, in order to recognize that such a shift has actually occurred within the history of relativism, one would need a workable definition of relativism in general from which deviances could be identified, and such a definition is precisely what is at issue. Still, if opponents of relativism can sometimes take fairly unfavorable definitions of relativism as a starting point for objections, as Kölbel notes, then it would not be surprising if supporters should attempt to frame relativism in the most favorable light. I think it is appropriate to ask of such formulations or reformulations of relativism: what makes them relativistic? In the course of reformulating relativism, it seems to me that supporters must not only overcome prior objections to relativism, but they must also show why the new formulation still counts as relativism. In some cases, attempts to save a doctrine might amount to a refutation of that doctrine if they deviate too sharply from the original doctrine.

So I agree with Kölbel also that the definition of relativism that I offer here must be partly stipulative. A general definition of relativism, if accepted, would serve as a corrective not only to some putatively relativistic doctrines that stray too far from relativism to merit that term, if 'merit' can properly be used with regard to so reviled a notion as relativism, but also as a corrective to some doctrines that ultimately should count as relativism, even though their proponents may have shied away from that term due to its negative connotations.

3.1 Proposed Definition

Relativism is radical indexed pluralism. This definition is brief, some may think it too brief, but I suggest that it adequately captures the nature of relativism. I am generally suspicious of short and simple definitions of complex notions, since they risk oversimplification and ultimately misunderstanding. Yet the merit of this proposed definition, I think, is that it allows the full complexity of the notion of relativism to be developed from out of this simple definition, as I will shortly explain. First, though, I will attempt to offer some justification for the three key terms in the proposed definition.

Pluralism: I claim that relativism is a species of pluralism, as discussed in section 2.3. With regard to theories, pluralism holds that for some domain of discourse there is more than one different theory or account that is adequate or true. Since relativism likewise posits more than one adequate theory, it thus seems to count as a variety of pluralism. Typically when pluralism is discussed, it seems to be a non-relativistic form of pluralism that is intended, but given that pluralism and relativism would share a common fate if it could be shown that there is just one adequate theory where pluralism and relativism posit more than one, it seems proper to link the two together. Pluralism seems to be the more general doctrine, since relativism displays additional features that pluralism in general lacks, as I will suggest next.

Indexed: The key difference between pluralism and relativism is that where pluralism accepts a simple plurality of theories, relativism constrains that plurality by relativizing those theories to some factor, such as cultures or individual persons. Relativism is an indexed pluralism, since each of the multiple theories is indexed to some element in the relativizing domain, where this indexing relation is more than a mere arbitrary assignment of theories to elements. Note that this sort of indexing is not the same as indexicality, which concerns certain context-sensitive features of language, as discussed in section 2.2, but indicates a stronger relationship between the theories and the relativizing domain.

Radical: There are other forms of indexed pluralism, such as contextualism and relativity in physics. What distinguishes relativism from these others is the depth of the relation between the theories and the relativizing domain. Roughly speaking, in a case of relativism, indexed pluralism is not a mere surface appearance, but runs closer to reality, going all the way down to the root of the matter, as suggested by the word 'radical'. It may seem that this difference in depth may be a question of degrees with no strict delimiting point between relativism and contextualism, but as I shall soon point out, there does seem to be a fairly clear test to distinguish cases of radical indexed pluralism from less radical versions.

This word-by-word analysis has been fairly cursory, but a deeper and more useful analysis of the proposed definition of relativism can be derived from a consideration of the terms in combination, namely in pairs. This pattern of analysis yields three substantive theses of relativism that elaborate on the proposed three-word definition of relativism, and these are precisely the three theses identified in the previous chapter, namely the formal requirements for relativity, the thesis of objective equity, and the thesis of incommensurability.[1] Each of the three theses requires extensive analysis, which will follow in subsequent chapters. Here I merely indicate the role that each thesis plays in the definition of relativism.

3.1.1 Indexed Pluralism: the Formal Requirements for Relativity

Indexed pluralism merely indicates a general case of relativity, one in which it is said that something is relative to something else. This general pattern of relativity sets a formal requirement for relativism, since it can be articulated on merely formal grounds according to the formula "x is relative to y".

First, there must be a set of theories adequate to some domain of discourse, whether that domain is morality, cultural practices, or whatever. In the terminology established at the beginning of the

---

[1] Compare these theses with a list by F. C. White of three things that must be shown to demonstrate that set of beliefs is relative: "one, that there exists, or may exist, an alternative set of beliefs which is different from and not complimentary to the initial set; two, that we have no means of deciding rationally which set is correct, or that neither is correct; three, that it does not even make sense to say that this or that set is correct to the exclusion of the other; or again that neither is correct" (White, 1982, p. 4). I think that White captures most of my proposed definition, except for incommensurability. I intend to motivate and substantiate my list of three theses to show why all of these theses are needed in an instance of relativism.

previous chapter, this set of theories is the *range of relativized sub-theories*. The topic of theories in this range stands in the x place of the formula "x is relative to y".

Second, there must a set of factors that relativize the theories, such as a set of cultures in a case of cultural relativism, or a set of individual persons in a case of Protagorean relativism. I have called this set of factors the *relativizing domain*. Elements in this set stand in the y place of the formula "x is relative to y". Thus once it is determined which element in the relativizing domain applies in a given case, it is thereby determined which theory in the relativized range of theories applies in that case.

Third, there needs to be some variance in the relation between the elements of the relativizing domain and the relativized sub-theories. It would seem improper to say that x is relative to y, if there were only one y or even none at all. Such a case would merely be an instance of pluralism, since there would be no relativization from sub-theories to different elements in the relativizing domain. Likewise, each of the relativized sub-theories cannot be identical, so that for any element of the relativizing domain, there would then be no difference in the corresponding theory. Such a case would not be relativism or even pluralism, but an ordinary non-relativistic single theory.

Other formal requirements for relativity will be discussed in greater detail in the following chapter.

I will sometimes speak of perspectives in discussing either the relativized sub-theories or the relativizing domain, but I do not intend these to be mysterious abstract entities. For the purposes of this study, perspectives are merely sub-theories that are indexed to some element in the relativizing domain. Thus perspectives merely provide a convenient way of talking indifferently about elements in the relativizing domain or the sub-theories that are indexed to them.[2]

---

[2] I will occasionally speak loosely of perspectives *holding* theories, but I do not intend to mean by this that a relativized sub-theory is whatever some group happens to believe, that there is no difference between truth and belief. Rather, I take holding in this sense simply to be equivalent to indexing, namely that a particular sub-theory is true or valid for some group, whether that group actually knows or believes the theory. So a theory may be indexed to a group that explicitly endorses some other theory, in which case it could be claimed that the group should properly hold a different theory. Consequently, I take it that there is still some room for normativity within relativism.

3.1.2 Radical Indexing: the Thesis of Objective Equity

It is common to hear in accounts of relativism the claim that none of the relativized sub-theories is any better than the others. Since the term 'better' has moral connotations that tend to influence the evaluation of relativism, particularly with regard to moral relativism and the question of the relationship between relativism and tolerance (Harrison, 1976), I prefer to speak more blandly of *objective equity* to describe this observation. In relativism, then, each of the relativized sub-theories thus shares a state of objective equity with every other relativized sub-theory. It is thus impossible to order the sub-theories uniquely according to any objective preference such that one sub-theory is preferable over all of the others.

The key notion here is clearly objectivity, since it is easy to order the sub-theories on subjective grounds, namely by placing them in whatever order by which I personally prefer them. The problem of course is that other people's subjective preference will likely differ from mine, which is why the theories are part of a relativistic system. Yet leaving such subjective preferences aside, the notion of objectivity that is operative with regard to this thesis needs to be clarified further, since some objective orderings will cause similar problems. For example, placing the theories in alphabetical order according to the name that they are given seems perfectly objective. However, it is a contingent matter that theories are given the names they have, and some may have multiple names, so it would seem arbitrary to prefer one theory to another because its name comes earlier in some alphabetical order. Furthermore, there are different conceptions of objectivity available, not all of which are fully relevant to the kind of objectivity required here, and indeed many of these conceptions seem precisely opposed to relativism insofar as they seem to require a denial of pluralism. So this study will need to clarify what sort of objectivity is required in this case.

If, in a case of putative relativism, one relativized sub-theory were preferred over the others on some universal objective grounds, this would seem to subvert the kind of indexing that is posited by the formal requirement for relativity. In such a case, it seems that the preferred sub-theory should be preferred across the entire relativizing domain, since if the preference is made on objective grounds, those grounds will apply to every element in

3.1. PROPOSED DEFINITION

the relativizing domain. What seemed to be a case of relativism would thus ultimately seem to be an unusual presentation of a non-relativistic theory in which a range of incorrect theories is presented as relativized, but all under the shadow of a single correct theory that is objectively to be preferred over the others. Yet relativism is not typically concerned with relativizing errors, but in relativizing truths. For this reason, the thesis of objective equity suggests that the indexing of relativized sub-theories is radical rather than a surface phenomenon, and that the kind of objectivity operative in this thesis allows that each relativized sub-theory compares equally well or equally poorly according to that conception of objectivity. What seems most important to this requirement is ultimately the equity of relativized sub-theories, not the mere assertion of objectivity, and it is still important to qualify the kind of equity required by the particular notion of objectivity operative in relativism, which will be established in chapter 5.

3.1.3 Radical Pluralism: the Thesis of Incommensurability

Suppose that in a case of putative relativism it could be shown that each of the relativized sub-theories could be transformed into each other according to some rule, perhaps by means of some additional open parameter that is given a value from the relativizing domain. In such a case, the pluralism that was posited would seem to be merely apparent, since either the relativized sub-theories would appear to be fundamentally the same theory or there would be a single unifying theory that accounts for contextual differences in the relativized sub-theories according to the role played by elements in the relativizing domain. Such a case would not seem to be thoroughly relativistic, precisely because the pluralism involved was not radical but a mere surface phenomenon.

It is common in such a case to say that the relativized sub-theories are therefore incommensurable, so I have called the requirement for radical pluralism *the thesis of incommensurability*. However, it is not immediately clear how this sort of incommensurability relates to the use of the term in the work of Thomas Kuhn and other writers, nor what sort of incommensurability is specifically required in this case. Still, the term does seem appropriate and does appear within literature on relativism, so I adopt it pend-ing further clarification.

As discussed in section 2.6 above, one notable example of the denial of the thesis of incommensurability occurs in the special theory of relativity, in which Einstein uses the Lorentz transformations to transform measurements made in one inertial framework into measurements into another framework (Einstein, 1954, pp. 32–33). It is precisely because of this transformation that Einstein's theory is not a case of relativism, though it obviously counts as relativity. In Einstein's theory, there are not multiple different theories relativized to inertial frameworks, but a single theory encompassing the difference in measurements across frameworks. A more detailed understanding of the kind of incommensurability that is operative in relativism will be worked out in chapter 6.

As noted earlier, the definition of relativism proposed here will likely need to be considered a stipulative definition. However, it seems to me that a good definition of relativism, whether stipulative or otherwise, should enable a fruitful analysis of relativism both with regard to its past history and on a continuing basis in the future. Accordingly, in the remainder of this chapter, I will attempt to apply this definition to a number of key discussions of relativism, for the purposes of illustration, starting with the relativism of Protagoras as discussed by Plato in the *Theaetetus*. I then consider two analytic philosophers who have explicitly proposed and endorsed versions of relativism, Nelson Goodman and Gilbert Harman. Next I discuss the efforts of two contemporary philosophers who have sought to understand the nature of relativism, Joseph Margolis and Max Kölbel. Finally, I evaluate the postmodernism of Jean-François Lyotard, which some have thought to represent a form of relativism.[3] My intent in these discussions is to show that the proposed definition provides a useful framework for understanding and evaluating various claims of relativism.

Some of these discussions of relativism may not accord well with the proposed definition at all. It might seem that these instances would provide counterexamples to the proposed definition. However, as already noted, the aim of the proposed defi-

---

[3] There are a number of more contentious discussions of relativism, particularly with regard to the work of Thomas Kuhn, some of which I will discuss in later chapters, some of which I will merely mention in passing. In this chapter, however, I have sought to restrict my discussion to cases in which relativism is either explicitly endorsed or can clearly be demonstrated.

nition is not to provide a conception of relativism that will cover every actual use of the term 'relativism' by some philosopher or other. Rather the aim is to provide a useful understanding of relativism according to which various claims about relativism can be evaluated. Where the claims of certain thinkers do not accord with the proposed definition, perhaps those thinkers should not properly understand their doctrines to be instances of relativism. If there are already doubts concerning whether those doctrines should count as genuine cases of relativism, then it would seem that the proposed definition would thereby demonstrate its usefulness in identifying why such doubts may have arisen. Therefore, the following discussions should be considered exercises in application of the proposed definition of relativism in an attempt to demonstrate the usefulness of that definition.

3.2 Protagoras

It seems that Protagoras' "man is the measure" doctrine is the paradigm case of relativism. If this doctrine does not count as relativism, then it would seem that nothing does. Unfortunately, little of Protagoras' own writings on this doctrine survive beyond the barest outline: "a man is the measure of all things: of those which are, that they are, and of those which are not, that they are not" (Plato, 1973, p. 16, 152a). Plato analyses this doctrine in some detail in the *Theaetetus*, and whether or not Plato's understanding of Protagoras' doctrine matches Protagoras' intentions seems merely an academic concern, since it is Plato's analysis of the "man is the measure" doctrine that has been most influential with regard to the history of relativism. Consequently, I will focus on Plato's treatment of Protagorean relativism here and resist speculating on what Protagoras' true intentions may have been.[4]

An overview of the dialogue was presented in the preface of this study, but I will review some aspects here in order to apply the proposed definition of relativism given in the previous section. The theme of the *Theaetetus* is the question of what knowledge is. Socrates invokes Protagoras in the dialogue in response to Theaetetus' first proposed definition of knowledge as perception (151e). Immediately, Socrates equates this definition with Pro-

---

[4] For an attempt to reconstruct Protagoras' thinking, see (Zilioli, 2007).

tagoras' "man is the measure" doctrine, and no sooner has he presented this doctrine to Theaetetus, but he suggests that Protagoras also held a secret doctrine separate from his publicly available teachings, namely the doctrine of Heraclitean flux (152c–e). Later, Socrates claims to have shown that "the three theories have turned out to coincide" (160d).

Strictly speaking, though, Socrates has not shown that the three theories are identical. In the discussion from (158e) to (160e), he has shown only that given Heraclitean flux, Protagorean relativism follows, and that given Protagorean relativism, it follows that perception is knowledge. In order to show that the three theories are identical, he would have to demonstrate that chain of entailment in reverse. Yet since Socrates' main concern in this dialogue is the nature and meaning of knowledge, it is not particularly important for this purpose that the three theories are identical, only that they yield the same conclusions in certain situations. John McDowell claims "the suggestion that Protagoras secretly taught the doctrine which follows [namely Heraclitean flux] is almost certainly not meant to be taken seriously" (Plato, 1973, p. 121),[5] and he suggests the following reason for the inclusion of the doctrine of the flux in the dialogue, "that Plato takes the secret doctrine to be an implication of Protagoras' explicit doctrine, so that Protagoras ought, in view of his explicit doctrine, to have taught the secret doctrine" (p. 122).[6] However, given the direction of implication in the demonstration that the three doctrines coincide, this suggestion seems misplaced. Socrates shows that Protagoras' "man is the measure" doctrine is an implication of the secret doctrine, not the reverse.

I think a better interpretation of the relation of the three doctrines is that Protagorean relativism provides one possible ground for thinking that perception is knowledge, and in turn, Heraclitean flux provides one possible ground for believing in Protagorean rel-

---

[5] In McDowell's notes to his translation of the dialogue.

[6] It may seem puzzling why Plato would have Socrates make the suggestion of a secret doctrine at all, if it is not to be taken seriously, as McDowell claims. It is less puzzling once it is recognized that Plato himself held a secret doctrine that he maintained as an oral teaching for his students, separate from his writings. See (Reale, 1997) for a description of this doctrine and an argument that an understanding of this secret doctrine is important to interpreting Plato's writings.

3.2. PROTAGORAS

ativism.[7] So in addressing the Protagorean and Heraclitean doctrines, Socrates is attempting to undermine two possible reasons that Theaetetus might believe that all knowledge is perception. In any case, Socrates addresses each doctrine separately: Protagoras in (161b–179d), Heraclitus in (179d–184b), and Theaetetus' first definition of knowledge in (184b–187a). Consequently, I will focus just on Plato's discussion of Protagoras and ignore the rest of the dialogue.

It seems surprising that more of Protagoras' treatise *Truth* is not quoted in the *Theaetetus*, since both Socrates and Theaetetus seem to have read it (152a), and Socrates intends to convict Protagoras on the basis of his own words (169e). Yet perhaps Mi-Kyoung Lee is correct that Protagoras' treatise likely did not contain any sustained discussion of the doctrine (M.-K. Lee, 2005, pp. 22-29). While the "man is the measure" doctrine teases the imagination in the pithy form in which is has been transmitted through Plato and other ancient writers, perhaps it would seem less interesting if Protagoras' actual views concerning the doctrine were available. In any case, though, as quoted by Plato the statement of the doctrine itself is ambiguous in its meaning. First, the nature of a measure is not clear. Socrates begins by linking Protagoras' doctrine to Theaetetus' definition of knowledge as perception, yet he later extends the application of the Protagorean doctrine beyond perception, as Myles Burnyeat points out, to "a law or practice (167c) or someone's opinion (171a)" (1990, p. 21). Jonathan Barnes interprets the notion of a measure both in a phenomenological and in a judgmental sense (Barnes, 1979, pp. 240–242). Socrates clearly applies the notion of a measure in a judgmental sense, even if he occasionally uses terms that favor a phenomenological reading, in accordance with his main concern surrounding the supposition that knowledge is perception.

Second, the scope of the word 'man' is not clear. It may extend just to an individual person, as McDowell translates it (Plato, 1973, p. 119), or it may extend to all of humanity as opposed to other species, or even just to a social group.[8] Socrates, though, clearly understands the scope to extend to the level of an individual: "everything is, for me, the way it appears to me, and is, for you, the

---

[7] For a similar interpretation, see (M.-K. Lee, 2005, p. 90 ff).

[8] See (Balaban, 1999, pp. 299–304) for a discussion of these options.

way it appears to you; and you and I are, each of us, a man" (152a).

Third, precisely what is being measured is not clear. From the statement of the doctrine alone, it seems that the judgments being made are ontological only, in other words, judgments concerning what things exist: "of those which are, that they are, and of those which are not, that they are not" (152a). Barnes claims that this existential interpretation "has a superficial attraction" (Barnes, 1979, p. 242), but does not see how the Greek text can support it with regard to negative judgments. Socrates clearly understands the judgments made under Protagorean relativism to be not merely existential but also predicative judgments: "shall we say that the wind itself, taken by itself is cold or not cold?" (152b). What is measured here is not the wind's existence, but what qualities the wind has.

So as understood by Socrates, Protagorean relativism holds that any judgments are relative to individual humans. This understanding, then, seems to meet the formal requirements for relativity, according to the formula "x is relative to y", and therefore counts as a case of relativity. Indeed it seems that Socrates' self-refutation argument is directed precisely against these formal requirements and their global scope, since it seems that in asserting this doctrine, Protagoras must acknowledge that the judgment of those who disagree with the doctrine is true, with the result that the doctrine is not true for anyone, "since it's disputed by everyone" (171c). By positing a form of global relativity, Protagoras has obliged himself to be subject to its consequences, even when those consequences seem to count against the doctrine itself. So Protagoras must concede that in allowing those who disagree with the doctrine to be correct, he himself cannot acknowledge the truth of the doctrine, at least according to the argument. Note that in the version of the self-refutation argument presented by Socrates, the point is not that the doctrine itself is incoherent because it entails its own denial as a consequence, but that a person accepting the doctrine must acknowledge that the doctrine is false and must therefore reject it, whether it is coherent or not. I think this difference is important to how Socrates intends this argument to work against Protagoras.

Though Theodorus thinks that this argument successfully refutes Protagoras (179b), it is not clear that Socrates intends it to be a refutation in itself. First, as McDowell notes, the conclusion of the argument is dubious since the argument seems to shift from a qualified notion of truth, namely true-for-someone, to an unqualified notion of truth, which seems to undermine the argument on formal grounds, though McDowell admits that "it still leaves Protagoras in a vulnerable position" (Plato, 1973, p. 171). Gregory Vlastos suggests that this indicates a lack of care on Plato's part, "thereby inadvertently vitiating his own polemic" (Vlastos, 1956, p. xiv, n. 27). Burnyeat, however, thinks that there is a way to understand the argument so that it succeeds while also explaining why self-refutation counts as a problem for the theory (Burnyeat, 1990, p. 179), and in doing so gives Plato "the benefit of the doubt once, the first time he omits the qualifier" (p. 184) on the notion of truth.

Second, this argument does not close Socrates' discussion of Protagoras' doctrine, as might be expected if Socrates considered the self-refutation argument to provide a clear refutation of Protagoras. Instead, after engaging in a digression about the ineptitude of philosophers in the law courts (172b–177c), Socrates resumes the direct discussion of Protagoras with Theodorus, finally concluding several pages later at (179c) before proceeding to evaluate the doctrine of the flux. If the self-refutation argument had been intended to be definitive, then Socrates would seem to be beating a dead horse in these final stages of the discussion.

Third, the self-refutation argument considered as such does not seem to correspond to Socrates' usual pattern of argument. Typically, Socrates questions someone who claims to know something until he has obliged that person to agree to a statement that contradicts that alleged knowledge, then for that person to admit that he did not know it after all. This is the kind of self-refutation that Socrates usually seeks.[9] The self-refutation argument in the *Theaetetus* is one that Socrates might have worked out in isolation and written in a book, without questioning anyone. Indeed in his earlier defense of Protagoras, Socrates claims on his behalf, "when it's something of mine that you're investigating by putting questions, I'm refuted if the person who had the question put to him trips up because of giving the sort of answer I'd give; if he has given a different sort of answer, he's the one who is refuted — the person who had the question put to him" (166a–b). So the self-refutation argument would refute Protagoras if the person answer-

---

[9] This corresponds to what John Passmore calls *ad hominem* self-refutation, as will be discussed in section 8.1 below. This point is noted also in (Castagnoli, 2004, p. 20).

ing on his behalf, in this case Theodorus, gives the kind of answer that Protagoras himself would give. However, immediately after the self-refutation argument, Socrates imagines Protagoras popping up out of the ground to "convict me of talking a great deal of nonsense, and you [Theodorus] of agreeing to it" (171d).[10] Consequently, Socrates does not seem to think here that Theodorus is giving the kind of answers that Protagoras would give, and therefore that Protagoras is not really refuted by the self-refutation argument according to the kind of self-refutation that Socrates seeks.[11]

A fourth reason I would add for thinking that the self-refutation argument is not primarily intended by Socrates as a refutation of Protagoras is that the conclusion of the self-refutation argument does not match either the stated aim of the discussion in which it appears, or the ultimate conclusion that attains that aim. Once Socrates has finally managed to draw Theodorus into the discussion, the aim that he articulates at this point is to establish from Protagoras' own words "that some people are superior to others on the question of what's better or worse, and that it's those people who are wise" (169d). Socrates had proposed this claim as part of a defense of Protagoras, but this seems to be a somewhat shady defense, since it effectively refutes the scope of Protagoras' doctrine: if the judgment of some is superior to others in certain cases, then man is the measure not of all things, but at best only of some things. Clearly, Socrates is aware that "someone might perhaps rule that we haven't the authority to make admissions on his behalf" (169e), and rightly so, since this admission would seem to be a fatal one for Protagoras to make. So the aim in the discussion is to get this admission from Protagoras' own words.

Furthermore, the conclusion of the self-refutation argument does not strictly meet this aim. The conclusion of the argument in

---

[10] The imagery here is peculiar, with Protagoras popping out of the ground only from the head up, then ducking down and rushing off again. See (Ford, 1994) for a discussion of various interpretations of this imagery and a novel interpretation of his own. For my preferred interpretation, see the preface above.

[11] No doubt there are interpretations that may overcome these problems and establish the self-refutation argument as Socrates' chief refutation of Protagoras. However, I will suggest below a different interpretation that subordinates the self-refutation argument to a broader strategy on Socrates' part, one that makes sense of a number of puzzling features of this section of the dialogue and that involves more of my proposed definition of relativism than the mere formal requirements for relativity.

itself is "that Protagoras' *Truth* isn't true for anyone: not for anyone else, and not for Protagoras himself" (171c), but the intended conclusion of this general line of discussion is "that anyone whatever will admit at least this: some people are wiser than others, some more ignorant" (171d). However, while Theodorus agrees to this last point, Socrates has not shown that Protagoras himself admits this, as Socrates himself recognizes, since he has just invoked Protagoras from out of the ground to disagree with the self-refutation argument. So this argument does not seem to have met Socrates' stated aim to get an admission from Protagoras' own words that some people's judgments are better than others at this point.

This aim relates precisely to what I have called the thesis of objective equity. If man is the measure of all things, then there is no other measure of the judgments of people than those same judgments and those who make them, and therefore no one judgment is better than any other, objectively speaking, neither of men nor of gods (162c). So I argue that Socrates' main objective in this portion of the dialogue and his main refutation of Protagoras' doctrine is to get Protagoras himself to deny the thesis of objective equity by acknowledging that some people's judgments are better than others, and that it is by virtue of knowledge that some judgments are better. Indeed, Socrates does finally succeed in this goal when he gets Theodorus to testify that Protagoras himself admitted that he was better than others in determining what would be most effective in courts of law (178e). Once this admission on Protagoras' part is made, the discussion of Protagoras' doctrine is quickly brought to a close, indicating that Socrates' primary objectives have been met by this admission.

According to this interpretation, then, the status of the self-refutation argument would need to be re-evaluated. I suggest that Socrates and Plato clearly understood the force of the argument of self-refutation as well as its limitations.[12] Yet a bare argument that the doctrine is self-refuting does not properly fit into Socrates' general methodology, as already noted. For Socrates, it is not the formal self-refutation of a doctrine that counts, but that the holder of the doctrine should refute himself by means of his own admissions. Perhaps Plato and Socrates could not find a way to get Protagoras to make such an admission without an illicit shift in

---

[12] Though for doubts on this point, see (Waterlow, 1977, p. 29).

the relativistic qualifiers on the notion of truth, as noted earlier, but still wanted to present the self-refutation argument for what value it does have, namely in casting doubts on the coherence of the doctrine. Yet the argument would still serve a role if it could provoke Protagoras through his defender Theodorus to point out what was wrong with the argument. If Protagoras could be made to admit that his judgment concerning the self-refutation argument was better than Socrates', then he will thereby have denied the thesis of objective equity in at least one instance.[13] If Protagoras corrects Socrates at this point, then his very correction would seem implicitly to constitute a claim that his judgment was better than Socrates'. If Protagoras thereby denies the thesis of objective equity, then insofar as Protagoras is endorsing relativism in his "man is the measure" doctrine, according to the proposed definition of relativism in this study, he will thereby have denied the very relativism he claims to be endorsing. This is precisely the kind of denial that would match Socrates' stated aim and conclusion in this section.[14]

Strictly speaking, of course, the self-refutation that Socrates elicits from Protagoras by means of Theodorus' testimony does not disprove the thesis of objective equity with regard to Protagorean relativism, since Protagoras' claim that he is better than others at determining what is best to say in a courtroom is still a distinctly subjective judgment, and does not establish that his judgments are in some way objectively to be preferred to the judgments of others. However, it is certainly embarrassing for the proponent of a doctrine to assert something contrary to that doctrine, and that is all that is required for the purposes of the Socratic method. That Socrates frames his refutation of Protagoras against the thesis of objective equity at all demonstrates that this thesis forms an important component of Protagorean relativism, and this demonstration is my main purpose here.

Given the nature of Protagoras' doctrine, it is not surprising

---

[13] This kind of provocative or ironic interpretation of the self-refutation argument is not new with me, but seems to have originated with Edward N. Lee (1973). Burnyeat also seems to appreciate the potential for the interpretation, even if he does not fully adopt it (Burnyeat, 1976b, p. 191). It is likewise noted in (Castagnoli, 2004, pp. 23–24).

[14] The preface above offers a full textual reading of this section of the *Theaetetus* that aims to substantiate this interpretation.

3.2. PROTAGORAS

that the theme of measurement arises several times in the dialogue. Besides the reference to measure in the articulation of the Protagorean doctrine, Socrates echoes Protagoras' language when he considers "if what we measure ourselves against or touch had been large, white, or hot, it would never have become different by bumping into a different person" (154b). Furthermore, in discussing the nature of vision, he mentions "an eye, then, and something else, one of the things commensurable with it" (156d). Earlier in the dialogue, Theaetetus relates how he and his friend classified various numbers with similar characteristics under a single name, including his classification of incommensurable magnitudes (147d).

It is tempting to see in Plato's mention of incommensurable numbers some reference to incommensurability with regard to Protagorean relativism. Perhaps just as Theaetetus was able to show that various kinds of incommensurable magnitudes can still be described together according to a single account of incommensurability, so will Socrates be able to show that he can evaluate apparently incommensurable judgments resulting from the "man is the measure" doctrine by a common measure, namely knowledge. However, this temptation may be stretching the interpretation too far and seems more like an overzealous attempt by a commentator to read his favored definition of relativism into the dialogue.[15]

While it is not immediately obvious that the mention of measure or incommensurables appearing in the dialogue indicates that the notion of incommensurability plays a significant role in Protagoras' doctrine according to what I have called the thesis of incommensurability in the proposed definition of relativism, I think that a role can be inferred. The question with regard to the thesis of incommensurability is whether there is a single theory that can account for the differences in the various relativized judgments, whether there is some path from one judgment to another.[16] There is clearly a difference between various relativized

---

[15] Though interestingly, another commentator on Protagoras has also cautiously invoked incommensurability: "I will not claim that any form of incommensurability is formulated in any section of the Platonic dialogues that concern Protagoras; what I wish to do is to get a better grasp of Protagorean relativism by attempting to make his doctrine a more coherent one through the use of the notion of incommensurability" (Zilioli, 2007, p. 70).

[16] Again, this question will be discussed in more detail in chapter 6.

Protagorean judgments discussed in the dialogue, such as judgments concerning whiteness or hotness, but it is not clear that these different judgments are thereby incommensurable. It may be that there is a common account including some open contextual parameter that could explain why one person makes a particular judgment and another person makes a contrary judgment. If such were the case, then it would seem that the Protagorean doctrine would not be particularly radical, but would amount to a kind of contextualism, though it would certainly be anachronistic to read a distinction between relativism and contextualism into Plato's dialogue. Yet if there were some kind of transformation between relativized Protagorean judgments comparable to the Lorentz transformations in the special theory of relativity, then the thesis of incommensurability would thereby be denied, and according to the definition of relativism proposed in this study, the Protagorean doctrine would not count as a variety of relativism.

Indeed Socrates' reference to the commensurability between the eye and its objects when giving an account of vision (156d) suggests that such an account might be given, since once it is recognized that vision only occurs with regard to objects commensurable with the mechanism of the eye, judgments based on vision can be understood in terms of the nature of the eye and the objects of vision. Even if there were a common account of vision, this alone would not invalidate the doctrine that man is the measure, but this account would certainly show that the doctrine is not as radical as Protagoras may have thought it to be.[17] Nor would this account of vision refute the radical relativity of non-sensory judgments, such as judgments concerning what is best for the state (172a), which would require a separate account explaining the differences in non-sensory judgments. Yet these considerations do suggest that Protagorean relativism does in fact require the thesis of incommensurability to prevent explanations of the variance in judgments from explaining the relativism away altogether. A common account of judgments would show that man is not primarily the measure of all things, but that there is a more fundamental

---

[17] So perhaps it is therefore understandable that Socrates' refutation of Protagoras would be on the basis of the thesis of objective equity, as I have argued earlier, rather than on the basis of incommensurability, since a failure of objective equity would more effectively refute Protagoras, rather than merely weaken his doctrine to a kind of contextualism, as I understand it in this study.

measure of all things by which men judge things to be true, and that it is this more fundamental measure that is crucial for understanding the nature of knowledge.

So while it seems fairly easy to identify the role of the formal requirements for relativity and the thesis of objective equity in Plato's discussion of Protagoras in the *Theaetetus*, the role of incommensurability needs to be deduced with some effort. Still I suggest on the basis of the evaluation offered here that all three theses play a role in understanding this early paradigm case of relativism. If any one of these theses were denied, the claim of relativism would thereby fail. According to the interpretation offered here, it is the failure of the thesis of objective equity that provides the basis for Socrates' refutation of Protagoras, rather than the self-refutation argument directed against the formal requirements for relativity.

3.3 Nelson Goodman

Nelson Goodman describes his notion of worldmaking as "a radical relativism", though one with "severe restraints" to prevent an attitude of "anything goes" in the process of worldmaking (Goodman, 1978, p. 94). By worldmaking, Goodman means the process of creating multiple versions of the world as various descriptions or depictions of the world, rather than discovering the single nature of a unitary world. A notable feature of Goodman's constructivism is his inclusion of works of art along with more prosaic theoretical descriptions of the world: "Worlds are made by making such versions with words, numerals, pictures, sounds, or other symbols of any kind in any medium" (p. 94). How are worlds made? "Not from nothing, after all, but from other worlds" (p. 6), and Goodman outlines several means by which worlds can be created from other worlds: composition and decomposition, weighting, ordering, deletion and supplementation, and deformation (pp. 7–16).

It seems that Goodman understands the radical nature of his relativism in much the same way as I do, namely in terms of the depth of the phenomenon: "My relativism, which nevertheless recognizes the difference between right and wrong versions, does not stop with representation and vision and realism and resemblance but goes through to reality as well" (1983, p. 269). The question remains whether Goodman understands relativism in general the same way that I do, namely as a radical indexed pluralism.

In describing the opponent of the kind of worldmaking that he and Ernst Cassirer espouse, Goodman seems to present the rejection of relativism precisely in terms of the theses that I have used to analyze the general notion of relativism: "His typical adversary is the monopolistic materialist or physicalist who maintains that one system, physics, is pre-eminent and all-inclusive, such that every other version must eventually be reduced to it or rejected as false or meaningless" (1978, p. 4). By identifying one pre-eminent system to which all other true versions of the world must be reduced, the opponent of worldmaking denies the thesis of incommensurability, since if alternative world versions can all be reduced to physics, they cannot therefore be incommensurable. Likewise, by identifying one world version as pre-eminent and rejecting all other versions that do not reduce to it as false, the opponent of worldmaking denies the thesis of objective equity, since clearly false versions cannot objectively be on an equitable basis with a true version. So by identifying these theses with regard to what his opponent denies, Goodman implicitly seems to endorse them in his own account.

Furthermore, Goodman seems to affirm these two theses in positive characterizations of his relativism as well. Though he does not use the term 'incommensurability', Goodman cites the failure of reduction as a reason for maintaining the plurality of worlds:

> If all right versions could somehow be reduced to one and only one, that one might with some semblance of plausibility be regarded as the only truth about the only world. But the evidence for such reducibility is negligible, and even the claim is nebulous since physics itself is fragmentary and unstable and the kind and consequences of reduction envisaged are vague. (How do you go about reducing Constable's or James Joyce's world-view to physics?) (1978, pp. 4–5)

Thus while recognizing that reduction to a single world version would provide grounds for denying the radical kind of pluralism he advocates, he denies such a reduction, particularly in the case of works of art where the very notion of a reduction makes no sense. Stated somewhat more positively, "many different world-versions are of independent interest and importance, without any requirement or presumption of reducibility to a single base" (p. 4), and this independence seems to be precisely what the thesis of incommensurability is designed to establish.

Goodman is still more explicit in affirming the thesis of objective equity: "I maintain that many world versions — some conflicting with each other, some so disparate that conflict or compatibility among them is hardly determinable — are equally right" (1980, p. 111). Throughout his various presentations of worldmaking, he is careful however to distinguish right versions from wrong versions, claiming that "the multiple worlds I countenance are just the actual worlds made by and answering to true or right versions" (1978, p. 94). So while not every version of the world is true or right, there are multiple right versions, each of which determines a world, and all right versions are equally right.

An interesting feature of Goodman's support for this claim is his analysis of the realism of representations. "If we can with some confidence grade ways of seeing or picturing the world according to their degrees of realism, of absence of distortion, of faithfulness in representing the way the world is, then surely by reading back from this we can learn a good deal about the way the world is" (1972, p. 27). Such an ordering of world versions according to degrees of realism would certainly constitute a denial of the thesis of objective equity, if it were possible. However, the problem that Goodman notes is that not only are there several senses of 'realism' with regard to representations (1978, p. 130, 1983), but according to one prominent sense of the term, realism seems to be judged according to a system of representation. "Realistic or right representation in this sense, like right categorization, requires observance of custom and tends to correlate loosely with ordinary judgments of resemblance, which likewise rest upon habit" (1978, p. 130). Even in the case of what seems to be the paradigm of realism in representation, the color photograph, differences in perspectives can lead to distortions (1972, pp. 27–28). Realism itself seems to be a matter of convention for Goodman, and there seems to be no objective choice between conventions.

Curiously enough, the hardest of the three theses to establish with regard to Goodman's relativism are the formal requirements for relativity, for while Goodman clearly espouses a form of pluralism, it is not clear that these various world versions are relative to anything definite. In other words, it is somewhat difficult to identify a relativizing domain within Goodman's relativism. He seems to satisfy the formal requirements when he claims: "The dramatically contrasting versions of the world can of course be relativized: each is right under a given system — for a given science, a given artist, or a given perceiver and situation" (1978, p. 3). The problem is that the putative relativizing domain he seems to offer in this passage is fairly disparate, and it is not clear that saying that world versions are right under a given system is any different than saying that the version is right in and for itself. For similar reasons, Maria Baghramian takes Goodman to be a pluralist rather than a relativist (Baghramian, 2004, p. 231).

However, I think a more definite relativizing domain ultimately does emerge from Goodman's account according to which his notion of worldmaking qualifies as genuine relativism and not merely pluralism. He speaks for instance of "substance dissolved into function" (Goodman, 1978, p. 7), and that "in other cases, worlds differ in response to theoretical rather than practical needs" (p. 9). These passages suggest that the relativizing domain consists of functions, needs, or purposes, thus placing Goodman firmly within the pragmatist tradition. This pragmatist conception of Goodman's relativism seems to accord well with his emphasis on rightness and wrongness of fit over truth and falsity (pp. 19, 132). Yet not just any set of purposes would seem to suffice for a relativizing domain. "In one world, there may be many kinds serving different purposes; but conflicting purposes may make for irreconcilable accents and contrasting worlds, as may conflicting conceptions of what kinds serve a given purpose" (p. 11). It seems that not only conflicting purposes would determine a relativizing domain, but also conflicting conceptions of how best to serve those conflicting purposes. This combination of factors seems to yield a fairly unwieldy relativizing domain, as a set of ordered pairs of purposes and conceptions, but perhaps this combination could be understood in terms of a case of pluralism nested within relativism. World versions are relativized to conflicting purposes, but for each conflicting purpose, there are several adequate world versions according to differing conceptions of how best to serve that purpose, and it does not matter which conception is adopted for that purpose. In any case, it does seem that purposes can be used to define a relativizing domain with a corresponding variance in world versions, thus satisfying the formal requirements for relativity. Consequently, it does seem that Goodman's relativism can be understood fairly clearly in terms of the three theses that emerge from my proposed definition of relativism.

3.4 Gilbert Harman

The kind of moral relativism espoused by Gilbert Harman is fairly uncomplicated. Just as judgments about the mass of an object are relative to an inertial framework according to Einstein's special theory of relativity, so are moral judgments relative to a moral framework (Harman & Thomson, 1996, p. 3).

In his earliest presentation of moral relativism, Harman focuses on what he calls "inner judgments", namely "judgments in which we say that someone should or ought to have done something or that someone was right or wrong to have done something" (Harman, 1975, p. 5). The use of the word 'ought' in inner judgments is distinguished from other uses, such as the assessment that a certain state of affairs is bad, as in the statement "No one ought to starve to death in our affluent society", which do not fall under Harman's analysis. This moral use of 'ought' in inner judgments gets treated by Harman "as a four-place predicate (or 'operator'), 'Ought (A, D, C, M),' which relates an agent A, a type of act D, considerations C, and motivating attitudes M" (p. 10), where the considerations C represent extenuating circumstances. Yet it is not primarily to extenuating circumstances but to motivating attitudes M that Harman makes inner judgments relative:

> In order to be somewhat more precise, then, my thesis is this. "Ought (A, D, C, M)" means roughly that, given that A has motivating attitudes M and given C, D is the course of action for A that is supported by the best reasons. In judgments using this sense of "ought," C and M are often not explicity [sic] mentioned by are [sic] indicated by the context of utterance. Normally, when that happens, C will be "all things considered" and M will be attitudes that are shared by the speaker and audience. (p. 11)

On the basis of this analysis, Harman argues for moral relativism. With regard to inner judgments, Harman notes two characteristics: "First, they imply that the agent has reasons to do something. Second, the speaker in some sense endorses these reasons and supposes that the audience also endorses them" (p. 8). These reasons constitute the motivating attitudes M that are shared by speaker and audience in Harman's analysis of the moral use of 'ought'. If these reasons are shared by everyone, then it seems that morality would be absolute rather than relative, but Harman argues that such reasons are not in fact shared universally through a series of thought experiments. Consider the following:

> Again, suppose that a contented employee of Murder, Incorporated was raised as a child to honor and respect members of the "family" but to have nothing but contempt for the rest of society. His current assignment, let us suppose, is to kill a certain bank manager, Bernard J. Ortcutt. Since Ortcutt is not a member of the "family," the employee in question has no compunction about carrying out his assignment. In particular, if we were to try to convince him that he should not kill Ortcutt, our argument would merely amuse him. We would not provide him with the slightest reason to desist unless we were to point to practical difficulties, such as the likelihood of his getting caught. Now, in this case it would be a misuse of language to say of him that he ought not to kill Ortcutt or that it would be wrong of him to do so, since that would imply that our own moral considerations carry some weight with him, which they do not. Instead we can only judge that he is a criminal, someone to be hunted down by the police, an enemy of peace-loving citizens, and so forth. (pp. 5–6)

Since this is a case in which a difference in reasons and motivating attitudes leads to a difference in inner judgments concerning whether the mobster ought or ought not to kill Ortcutt, Harman claims that such inner judgments are relative. It might be claimed that the event of Ortcutt's murder by the mobster ought not to occur, regardless of whether motivating attitudes are shared or not, but this claim embodies a different sense of 'ought' than in the inner judgments that concern Harman here.

3.4. GILBERT HARMAN

In later formulations, Harman extends his account of moral relativism beyond inner judgments to any moral judgment, resulting in the following general definition of moral relativism:

> For the purposes of assigning *objective* truth conditions, a judgment of the form, *it would be morally wrong of P to D*, has to be understood as elliptical for a judgment of the form, *in relation to moral framework M, it would be morally wrong of P to D*. Similarly for other moral judgments. (Harman & Thomson, 1996, p. 43)

These moral frameworks are determined by the values, standards and principles of people who adhere to those moral frameworks, though "there is no single agreed on answer on how a given person's values determine a moral system" (p. 14). Harman's suggestion is that "It is likely that most people's values reflect conventions that are maintained by continual tacit bargaining and adjustment" (p. 22), similarly to the way that two people rowing a boat adjust their rowing rate to remain synchronized. "It is necessary to suppose that, in order to further our interests, we form certain conditional intentions, hoping that others will do the same. The others, who have different interests, will form somewhat different conditional intentions. After implicit bargaining, some sort of compromise is reached" (Harman, 1975, p. 13). From this process of implicit bargaining and adjustment, a common framework of reasons and motivating attitudes emerges among a group of people, making it possible for moral judgments to be made and understood between people who share that common framework. For those who do not share a common framework, moral disagreements emerge. Harman's claim is that moral relativism resulting from this process of implicit bargaining best explains moral disagreements and the diversity of moral judgments.

With regard to my proposed definition of relativism, Harman's moral relativism seems to meet the formal requirements for relativity, since he recognizes a difference in moral judgments corresponding to a difference in moral frameworks. Yet Harman's reference to conventions would seem to question these formal requirements, in accordance with the discussion of conventionalism in section 2.4. If morals did reflect conventions, then insofar as it is recognized that those conventions may have been different, the kind of non-arbitrary relations between the relativizing domain and the range of relativized sub-theories would seem to be missing, in which case the formal requirements would not be met. However, given Harman's account of how such conventions arise, the relativizing domain might more properly be taken to represent a given set of individuals with specific interests and intentions. While there may be some freedom with regard to the way that specific conventions can arise among these individuals, given those individuals and their actual interests, the range of conventions that can arise are thereby restricted. Consequently, this would seem to be a case of the relativization of conventionality as discussed in section 2.4, where I suggested that such a case would primarily represent an instance of conventionality, though one where the conventionality itself was relativized. For Harman's account to qualify as relativism according to the proposed definition, he would need to understand the notion of moral frameworks differently from a conception of conventions, and insofar as Harman seems to suggest the model of conventions simply as a proposal, perhaps it could be granted that there may be such a conception of moral frameworks on Harman's account according to which it would qualify primarily as relativism rather than conventionalism.

In his early presentation, he claims, "I am not denying (nor am I asserting) that some moralities are 'objectively' better than others or that there are objective standards for assessing moralities" (Harman, 1975, p. 4), which would make it difficult to determine whether he accepts the thesis of objective equity with regard to inner judgments. Yet it seems that Harman had mainly wished not to complicate his discussion of inner judgments in that earlier article, since in his later arguments for moral relativism, Harman clearly endorses the thesis of objective equity: "There is no single true morality. There are many different moral frameworks, none of which is more correct than the others" (Harman & Thomson, 1996, p. 5).

Einstein's special theory of relativity provides a guiding metaphor for Harman's moral relativism. Yet as I noted earlier, Einstein's theory does not seem to qualify as relativism, given the role of the Lorentz transformations in coordinating measurements of space and time between alternative inertial frameworks. These transformations provide a form of commensurability that genuine relativism denies. Unfortunately, Harman does not discuss this aspect of the special theory of relativity with regard to his version of moral relativism, so it is not immediately clear from Harman's arguments whether he endorses the thesis of incommensurability. If the moral frameworks in Harman's account are commensurable, if the reasons embodied in the various motivating attitudes can be coordinated into a common account, such as an account of the general conventionality of values, then it seems that Harman's moral relativism would count as a form of moral contextualism rather than genuine relativism.

It is true that Harman argues against the universality of practical reasons (Harman & Thomson, 1996, pp. 45–56), but failing to hold the same practical reasons does not thereby indicate that those differing practical reasons are not commensurable in some way. This is a point that will need to be clarified when the thesis of incommensurability is investigated in greater detail in chapter 6. Yet it is not reasons alone that determine the moral frameworks on which Harman's moral relativity depends, but individual reasons, values and principles entering into a process of implicit bargaining between people holding different reasons, resulting in a common moral framework. It does seem that this process of moral bargaining may provide some grounds for thinking that the moral frameworks in Harman's account may be incommensurable, since the process of bargaining does not seem to determine a fixed output from a given set of inputs. Consider two people with different reasons and values who work out a common moral framework in a process of moral bargaining. Next consider two different people with the same set of reasons held by the first two people. Why should it be expected that the moral framework derived from the process of moral bargaining between the second set of people be identical with the moral framework derived by the first set of people, even though the starting set of reasons is the same? Nor is it clear that the resulting frameworks would be explainable according to a common account, despite the identity of reasons from which the two bargaining processes began. It may be that the process of moral bargaining is too complex to admit of a single definitive account that would provide any grounds for supposing the commensurability between resulting moral frameworks. Yet Harman is not clear on these points, and perhaps he would not even wish to espouse relativism in the radical sense in which this study understands it, if he ultimately denies the thesis of incommensurability with regard to moral frameworks.

So the case of Gilbert Harman's putative moral relativism does not completely align with the proposed definition of relativism and its three theses. Not only does the question of the possible commensurability between different moral frameworks suggest that Harman may be espousing a form of moral contextualism rather than relativism, but his use of conventions casts doubt on whether his account properly constitutes an instance of relativity in the first place. Rather than representing a counter-example to the proposed definition of relativism, I would suggest that this discussion demonstrates the fruitfulness of the proposed definition. If Harman's moral theory relies significantly on conventions, then it will have different formal requirements than relativism. If it allows for commensurability between different moral frameworks, then it does not represent a particularly radical claim and can be treated as a form of contextualism.[18] The definition can be used in this case to clarify the proposal and possibly to redirect criticism of it to more pertinent considerations than those surrounding the connotations of the word 'relativism'.

3.5 Joseph Margolis

Joseph Margolis advocates and defends what he calls 'robust relativism', which he proposes in contrast to what he calls 'relationalism', according to which "truth-values or truth-like values are themselves relativized or, better, *relationalized*, so that (for instance) 'true' is systematically replaced by 'true in L_k' " (Margolis, 1991, p. 8), where L_k is some relativizing language or subsystem. Margolis concedes that this form of relativism "is admittedly prone to insoluble paradox, incoherence, self-contradiction when taken to range over genuine truth-claims" (p. 9). While relationalism may appear to represent the canonical formulation of relativism, Margolis thinks this is mistaken, claiming that what char-

---

[18] Of course, Harman may not especially care whether his account qualifies as genuine relativism. In fact, he might be relieved to distance his moral theory from the negative connotations of the term 'relativism', and I would be pleased to offer him this service by means of the proposed definition.

acterizes relativism in general is what he calls "the least form of relativism", namely, "Any doctrine counts as a form of relativism if it abandons the principle of excluded middle or bivalence (and *tertium non datur*), or restricts its use, so that, in particular sectors of inquiry, incongruent claims may be validated" (p. 17).

Accordingly, robust relativism is "a relativism that, for cause and with regard to carefully selected contexts of substantive inquiry, replaces bivalent truth-values with many-valued values and is prepared to entertain incongruent claims where, otherwise, on the bipolar model, only contradiction and inconsistency would pertinently arise" (p. 157). Whereas relationalism replaces the value 'true' with 'true-in-L', robust relativism does not relativize the values 'true' and 'false' at all, but replaces those bivalent values with "a logically weaker set of many-valued truth values or truth-like values" (p. 8), thus avoiding the contradictions that bivalence would entail in Margolis' view. To understand Margolis' view fully, however, several points must be clarified.

First, the simple addition of a third truth-value such as 'indeterminate' does not count as robust relativism for Margolis (1995, p. 4). Rather the kinds of weaker truth-like values that interest Margolis are 'plausible', 'apt', 'reasonable' (p. 6), 'compatible' (1983, p. 561), or even 'probable' (1976, p. 37). Yet Margolis resists the suggestion that these truth values are epistemic concessions, "as, for example, in introducing probabilistic truth-values that remain, in principle, tethered to overriding bivalent values" (1991, p. 9). So 'probable' is not equivalent to 'probably true' or 'true with n% certainty', but counts as a truth-like value independent of 'true' (p. 13). Thus it seems that the values 'true' and 'false' are retained in some sense by Margolis, but their exclusive use is denied under robust relativism in favor of weaker values.

Second, not every application of these weaker truth-like values counts as robust relativism, only the application to incongruous claims, meaning "truth- or truth-like claims that, on the bivalent model but not now, would be inconsistent, incompatible, or contradictory" (1991, p. 13). So unless these weaker truth-like values are applied to cases that would count as contradictions according to bivalent truth-values, their application does not thereby count as relativism. Yet since values weaker than the bivalent ones are applied in these cases, the contradictions are avoided.

Third, by admitting these weaker truth-values, Margolis allows that truth and falsity may be treated asymmetrically, namely that "interpretations can be shown to be false (as not according with pertinent evidence) but can no longer be shown to be true (since retaining truth would lead inevitably to contradiction)" (1995, p. 6). This asymmetric treatment seems required to reinforce the separation of weaker truth-like values such as 'probable' from dependence on the value 'true', where it might be thought that probable means just 'probably true' (1982, pp. 93–94). Thus if a statement can be shown to be false, under Margolis' asymmetrical treatment, that does not thereby show that the contradictory statement is true or even that the probability of its truth is high, as would be expected under a bivalent treatment.

Last, Margolis does not claim that robust relativism applies in every field, but holds that its viability in any given domain must be demonstrated "on an analysis of the pertinent properties or peculiarities of that domain, and cannot reasonably be decided one way or the other solely on the basis of the formal properties of judgments or claims as such" (1982, pp. 96–97). Indeed, Margolis begins his formulation of robust relativism within the field of aesthetics, where he aims to identify "what it is about the nature of art and judgment that sustains a relativistic thesis" (1976, p. 38). Thus Margolis does not espouse a form of global relativism based simply on a non-bivalent account of truth in general. Rather, the applicability of the weaker truth-like values that Margolis espouses must be demonstrated in any particular field, thus leaving certain fields such as mathematics free to conform to the usual bivalent truth-values.

With regard to the proposed definition of relativism, Margolis' account of relativism does not seem to align very well at all. First, incommensurability figures as a recognized form of relativism for Margolis, namely one that "emphasizes epistemic considerations", but is not essential to relativism in general, given that other forms may be concerned with "ontic considerations" (1991, p. 18). If indeed incommensurability is merely an optional factor in robust relativism, then obviously the scope of robust relativism includes versions of relativism that deny incommensurability.

Second, Margolis denies what I have been calling the thesis of objective equity, since he explicitly claims "relativism need not be committed to the thesis that all alternative claims are equipotent" (Margolis, 1984, p. 319). Furthermore, he asserts that the kinds of truth-like values he espouses "provide for comparing and appraising the relative strength of competing claims" (1983, p. 561). While in this passage he seems more concerned to deny that robust relativism is a theory in which anything goes, by allowing weaker truth-like value such as 'probable' and 'apt', Margolis nowhere supports the claim that every judgment that is probable or apt is equally probable or apt. Although equity could have applied just as much to Margolis' weaker truth-like values as with bivalent values according to the thesis of objective equity, equity seems to play no part in robust relativism.

Therefore, on my proposed definition of relativism, Margolis' robust relativism does not count as relativism at all. Herein would seem to lie a problem, namely whether my proposed definition is defective for not including robust relativism, or whether Margolis is incorrect in calling his proposal a version of relativism. Of course I am not the only one to question whether Margolis is properly espousing relativism or not. Rom Harré and Michael Krausz claim that "the abandonment of bipolarity alone does not lead to relativism" (Harré & Krausz, 1996, p. 147), Richard Beatch claims that "Margolis' relativism is only partially a relativism" (Beatch, 1996, p. 91), and Brandon Cooke claims that Margolis espouses anti-realism rather than relativism (Cooke, 2002, p. 304). Indeed, Margolis seems sensitive to such charges, but understands this denial of the attribution 'relativism' to his account to be part of a strategy for dismissing relativism in general by simply ignoring a perfectly coherent version of relativism (Margolis, 1991, p. 11). Yet I do not count myself an enemy of relativism, and am not interested in dismissing relativism, but still wonder why Margolis thinks that the key feature of relativism is the abandonment of the principles of excluded middle and bivalence.

For my part, the most telling feature of Margolis' robust relativism that makes me think that he has incorrectly identified his view as relativism is that Margolis does not seem to support what I have been calling the formal requirements for relativity, namely whatever is required properly to make the claim that "x is relative to y" for some x and y. Nowhere does Margolis claim that interpretation in aesthetics, for example, is relative to some factor. Indeed, such a claim would be tantamount to espousing relationalism in Margolis' view, which he frequently acknowledges to be incoherent. Robust relativism, on the other hand, permits the same culture or individual or any other member of some potentially relativizing domain to claim that conflicting judgments are probable or apt, or indeed all members of any relativizing domain to make the same truth-like judgments. There is accordingly no clear relativizing domain identifiable within robust relativism, and therefore there is no relativity in robust relativism.

It thus seems mistaken to label a claim as relativism where there is no relativity. The very linguistic roots seem to demand relativity within any claim of relativism; else what justifies the use of the term 'relativism' other than by fiat or stipulation? Perhaps Margolis could justify his usage from the adverb 'relatively', in which a statement is affirmed but only weakly. So perhaps a statement like "It is relatively hot today" suggests the kind of robust relativism Margolis has in mind, by assigning the statement "It is hot today" a truth-like value weaker than true. However, this adverbial usage is dependent on an underlying relativity, such that it is proper to ask, "It is hot today, relative to what?" where the response might be "Relative to the current temperature in Antarctica". Yet this underlying relativity serves to identify a relativizing domain, and this would seem to lead to an incoherent relationalism according to Margolis.

I think Margolis' path to robust relativism can be traced starting from his understanding of the relativism of Protagoras, and this path likewise traces the way in which I think he deviates from traditional relativism. Margolis claims to "favor the doctrine of the flux" (Margolis, 1996, p. 99), and furthermore claims "Protagoras is best characterized as the philosopher of the flux" (1991, p. 82). As noted earlier in the discussion of Protagoras in the *Theaetetus* in section 3.2, Socrates introduces the notion of the flux on a speculative basis, as a secret doctrine that Protagoras might have taught to his pupils outside of his published doctrines. It seems that Margolis takes this notion of a secret doctrine seriously, whereas John McDowell and other commentators find no reason to believe that Protagoras actually held what Socrates speculatively attributes in that passage. Yet the relativism explicitly embodied in Protagoras' "man is the measure" doctrine does not require an underlying doctrine of the flux, so by preferring Socrates' mere suggestion of a secret doctrine over Protagoras' explicitly stated, though laconic, doctrines, Margolis seems to take his first steps away from relativity and relativism.

3.5. JOSEPH MARGOLIS

Further, Margolis might be more influenced by Aristotle's treatment of Protagoras than by Plato's, in a way that he does not explicitly acknowledge. Whereas Plato takes the relativization of truth to individuals fairly seriously and seeks to understand what it might mean for something to be true for someone, Aristotle in the *Metaphysics* tends to ignore the relativization of truth-values and to consider the assignment of truth-values to statements without reference to the individuals or groups that may have valued those statements differently (Aristotle, 1984, pp. 1593–1597, 1009a–1011b). In this way, Aristotle finds Protagoras guilty of a violation of the law of non-contradiction. Likewise, it seems that Margolis is focused on the direct valuation of statements without reference to whoever is valuing those statements. His characterization of the least form of relativism as a simple denial of excluded middle and bivalence represents this focus clearly. With the doctrine of the flux working in the background, Margolis can therefore consider the valuation of contrary statements in response to Aristotle's charge of contradiction. Yet focusing on the direct valuation of statements seems to leave no room for any form of relativity. Margolis charges that Aristotle's "argument presupposes a very special sort of baggage" (Margolis, 1991, p. 70), namely the doctrines that Aristotle propounds in the *Metaphysics*; yet while Margolis criticizes this baggage, he nevertheless follows Aristotle's strategy of direct valuation without much consideration whether that strategy makes it possible to treat Protagoras' claim adequately.

Finally, Margolis characterizes robust relativism in terms of three desiderata: "a version of relativism, that *saves* an essential part of what the cultural relativist wishes to hold on to, that does not abandon the difficult concession that the claims in question *are* truth bearing (take truth-values), and that *remains* formally self consistent for all that" (1991, p. 63). I think the first desideratum is the most questionable one in Margolis' case, not only because it might not be clear what any given cultural relativist wishes to hold on to, but also because what may preserve the key insight of the cultural relativist, as understood by Margolis, may not ultimately be a form of relativism. Efforts to preserve a perceived insight within a doctrine may end up destroying that doctrine itself in favor of a quite different one. By holding to the doctrine of the flux and focusing on the direct valuation of statements, Margolis may have saved what he considers worthwhile in Protagoras' doctrine, but by denying the need to formulate that doctrine in terms of a relativity claim, I think he has forfeited the right to call his robust relativism by the term 'relativism'. It would seem much clearer for Margolis to identify his proposal as a kind of anti-realism or pragmatism, which is where he seems to be tending in any case, rather than to confuse the issue of relativism any further.

Here again I suggest that the proposed definition of relativism has demonstrated its fruitfulness in this discussion, by substantiating the suspicions that Margolis' account does not represent an instance of relativism.

3.6 Max Kölbel

Max Kölbel distinguishes between indexical and genuine relativism, as already noted, where "Indexical relativists locate all relativity at the level of sentences, while genuine relativists claim that there is relativity also at the level of utterances and the contents or thoughts thereby expressed" (Kölbel, 2004, p. 297). Yet Kölbel also proposes a general definition of relativism, as follows, where F is some feature or predicate, and P some set of relativizing parameters:

> We can then define relativism as follows:
> (DR) For all F: a view counts as relativism about F-ness just if it is committed to claims of the form (i)–(iii). (p. 300)
> (i) It is relative to P whether a thing has feature F. (p. 299)
> (ii) There is at least one x and parameters p_i, p_j which belong to P, such that x has F in relation to p_i, but not in relation to p_j. (p. 299)
> (iii) There is no uniquely relevant choice of parameter. (p. 300)

With Kölbel's definition presented in this formal manner, it is fairly easy to evaluate it with regard to my proposed definition. Clauses (i) and (ii) seem to represent what I have called the formal requirements for relativity. Kölbel includes clause (ii) to eliminate a trivial case "where all parameters in range P are unanimous"

(p. 299). Yet it seems to me to be part of what it means for something to be relative to something else that there is a difference between sub-theories across a relativizing domain, as I will discuss later in section 4.2, so clause (ii) seems a little redundant to me. Clause (iii) seems to represent what I have called the thesis of objective equity, where Kölbel uses the notion of unique relevance to capture what I would characterize as objective preference. Unfortunately, he does not clarify what should count as relevance with regard to a choice of parameter, but as I will discuss later in chapter 5, the question of relevance with regard to objective preference is a definite concern in making this thesis clear.

Notably absent from Kölbel's definition is the thesis of incommensurability. In an earlier presentation of this definition, Kölbel includes Einstein's special theory of relativity in a list of sample cases of relativism (Kölbel, 2002, pp. 116–117), suggesting that he makes no distinction between relativity and relativism, as would be expected given the absence of incommensurability from a definition of relativism. I have argued that incommensurability is needed to distinguish between fairly shallow cases of relativity such as contextualism and the more radical case of relativism. Kölbel's distinction between indexical and genuine relativism seems sensitive to the same kind of concern, where indexical relativism seems definitely less radical than genuine relativism. The difference between Kölbel's and my proposed definitions may therefore primarily be a difference in emphasis.

The emphasis in Kölbel's case seems to be firmly within the philosophy of language, as indicated by the key role of sentences, utterances, contents and thoughts in his distinction between indexical and genuine relativism, whereas my emphasis is rather on the structural form of relativism as a means toward the formulation of the logic of relativism. Furthermore, Kölbel's main concern in the book in which he initially presents his definition of relativism seems to require only relativity rather than relativism in the sense in which I have distinguished the two. "The aim of this book is to show how the assumption of global truth-evaluability *can* be made compatible with the view that not everything is objective" (2002, p. 19). The solution for which Kölbel argues relies on the adoption of relative truth, where global truth-evaluability of statements under a conception of relative truth allows for faultless disagreement, which he takes to be the key indicator that something is not objective (p. 29, 2003). Yet the adoption of relative truth alone implies nothing about the commensurability of the various relativized sub-theories, as indicated by Kölbel's application of relative truth to the special theory of relativity, which does provide commensurability through the Lorentz transformations.

Therefore, the difference in emphasis between Kölbel's project and mine seems to account for the need to distinguish different features of relativity in formulating a general definition of relativism. Kölbel's emphasis on philosophy of language leads him to distinguish between indexical and genuine relativism, whereas my concern with the logical structure of relativistic systems leads me to distinguish between mere relativity and relativism as a more radical form of relativity.

I have discussed Kölbel in this chapter to show how the proposed definition of relativism aligns fairly closely with at least one contemporary attempt to define relativism, though other attempts such as Margolis' clearly fail to align.

3.7 Jean-François Lyotard

The question of relativism with regard to Lyotard arises with regard to the quasi-legalistic concept of a *differend*, which Lyotard defines as follows:

> As distinguished from a litigation, a differend [*différend*] would be a case of conflict, between (at least) two parties, that cannot be equitably resolved for lack of a rule of judgment applicable to both arguments. One side's legitimacy does not imply the other's lack of legitimacy. However, applying a single rule of judgment to both in order to settle their differend as though it were merely a litigation would wrong (at least) one of them (and both of them if neither side admits this rule). (Lyotard, 1988, p. xi)

Yet Lyotard's application of the concept of a differend is not restricted to legal contexts, but is extended to discourse in general, specifically with regard to conflicts between different genres of discourse. Nor should genres be understood narrowly in terms of literary genres. The following are examples of genres of discourse that Lyotard discusses: cognitive, metaphysical, speculative, logical, philosophical, ontological, dialectical, narrative, ethical, declarative, and economic.

Each genre has certain stakes or aims associated with it: "to persuade, to convince, to vanquish, to make laugh, to make cry, etc." (p. 84, ¶147). One might think that genres of discourse are determined by these aims, but Lyotard claims that this supposition reverses the situation: "We believe that we want to persuade, to seduce, to convince, to be upright, to cause to believe, or to cause to question, but this is because a genre of discourse, whether dialectical, erotic, didactic, ethical, rhetorical, or 'ironic,' imposes its mode of linking onto 'our' phrase and onto 'us' " (p. 136, ¶183).

What is at issue is the linking of phrases in discourse. Phrases occur, and they must be linked to other phrases, since even silence is a phrase for Lyotard (p. 29, ¶40), as well as other non-verbal phrases: "A wink, a shrugging of the shoulder, a taping [sic] of the foot, a fleeting blush, or an attack of tachycardia can be phrases" (p. 70, ¶110). Every phrase is formed in accordance with some regimen, or formation rule, such as "descriptive, cognitive, prescriptive, evaluative, interrogative" (p. 84, ¶147). What counts as a proper linking between phrases varies by genre:

> The stakes bound up with a genre of discourse determine the linkings between phrases. They determine them, however, only as an end may determine the means: by eliminating those that are not opportune. One will not link onto *To arms!* with *You have just formulated a prescription*, if the stakes are to make someone act with urgency. (p. 84, ¶148)

The perpetual linking of phrases, however, inevitably crosses genres of discourse, since no one lives solely within a single genre. "In this sense, a phrase that comes alone is put into play within a conflict between genres of discourse. This conflict is a differend, since the success (or the validation) proper to one genre is not the one proper to others" (p. 136, ¶184). According to this differend, judging the validity of linking phrases proper to one genre of discourse by the standards of another genre constitutes a wrong, namely "a damage [*dommage*] accompanied by the loss of the means to prove the damage" (p. 5, ¶7). The reason that this differend between genres constitutes a wrong is because the very proof of damage that could be offered with regard to judging a conflict between genres of discourse would be offered within the genre of proving, and this genre simply constitutes yet another genre of discourse that is itself in conflict with the genre on whose behalf the proof is offered. Lyotard initially motivates this notion of the stifling of the possibility for proof of damage with a consideration of victims of death camps, whose testimony of the existence of such camps is eradicated by the very function of such camps (Lyotard, 1988, pp. 3–4).

Of special interest to Lyotard is the differend between the economic genre in its capitalistic form and other genres, particularly because the very notion of a differend is judged unfavorably according to this genre. "The differends between phrase regimens or between genres of discourse are judged to be negligible by the tribunal of capitalism.... Time is at its fullest with capitalism. But if the verdict, always pronounced in favor of gained time, puts an end to litigations, it may for that very reason aggravate differends" (p. 178, ¶252). Not only might other genres be judged a waste of time according to the economic genre, since time is money, but the very concern with differends seems likewise a waste of time. The result is that the wrong occasioned by differends between genres is not even acknowledged if the economic genre is posited as primary over other genres, as Lyotard claims to see in contemporary society.

From this brief presentation of Lyotard's conception of the differend, I think all three of the theses that constitute my proposed definition of relativism are clearly recognizable. The rules for properly linking phrases are relative to genres of discourse, thus meeting the formal requirements for relativity. Furthermore, "The principle of an absolute victory of one genre over the others has no sense" (p. 138, ¶189), and "There is no genre whose hegemony over the others would be just" (p. 158, ¶228). Here Lyotard clearly affirms the thesis of objective equity, where objectivity itself for him would likely figure within one or more separate genres of discourse at the expense of others.[19] Lastly, Lyotard is quite clear about

---

[19] This would constitute an instance of equity by virtue of a failure of objectivity, which is one way that the thesis of objective equity can be affirmed, as will be

3.7. JEAN-FRANÇOIS LYOTARD

the role of incommensurability with regard to the differend: "The stakes implied in the tragical genre ..., and the stakes implied in the technical genre ... are, for their part, incommensurable, and they induce heterogeneous linkings, be they on the basis of the same phrase" (p. 128, ¶179), so Lyotard explicitly affirms the thesis of incommensurability. Therefore, Lyotard's doctrine of the differend clearly counts as a case of relativism under my proposed definition, though he does not specifically identify his position as relativism.

Lyotard defines postmodernism "as incredulity toward metanarratives" (Lyotard, 1984, p. xxiv), where a metanarrative is an overarching narrative framework for interpreting other narratives, such as the metanarrative of Marxism or Freudianism. The doctrine of the differend seems to underwrite Lyotard's incredulity toward such metanarratives, since metanarratives appear within a particular genre of discourse, but their function as metanarrative involves the application of that genre of discourse to other genres with the presumption that the genre of discourse of the metanarrative assumes predominance over the other genres. This is precisely the situation of a differend that Lyotard thinks constitutes a wrong, and therefore any metanarrative seems to embody a wrong within a differend across all genres to which the metanarrative is applied. However, it may be wondered whether the relativism embodied in the differend itself constitutes the kind of metanarrative that Lyotard seeks to avoid. Perhaps Lyotard's relativism is simply self-refuting.

Lyotard himself seems sensitive to this concern (Lyotard, 1988, pp. 135–136, ¶182), but his response is unclear at this point, seeming almost to accept the charge that he is merely propagating yet another metanarrative. In one sense, it may seem that the notion of a differend should count as a metanarrative insofar as Lyotard applies the notion to all other genres of discourse. However, in another sense, perhaps more importantly for Lyotard, the relativism of the differend does not seem to be a metanarrative at all, in the sense that a metanarrative will govern interpretation within another genre and predominate over it, as the Marxist metanarrative may govern other genres to produce Marxist philosophy of science or even Marxist erotic literature, for example. Yet the recognition

---

discussed in chapter 5.

of relativism between genres of discourse does not entail that relativism must be recognized within a particular genre of discourse, as would be the case if that relativism were an overarching metanarrative. Recognition of relativism by means of a differend between scientific discourse and erotic literature does not thereby produce relativistic science or relativistic erotic literature. Within any genre, different linkings of phrases are judged according to how well the linkings in question achieve the aims or stakes of that genre. In the economic genre, for example, one linking may be judged more conducive to economic aims than another absolutely, without recourse to any relativization. If there is relativity within a genre, it does not seem dependent upon the relativism of the differend between genres, but upon the aims and stakes of the genre itself. The exception may be within the ethical genre, where Lyotard's understanding of obligations arising from within genres of discourse may seem to entail moral relativism (pp. 116–117, ¶174–175), though Lyotard is not perfectly clear at this point.

Whether the relativism of the differend constitutes a metanarrative in any other sense is a question that ultimately exceeds the scope of this investigation. It is enough for my purposes to recognize that the apparent relativism in Lyotard's account aligns with the definition of relativism that I propose, further demonstrating the fruitfulness of the definition. Postmodernism has frequently been associated with relativism (Baghramian, 2004, pp. 104–117; Norris, 1997), and it might be wondered whether this association is proper. This discussion shows that the position of at least one prominent postmodernist does properly count as relativism, even if that relativism is not explicitly acknowledged.

I have endeavored in this chapter to provide some motivation for adopting the proposed definition of relativism as radical indexed pluralism. The motivation here would derive from the fruitfulness of that definition in the analysis of various discussions of relativism. For example, in the case of Harman, the failure to recognize any definite pattern of incommensurability in his account suggests that he may be advocating moral contextualism rather than moral relativism. In the case of Margolis, the failure to demonstrate the formal requirements of relativity suggests that he is not even advocating a form of relativity, let alone relativism. In the case of Lyotard, suspicions that his postmodernist account involves a form of relativism seem to be confirmed, even though

3.7. JEAN-FRANÇOIS LYOTARD

Lyotard does not explicitly use the term 'relativism'.

The usefulness of the proposed definition seems to result primarily from the articulation of the notion of radical indexed pluralism into three separate theses: the formal requirements for relativity, incommensurability, and objective equity. However, I have not yet described these three theses in any great detail, and each of these theses demands careful consideration to determine what is required in each case. The next three chapters are devoted to such careful considerations.

Chapter 4

Formal Requirements for Relativity

There would seem to be some minimal requirements for claiming that relativity[1] holds in a given case, simply in order to use the words 'relativity' and 'relative' properly. I take these requirements to be formal in nature, as suggested by the schema "x is relative to y" that is characteristic of claims of relativity. Given this schema, the formal requirements for relativity would seem to address three factors: (1) the theories on a given topic that are identified as relative, which take the x position in the schema, and which I have been calling *relativized sub-theories*, (2) the set of elements to which those theories are relative, which takes the y position in the schema, and which I have been calling the *relativizing domain*, and (3) the relation between the relativizing domain and the relativized sub-theories.

In my proposed definition of relativism, the formal requirements for relativity represent a claim of indexed pluralism, where the multiplicity of relativized sub-theories constitutes pluralism, and the identification of a relativizing domain and the relation between this domain and the sub-theories constitutes indexing. In order to identify precisely what is required in the formal requirements for relativity, I will discuss each of the three factors identi-

---

[1] In this chapter, I speak of relativity rather than relativism, according to my earlier distinction between the two notions. Since I take relativism to be a species of relativity, the formal requirements for relativity are shared between them, while the success or failure of the thesis of incommensurability serves to distinguish them in any given case.

fied in the last paragraph separately, starting with a consideration of the relativizing domain.

4.1 Relativizing Domain

In any claim of relativity, a set of elements must be identified to which theories on some topic are taken to be relative. For example, in a claim of cultural relativity, a set of cultures must be identified. In a claim of conceptual relativity, a set of conceptual schemes must be identified. The contents of the relativizing domain will vary according the particular kind of relativity that is claimed; however, from a formal point of view, it seems that there must be some restriction on the nature of the relativizing domain insofar as the elements of the domain must be capable of entering into the relation of relativization with the relativized sub-theories.

I take this restriction to be that the elements of the relativizing domain must constitute a perspective, by which I mean that something about the elements of the domain must enable them to be indexed non-arbitrarily to a theory, in accordance with the conception of a perspective I presented in section 3.1.1, where the nature of this non-arbitrary indexing relation needs to be clarified by the overall relative system. Where the elements of the domain are persons or groups of persons, this requirement seems easily met, since individual people and communities are clearly the sorts of entities that hold theories and therefore can constitute perspectives. Where the elements of the domain are somewhat more abstract, it seems that the requirement would need to be met by linking those abstract elements with persons or groups of persons. For example, where the relativizing domain consists of conceptual schemes, those schemes can be understood as being adopted by people and thereby as constituting a perspective. In the special theory of relativity, the relativizing domain consists of a set of inertial frameworks, and a perspective results when an individual person is placed within some inertial framework, though a person need not actually be placed in every inertial framework, only that those frameworks are capable of forming perspectives by positing a person in that framework who would make spatial and temporal measurements. For other abstract elements that might be proposed in a relativizing domain, it is not clear how a per-

4.1. RELATIVIZING DOMAIN

spective could be recognized, for example, if the relativizing domain is taken to be the set of natural numbers, it is not clear how any particular number could represent a perspective, unless individual people were numbered in some way, such as according to birth order. In this case, however, it would seem that the relativizing domain has been misidentified, and that the proper domain would consist more properly of individual people rather than natural numbers.

This requirement also depends partly upon the requirements surrounding the indexing relation between the relativizing domain and the relativized sub-theories, which will be discussed below. Perhaps it is not feasible to delineate in advance of any particular proposed case of relativism precisely what is required to meet the requirement of constituting a perspective, since any rigid rule risks eliminating by fiat some novel form of relativization that might be devised in the future. For example, in a system of moral relativism, a perspective could be the adoption of, endorsement of, or attribution to some group or individual, a particular theory of morality. However, in the special theory of relativity, a perspective would simply be the emergence of spatial and temporal measurements from a given inertial framework. In each case, the overall theory determines what it would mean to constitute a perspective according to the indexing relation posited by the overall theory, so the nature of constituting a perspective cannot be described in any greater detail here other than as the mere indexing between relativized sub-theories and relativizing domain, as indicated in section 3.1.1 above. Rather, I would simply note that any proposed instance of relativity must demonstrate convincingly how the elements in its relativizing domain can constitute a perspective by entering into the overall theory's indexing relation.

Another proposed restriction on the contents of the relativizing domain is that the domain as a whole should constitute a kind. Typically, instances of relativity contain relativizing domains such as cultures, individuals, and conceptual schemes that do constitute kinds. It would be strange to claim that something is relative to the following set: {the author of this study, the number 42, John Coltrane's album *Blue Train*, Donald Davidson's corpse, the last word spoken by the Pharaoh Ramses II}. Even if some story could plausibly be told concerning how each of the elements of such an odd assemblage of items could constitute a perspective, it would not be clear how perspectives could be shifted across this disparate domain, as a shift in cultural relativism could be made by entering a region where a particular culture was dominant. If an account of shifts of perspective could be given, then I suspect that the relativizing domain might be reformulated more clearly so that it does constitute a kind. As will be discussed in section 6.6, the thesis of incommensurability concerns the difficulty by which a shift in perspective can occur. If the relativizing domain represented radically different kinds of perspectives, the thesis of incommensurability would appear to be granted by default, by virtue of the difficulty or even impossibility of incorporating a disparate relativizing domain into any proposed transformation between sub-theories. Yet this default recognition of incommensurability seems suspect, since the thesis of incommensurability was intended as an additional requirement above the formal requirements for relativity, not a consequence of certain formal aspects of those requirements. Thus it seems necessary to require that the term y in the formula "x is relative to y" be a kind term.

Besides restrictions on the nature of the relativizing domain, there seems to be at least one restriction on its size, namely that there must be more than one element in the domain.[2] An empty relativizing domain would make something relative to nothing, whereas a relativizing domain with a single element would make something relative to just one thing. In either case, there would seem to be nothing to distinguish such a case of relativity from simple pluralism, if the multiplicity of theories were all indexed to one thing or to nothing at all. For the notion of indexing in indexed pluralism to make any sense, it seems that the relativizing domain must have more than one member. It might also seem strange for there to be only a very few elements in the domain, such as just two or three, but the nature of the particular variety of relativity proposed must ultimately dictate the size of the relativizing domain. For example, it does not seem immediately absurd to propose a case of relativity of something to gender, which might contain a small relativizing domain of just two or three genders, depending upon how one counts genders.

Furthermore, since the relativizing domain is a set, it thereby

---

[2] Max Kölbel also includes such a restriction to preclude what he calls a "trivial limit case" (Kölbel, 2004, p. 299).

4.1. RELATIVIZING DOMAIN

must contain discrete members. It must be possible to identify a definite member from the domain to which a relativized sub-theory gets indexed. Where the proposed domain may have indefinite boundaries between members, this kind of indexing would be problematic. As an example, consider the set of colors as a relativizing domain. If colors are considered as color names, it may seem that the members in the domain are discrete enough, but the application of those color names to particular hues may be problematic, given the availability of shades of color between shades corresponding to any two color names. If colors are taken to be elements in a relativizing domain, they must be understood as something more discrete, possibly as wavelengths of light.

Finally, there is a question concerning the modal status of elements in the relativizing domain, namely whether the elements must all be actual or whether they can be merely possible. Consider a proposed relativizing domain that consists of persons, but where some relativized sub-theories are indexed to merely possible persons, not actual ones. If every actual person in the domain were indexed to the same sub-theory, whereas merely possible persons were indexed to different sub-theories, I would consider it inaccurate to claim that some topic *is* relative to persons. Since there is only one theory indexed to every actual person, the topic in question would seem to be actually absolute with regard to those persons, since there is no actual alternative person indexed to a different theory to provide the grounds for a relativity claim. Rather it seems to me that the claim with regard to such a relativizing domain must be understood to be that the topic *is possibly* relative to persons, given the possibility of other persons that do not exist that might be indexed to some different sub-theory. Consequently, I would suggest a further requirement that if the claim is that x is actually relative to y, then the relativizing domain that stands for y must consist entirely of actual entities. If the relativizing domain contains possible entities, then the relativity claim must be understood as primarily making a possibility claim.[3]

Note that abstract entities do not seem to be affected by this

---

[3] In section 7.2 below I consider a strategy for combining the modalities of relativity and possibility, based on a proposal by Steven D. Hales, though I do not implement it in the proposed relative systems in this study. Note that a claim of possible relativity is different from a claim of relative possibility, as will be considered in the discussion below.

proposed requirement, since there does not seem to be a significant difference between an actual abstract entity and a merely possible one. For example, if languages are considered to be abstract entities, then it seems that languages can be recognized as actual in a sense whether or not anyone actually speaks the language or indeed whether the grammar of the language has actually been formulated by anyone. Yet this admission of abstract entities may seem to undermine the proposed restriction on possible entities in the relativizing domain, since in the example used in the previous paragraph, persons might be likewise be considered as abstract entities rather than considered in terms of actual or possible persons. However, I do not think that this consideration poses a counterexample to the proposed requirement, but rather merely forces an addition obligation on whomever makes a relativity claim to clarify the intended modal status of entities within the relativizing domain, whether they be actual, possible or abstract. Once this clarification is provided, then proposed requirement would remain in force.

Against my proposed exclusion of merely possible entities from the relativizing domain, it might be objected, for example, that if morals are relative to actual persons, and I subsequently kill every actual person who disagrees with my morals, then the exclusion of possible entities from the relativizing domain would mean that I have thereby made morals absolute by an act of genocide. Any relativism or absolutism in this case would be merely accidental according to the current state of the relativizing domain. Yet it seems to me that if such an instance of relativism were understood in terms of abstract persons in the relativizing domain, then no change in the actual instantiations of those abstract persons would change the relativity in question. Rather than counting against my exclusion of possible entities from the relativizing domain, the objection simply suggests to me that the instance of relativism in the example may be poorly formulated in terms of actual or possible persons, and would better have been formulated in terms of abstract persons. This consideration might further suggest that every relativizing domain should contain only abstract entities, precisely to prevent this sort of accidental relativism. However, I think that such a requirement would be excessive, since there may be forms of relativism in which the status of such relativity could plausibly change over time. In the example used in the objection, it would seem to be the case that morals had once been relative to actual persons, but after the genocide, morals became absolute, which would indicate a further aspect of relativity of the status of relativism according to time. While such a situation might seem implausible with regard to morals, I would not want arbitrarily to exclude other such cases from qualifying as relativism by requiring the relativizing domain to contain only abstract entities. Rather, I think all that should be required in this case again is that a proposed instance of relativism should clarify the modal status of the relativizing domain, and that if the case for relativism depends critically upon merely possible entities in the relativizing domain, then that instance of relativism should be understood more properly as a case of merely possible relativism.

As a final argument against the inclusion of merely possible entities in the relativizing domain, note that if these possible entities were not excluded, then relativism would come far too easily. Consider moral relativism. Unless I am a Kantian deontologist concerning morals, I might recognize that there are other possible systems of morality that could be linked with some merely possible culture or species of rational creature. If I include these possible cultures into a relativizing domain, then morality can easily be shown to be relative, even if it is in fact actually absolute. While this kind of facile demonstration of relativity might be blocked by stipulating that only certain kinds of possibility should enter into specific arguments for relativity, I think it is far clearer and less controversial to demand that the two different modalities of possibility and relativity be kept separate, as will be discussed in chapter 7.

To review, I have proposed the following requirements related to the relativizing domain:

- The elements in the domain must be able to constitute perspectives.

- The domain as a whole should constitute a kind.

- The domain must contain more than one element.

- The domain must contain discrete members.

- The domain must contain actual or abstract entities unless it forms part of a claim of possible relativity.

4.2 Range of Relativized Sub-Theories

For the purposes of this study, a theory is a set of sentences in a formal language closed under entailment, sentences that are held to be true according to the theory. However, the conception of entailment is something that itself might be considered to be relative, so the conception of entailment used here cannot be an absolute conception imposed across all relativized sub-theories in the overall relative system. Rather it would seem to be a requirement on relativized sub-theories that they be closed under some conception of entailment. For the sake of consistency, it might be thought that the conception of entailment under which the theory is closed should not conflict with any explicit endorsement of a different conception of entailment. A theory that was explicitly committed to one conception of entailment but entered into an overall relativistic system by virtue of being closed under a different conception of entailment would seem to be hypocritical. However, it is not clear that this is a requirement that should be demanded in every case of relativism, particularly since the relativism in question might involve disagreement over whether such consistency should be counted as a virtue.[4]

Since relativity and relativism are species of pluralism, a second requirement for the range of relativized theories is that there must be multiple theories, not just one. Yet a multiplicity of theories seems to imply a multiplicity of different theories, not a repetition of the same theory, which raises the question of what makes one theory different from or identical to another theory. Quine was concerned with this question in the middle of his career, and proposed the following criterion to individuate theories: "two formulations express the same theory if they are empirically equivalent and there is a reconstrual of predicates that transforms the one theory into a logical equivalent of the other" (Quine, 1975, p. 320), effectively making theories "classes of theory formulations" (p. 321). This proposal and other related doctrines of Quine's has prompted controversy over the notion of empirical equivalence, notably a challenge by Larry Laudan and Jarrett Leplin rejecting "both the

---

[4] Those who would find this sort of hypocrisy objectionable would likely find any suggestion of relativism concerning the value of consistency objectionable. The key point of dispute would thus be the truth of such relativism, not whether hypocrisy over conceptions of entailment should properly count as relativism.

4.2. RANGE OF RELATIVIZED SUB-THEORIES

supposition of empirical equivalence and the inference from it to underdetermination" (Laudan & Leplin, 1991, p. 449). Toward the end of his career, though, Quine would write: "Effort and paper have been wasted, by me among others, over what to count as sameness of theory and what to count as mere equivalence. It is a question of words; we can stop speaking of theories and just speak of theory formulations" (Quine, 1992, p. 96).

In the same spirit, I suggest that the response to the question of what constitutes a difference between theories need not be complicated. Any difference in theory formulations will suffice as a difference in theories for the purpose of this study, even a difference as trivial as a difference in the symbols used to formulate the theories. I make this suggestion since the thesis of incommensurability seems to do the required work that Quine had originally sought in order to individuate theories, without relying on empirical equivalence. For the purposes of a formal requirement for relativity, a trivial difference in theories will merely indicate a trivial sort of relativity, as indicated by the ease by which a transformation can be devised to show commensurability between those theories and thus to deny the thesis of incommensurability. Therefore such a trivial difference would indicate that the proposed relativity does not meet all three major theses for establishing a case of relativism. Since this study will investigate relative systems generally, besides specifically relativistic systems, I do not think that trivial cases of relativity should be excluded from consideration by virtue of their triviality, but rather that all cases of relativity should be included in a general account and an explanation should be provided to show precisely why trivial cases are trivial. In this case, the ease of demonstrating commensurability serves as such an explanation, since it does not take any special genius to substitute one set of symbols for another, whereas the formulation of the Lorentz transformations required significant effort and insight, for example.

A third proposed requirement for the range of relativized theories is that each of the theories must address the same topic, that they must be rival theories. In the schematic motto "x is relative to y", x represents theories on a certain topic. A theory concerning domestic plumbing does not properly compete with a theory of morality. Where theories on different topics are considered, it does not seem proper to characterize that situation in terms of relativity.

Before investigating what constitutes rivalry among different theories, I should note that the issue of rivalry seems to form the basis for a general challenge to relativism, such that the very articulation of the requirements for relativism in terms of rivalry seems to provide the means for relativism's own destruction. Addressing Kuhn's account of scientific revolutions, Dudley Shapere notes,

> if "the differences between successive paradigms are both necessary and irreconcilable" (p. 102), and if those differences consist in the paradigms' being "incommensurable" — if they disagree as to what the facts are, and even as to the real problems to be faced and the standards which a successful theory must meet — then what are the two paradigms disagreeing about? (Shapere, 1984, p. 45; page reference is to Kuhn (1996))

Similarly, William Newton-Smith raises the following challenge with regard to relativism about truth:

> Schematically expressed the relativist thesis is:
>
> something, s is true for ψ and false for ϕ.
>
> But what is the something? The trick is to find some one thing the truth of which can vary giving us an interesting version of relativism without lapsing into incoherence. Clearly it is just boring to take the something as a sentence. The sentence 'grass is good to smoke' is false in the ideolect of my farming friends in Wales but true in the ideolect of some communes in my neighbourhood. We can understand how this happens and while the Welsh hill farmers and hippies live in different worlds they do not do so in any substantial metaphysical sense. The truth of a sentence depends on both what it means and on how the world is. A sentence can vary in truth-value from group to group in view of variation in the former without any variation in the latter. Alternatively one might say in the interest of avoiding triviality that it is propositions and not

sentences that vary in truth-value. But this is to take the short road to incoherence. For propositions are individuated in terms of truth-conditions. It is just incoherent to suppose that the same proposition could be true in ψ and false in ϕ. (Newton-Smith, 1982, pp. 107–108)

The force of the rivalry objection as a general refutation of relativism seems to demand that relativized sub-theories form genuine rivals to each other, to disagree on some definite point, then to show how relativism fails to demonstrate such disagreement. Yet the challenge of the rivalry objection would seem to apply equally to instances of relativity as well as to relativism, even to the scientifically reputable special theory of relativity. If an account is available of how the special theory of relativity avoids the rivalry objection, then why would that account not apply to relativism as well? Perhaps the role of the thesis of incommensurability would play a part. Perhaps, though, there is something misguided in the rivalry objection when used as a general refutation of relativism.

Shapere's use of the rivalry objection is not in fact part of a general refutation of relativism, but rather he uses the issue of rivalry precisely to demonstrate that relativism is inherent in Kuhn's position with regard to the question of scientific progress.[5] "The logical tendency of Kuhn's position is clearly toward the conclusion that the replacement [of one paradigm by another] is not cumulative, but is mere change: being 'incommensurable,' two paradigms cannot be judged according to their ability to solve the same problems, or deal with the same facts, or meet the same standards" (Shapere, 1984, pp. 45–46). Thus for Shapere the point is not that relativism is incoherent because it fails to demonstrate disagreement on a common topic, but that failure to demonstrate such disagreement itself constitutes a form of relativism. I will return to this point shortly.

Newton-Smith, however, does seem to use the rivalry objection as part of a general attack on relativism.[6] Yet note that the

---

[5] Kuhn's account will be discussed in chapter 6 on incommensurability, since that notion plays an important role in Kuhn's arguments.

[6] Newton-Smith restricts his remarks to relativism concerning truth and reason, not explicitly addressing relativism in ethics (Newton-Smith, 1982, p. 107); however, the question of assigning varying truth-values to sentences or propositions would seem to apply to any form of relativism.

incoherence he finds in relativism is dependent on taking the locus of disagreement in relativism to be at the level of propositions, rather than that of sentences, which he finds boring, uninteresting and trivial. Indeed the relativity of truth-values of sentences to interpretation in a formal system is well-known and perhaps boring, but Newton-Smith cannot simply rely on this kind of relativity to reject sentences as the bearers of truth-values in any instance of relativism. He must argue that no variation of truth-values at the level of sentences can occur in a philosophically significant way, and dismissing one well-known instance of truth variation of sentences does not preclude other accounts, perhaps not yet formulated. With regard to the question of differences in theories, I am perfectly content to accept trivial cases of relativity, so it should be no surprise that I am similarly content to accept triviality with regard to the locus of disagreement. Again, for the purpose of this study, theories are sets of sentences not sets of propositions. Recall that in order to formulate a general definition of relativism, the methodology of this study was to consider instances of relativism as formal, structural phenomenon and to abstract away from particularly substantive features of particular forms of relativism, as described in the introduction. The formal requirements for relativity aim precisely to outline such structural features, so I do not consider the characterization of formal features as boring or trivial to be a significant objection. However, I take the supposition of the existence of propositions to be a substantive metaphysical claim, not a structural claim.

If Newton-Smith is correct that the claim of disagreement at the level of propositions leads to incoherence in relativism, then perhaps the incoherence results from his substantive metaphysical claims and not from the formal nature of relativity or relativism as such. So if the rivalry objection were not understood to challenge the special theory of relativity under Newton-Smith's analysis, it may be because there is some way to understand propositions such that they do not vary according to inertial frameworks, else the variance of truth conditions for propositions under special relativity would lead to the incoherence of that theory as well as relativism in general. However, this strategy not only relies on a substantive account of the role and nature of propositions, it seems to undermine the kind of relativity asserted by the special theory of relativity by focusing on the invariance of propositions. In order to

4.2. RANGE OF RELATIVIZED SUB-THEORIES

regain the sense of relativity, I think it is necessary to bracket any substantive metaphysical claims and to focus on the difference of truth assignments to sentences and not to propositions, however trivial and boring that may be. My aim here is precisely to outline the formal requirements for relativity, so a concern with sentences as a formal feature seems perfectly appropriate, which thereby seems to nullify the force of Newton-Smith's rivalry objection, at least in this context. Consequently, I do not take this particular rivalry objection to pose a challenge to the formal requirements for relativity.[7]

It remains however to explicate a positive account of the rivalry requirement for relativized sub-theories. As a starting point, consider Shapere's use of rivalry to demonstrate the relativism in Kuhn's position. How can the absence of rivalry between paradigms indicate relativism, when I have claimed that rivalry is required for relativity and therefore for relativism? I think these apparently contrary claims can be reconciled by considering Shapere's conception of a domain in science.[8]

> A "domain" can be defined roughly, for present purposes, as a body of information which is problematic in certain respects, and the items of which we have reason to believe are related in the sense that a unified account of them (with regard to their problematic aspects) can be expected. Domains, in this sense, can be as broad as the subject-matters of fields like electro-

---

[7] Newton-Smith's paper is heavy on rhetoric. For example, "If relativism held with regard to reason even if it failed with regard to truth and logic, this would be a victory for the Kingdom of Darkness" (Newton-Smith, 1982, p. 110). With regard to his argument based on the rivalry objection, he claims "One's opponent is likely to remain unconvinced, muttering that there is some mistake, he knows not what, in the argument" (p. 113). If I may indulge myself with some counter-rhetoric, the mistake is in dismissing considerations that would undermine the argument simply by calling them boring, uninteresting, or trivial. The mistake is in expecting rhetoric to carry the weight of the argument. If relativism is in fact incoherent, self-defeating, or necessarily false, I would expect this incoherence to be demonstrated as a result of a careful and comprehensive examination of the nature of relativism, not by the judicious placement of derogatory adjectives. This study aims precisely to provide such a careful, comprehensive examination.

[8] Of course Shapere's use of the word 'domain' should not be confused with my usage of the word when I refer to relativizing domains. Shapere's usage relates to the ordinary notion of a "scientific field" (Shapere, 1984, pp. 320–324).

> magnetism, genetics or organic chemistry, or as narrow as the specialized interests of individual research workers. (Shapere, 1984, p. 263)

The rivalry that Shapere finds lacking in Kuhn's account of paradigms is at the level of problems, facts, and standards that Kuhn claims are dependent upon paradigms. However, it seems that Shapere does recognize that competing paradigms are still part of the same general domain, for example, as competing paradigms of electromagnetism. Failure of rivalry of paradigms at the level of problems, facts, and standards leads to relativism because those paradigms are thereby rivals at the level of their domains. Indeed, paradigms can be said to succeed each other only within a given domain, since for example a paradigm of electromagnetism is not properly said to succeed a paradigm of genetics.

However, if facts are determined within a paradigm, it may seem incorrect to see such rivalry at the level of domains if domains are bodies of information, which might be considered to be the same as sets of facts. Yet Shapere does not equate facts and information:

> It is because theories and theory-determined entities, for example, can be or are parts of domains that I have preferred to speak of "items" or "elements" of domains rather than in more traditional terms like "facts," which have associations that make them unsuitable for covering the sorts of things that go together to form objects of scientific investigation. My talk of items of "information" (rather than, say, of "knowledge") is also partly motivated by the occurrence of theory-determined entities whose existence is merely proposed as a possibility.... (Shapere, 1984, p. 283)

Even if facts are theory-laden or parts of paradigms, Shapere still thinks that there is something more basic by which domains of inquiry can be grouped, and which helps explicate the concept of observation (Shapere, 1982).

So it seems plausible to understand the rivalry required among relativized sub-theories to be rivalry in terms of Shapere's conception of a domain. There must be some body of information for

4.2. RANGE OF RELATIVIZED SUB-THEORIES 115

which a unified account seems plausible, and there are different theories accounting for that information. However, Shapere characterizes this body of information as being problematic, which may not fit perfectly well with a general characterization of relativity. Some forms of relativity or relativism may address information that may not be taken to be problematic at all, at least from certain perspectives. Shapere seems to include this clause since the notion of a domain is intended to help explain scientific practice, and scientists tend not to investigate bodies of information that are not problematic in some way. Yet it is not clear that this clause needs to be part of a rivalry requirement with regard to relativity in general.

Furthermore, Shapere's clause relating to reasons for thinking that the information can be unified seems unnecessary for the purposes of determining the rivalry requirement for relativity. The possibility of unification of information seems needed to explain why a certain body of information is studied by physicists rather than by geneticists, but it is not clear that it is required for understanding relativity, particularly if such unification would threaten to undermine the very relativity that needs to be explained here by reducing the multiplicity of sub-theories in an instance of relativity to some single absolute theory.

To generalize, then, rivalry seems to require that theories attempt to account for the same information, in Shapere's sense. There may be a temptation to require further that rival theories account for all the same information, but I think that this requirement would be too strong, since some forms of conceptual relativity may group information so differently that what gets unified into a theory under one conceptual scheme is parsed differently under another scheme. To deny that these forms are genuine cases of relativity seems arbitrary. I would suggest that mere overlap in the information accounted under each theory should count as rivalry. This suggestion may seem too weak, since it might be thought for example that if a theory of domestic plumbing contains just one sentence representing a substantive ethical claim then it should not thereby be considered a rival for a fully articulated ethical theory on the basis of that single overlap. Yet I am not sure that this objection holds up, since if a theory of domestic plumbing contains one sentence with ethical import, then it should contain many more if it is closed under entailment. In any case, to avoid the need to articulate precisely how much overlap of accounted information is required in order to qualify as genuine relativity, I recommend that any overlap be considered sufficient. Certainly, global theories would count as rivals by virtue of their purported comprehensiveness, even if sub-groupings of information differ between them. Local theories would count as rivals by virtue of any overlap in information. Where local theories cover exactly the same information, they are clearly rivals with regard to that information. Where they cover only some of the same information, they would thereby seem to be rivals at least with regard to how that information gets parsed and classified.

To summarize, then, the following are required for the range of relativized sub-theories:

- Each theory must be closed under some conception of entailment.

- There must be multiple, different theories.

- The theories must be rivals.

4.3 Indexing

Indexing is the relation between relativized sub-theories and the elements of the relativizing domain. Again, indexing here is not to be confused with indexicality, as discussed in section 2.2. Whereas indexicality was concerned with the meaning and reference of individual terms, phrases, or sentences, indexing in relativity associates entire theories with some element of the relativizing domain, not to indicate the meaning of the theory, but to indicate the ownership or applicability of that theory, so to speak. A relativized sub-theory is a theory on a particular topic for some group, and indexing embodies this "for" relation. Susan Haack claims that there is a difference in interpretation in the phrase "is relative to" among various forms of relativism (Haack, 1996, p. 298), suggesting that there may be multiple kinds of indexing, but she seems to be considering the substantive metaphysical positions of various instances of relativism. From a purely structural perspective, I think several requirements for indexing can be identified across all instances of relativity by focusing on the formal relation between the relativizing domain and the relativized sub-theories. At the very

4.3. INDEXING

least, every element in the relativizing domain should be associated with some relativized sub-theory, if indeed x is to be relative to y for some x and y.

Ideally, I think the relation would be a one-to-one relation between relativized sub-theories and elements of the relativizing domain. Every sub-theory would be associated with one and only one element of the domain, and every element in the domain would be associated with one and only one sub-theory. Yet it is not clear whether a one-to-one relation is strictly required.

Suppose that there are more relativized sub-theories than there are elements of the relativizing domain. In this case, it seems that the range of relativized sub-theories may simply be misidentified. Pluralism in general does not require that all possible theories on a given topic are true or valid, only that more than one theory is valid. If there is a sub-theory that is not associated with some member of the relativizing domain, then it seems that the sub-theory should simply be removed from the range of relativized sub-theories, since it is not a theory for some group. In this way, it seems that a one-to-one relation can be preserved in this situation.

Alternately, there might be more sub-theories than elements of the domain because multiple sub-theories are associated with the same element. This situation would suggest that there is an instance of pluralism embedded within the overall relativity, namely that the sub-theory indexed to some member of the relativizing domain was in fact a pluralistic sub-theory, itself composed of multiple sub-theories, each of which is indifferently valid for the element of the relativizing domain. Perhaps some culture has more than one system of morality that is right for it, and it does not matter which system members of the culture follow at any given time, so long as they follow one of the systems associated with the culture. Yet rather than removing theories from the range of relativized sub-theories, this alternative seems to require combining certain sub-theories into pluralistic sub-theories in order to preserve a one-to-one relation. In any case, a one-to-one relation can also be preserved in this situation.

Suppose on the other hand that there are more elements in the relativizing domain than there are relativized sub-theories. Here it does not seem plausible simply to remove an element from the relativizing domain in order to preserve a one-to-one relation, since as already noted, the elements of the relativizing domain need to form a kind. If there is one element in the domain representing a kind that does not have a theory at all on a given topic, then it seems incorrect to say that that topic is relative to that kind. However, it may be the case that for some element in the relativizing domain, the topic simply does not exist, as in a radical case of conceptual relativism. Perhaps for some culture, there is simply no theory of morals at all, since there is no concept in that culture even remotely similar to morality. The example may be implausible, but in this hypothetical case it seems that a null theory should be accepted within the range of relativized sub-theories. Morality would still be relative to culture in the example, but for some culture or cultures the theory of morality is empty. Here too a one-to-one relation could be preserved.

Alternately, though, there may be more elements in the relativizing domain than theories in the range of relativized sub-theories because one sub-theory is a theory for several different elements, for example, if several cultures held the same moral theory. It is not clear that this situation would be unacceptable in a case of relativity; however, I would strongly suspect that the relativizing domain has been misidentified in such a case. If a single sub-theory is associated with multiple elements of the relativizing domain, it may be because there is something shared among those elements such that the relativizing domain should properly be formulated at the level of that shared characteristic, rather than at the level of individuals that share it. For example, if the relativizing domain contained individual humans, and all the men shared the same sub-theory, and all the women shared a different sub-theory, it would seem more appropriate to identify the relativizing domain as a set of sexes. Yet since it is not clear that there would always be some shared characteristic in such a case, I am not sure that this suspicion counts as an argument against the association of single sub-theories with multiple elements of the relativizing domain. Therefore, in the end, I do *not* think that a one-to-one relation should be required in every instance of relativity. A one-to-one relation would still seem to be an ideal case for an indexing relation, but it does not seem necessary in order to count as an instance of relativity. In cases in which a large number of elements in the relativizing domain share the same theory, though, I would still suspect that the relativizing domain may not have been formulated correctly and would seek to redefine the relativizing domain.

4.3. INDEXING

Where this cannot be accomplished, I think it is incumbent upon the overall relative theory to explain why the failure of a one-to-one relation is needed within the theory.

There would seem also to be some further requirements on the nature of the indexing relation. For example, given some range of sub-theories and some domain of elements forming a kind, it would seem quite easy to make an arbitrary correlation between the two sets. Yet such a random, haphazard association seems insufficient to qualify as an instance of relativity. The relation between elements of the relativizing domain and the range of relativized sub-theories does not seem to be an random one, but rather a non-arbitrary relation, meaning that the nature of the element in the relativizing domain should determine which sub-theory gets associated with it, as suggested earlier in the discussion on conventionalism in section 2.4. If morals are relative to culture, it is something about cultures in general that makes morality relative, and it is something about a particular culture that makes a particular system of morality proper to it. From a purely formal or structural perspective, it seems that this non-arbitrary relation cannot be elaborated any further without introducing substantive philosophical claims, but there would seem to be a requirement on any proposed case of relativism to demonstrate that the determination of a given element of the relativizing domain also determines which relativized sub-theory is appropriate to it, and that the indexing relation is not merely arbitrary. If it is indifferent which sub-theory gets indexed to which element of the relativizing domain, then I think it would be improper to classify the situation as an instance of relativity, but rather should be understood either as conventionalism or pluralism.

If choice or convention were acceptable instances of an indexing relation, it would seem that there would be no difference between relativity in that case and pluralism. In a case of pluralism, multiple theories on a given topic are applicable for some group. Since those theories are different in some way, there will be some difference in application. Some theories may have different normative consequences, such that one cannot act on both theories simultaneously in every situation. Even in cases of trivial differences between theories, where the theories differ only in the set of predicate letters used in the formalization, for example, there seems to be some difference in application, since in using a formalization, one must use one set of predicate letters or another. These practical differences imply that a choice must be made between which theory is applied at any given time, even though it may not matter which theory is chosen. Yet if choice were acceptable as an indexing relation, then any case of pluralism would also be a case of relativity, thus undermining the distinction between the two concepts. Insofar as conventions are based on such choices, even if those choices become stable over time, it seems that conventions likewise cannot form the basis for an indexing relation in relativity.[9] For these reasons I argue that the relation between the relativizing domain and the range of relativized sub-theories cannot be understood in terms of a choice without collapsing into conventionalism or pluralism.

There may yet be some aspect of choice within a relative system, though still constrained by the requirement for a non-arbitrary indexing relation. For example, suppose that morals are relative to cultures, and I am born into a particular culture. According to the account of the indexing relation as a non-arbitrary relation, there is some moral theory determined to me by virtue of membership in that culture. However, I think it would seem wrong to say that I could not choose some different moral theory. What the indexing relation in relativity suggests, though, is that if I choose a different moral theory, I thereby essentially choose a different culture. Choice can be made within a relative system, but the choice is primarily a choice to align oneself with a different element in the relativizing domain in order thereby to choose a different relativized sub-theory. Perspectives can indeed be shifted, but shifts in perspective would seem to entail a change both with regard to the relativizing domain and the range of relativized sub-theories, in accordance with the conception of a perspective adopted in this study.

Lastly, one additional requirement on the indexing relation should be noted to address a somewhat unusual situation. It may be the case that the relativizing domain likewise contains sub-theories, that something is relative to theories, perhaps as meta-narratives in the sense used by Lyotard as discussed in section 3.7. So perhaps theories can be relative to other, more general interpre-

---

[9] And therefore, I would insist that the phrase "relative to convention" be understood more strictly as "according to convention", in order not to confuse conventionality with relativity.

tive theories, for example, Marxist philosophy of science or Marxist erotic literature, as suggested earlier, as opposed to Freudian philosophy of science or Freudian erotic literature. In such a case there should be a restriction on the indexing relations between sub-theories and metanarratives to prevent a case in which each relativized sub-theory is indexed only to itself. In such a case, it would seem that the range of relativized sub-theories is simply mapped back onto itself, in the form of Marxist Marxism and Freudian Freudianism, for example, without any other variance of theory to theory. Rather than representing an instance of relativity, this case would seem simply to constitute an instance of pluralism, where the multiplicity of theories in the range of relativized sub-theories are all valid or true. Consequently, if sub-theories are relativized to sub-theories, they cannot only be indexed to themselves.

Therefore, indexing seems to entail the following requirements:

- Every element of the relativizing domain must be associated with some theory in the range of relativized sub-theories.

- This association must be made on the basis of a non-arbitrary relation whereby the determination of an element in the domain likewise determines which sub-theory is proper to it.

- Relativized sub-theories cannot only be indexed to themselves.

4.4 Modeling Conceptual Relativism

The preceding three sections have outlined the formal requirements for relativity. These requirements provide a structure in which an instance of relativism can be modeled. Relativism as an overall theory or system comprises a plurality of sub-theories, each of which is indexed to a member of some relativizing domain indicating the applicability of that sub-theory. As noted throughout this study, the structural approach adopted herein seeks to abstract away from substantive metaphysical, epistemological or moral claims made within particular claims of relativism. However, one form of relativism needs to be discussed briefly before proceeding further, namely conceptual relativism, since this form of relativism seems to pose a potential obstacle, and this obstacle relates to the formal requirements for relativity, specifically the suppositions underlying the requirements concerning the range of relativized sub-theories.

Consider some relative system meeting the formal requirements for relativity outlined here with regard to its relativizing domain, its range of relativized sub-theories, and its indexing relation between them. The relativized sub-theories will be formalized according to the assumptions of this study outlined in the introduction, and the formalizations will be presented in some formal language. The logic of such a relative system would need to provide semantics for the two relativity terms 'relative' and 'absolute' based on the structural features of this system, where those two terms are applied as operators to sentences in the system. It is a further assumption of this study that a formal account of these relativity terms can be given. Suppose now that what is modeled in this system is an instance of conceptual relativism, according to which certain conceptual schemes in the relativizing domain may lack concepts appearing within other conceptual schemes. A potential problem is that the concepts of being relative or absolute might be missing entirely from some of conceptual schemes in the relativizing domain, and therefore might be missing from the corresponding relativized sub-theories. Consequently, the recognition of conceptual relativism may undermine the very possibility of providing an account of the logical behavior of the two relativity terms, where that relativism is directed precisely against the concepts embodied in those terms. How can an account of the relativity terms be imposed on conceptual schemes that lack the corresponding concepts without changing those schemes and thereby changing what was needed to be modeled in the first place?

In order to preserve the assumption that a formal account of the relativity terms can be provided, I propose that the language of any sub-theory that lacks one or more of the relativity notions be supplemented with new symbols for those terms, or perhaps with some designated symbol from the language of one of the sub-theories that does contain concepts for the relativity notions.[10]

---

[10] The designation of a symbol for a relativity operator from the language of one of the sub-theories is not intended as a denial of the thesis of objective equity

4.4. MODELING CONCEPTUAL RELATIVISM

The concern here is that adding new symbols into the language may thereby add a new concept to the theory and thus change the theory. However, since a theory is a set of sentences in a language, namely those sentences held true by the theory, then adding a new symbol would change the theory substantially only if atomic sentences containing that symbol were held to be true. Certainly the addition of new symbols should not change the truth-values of sentences in the original theory, but this requirement does not seem sufficient. If atomic sentences containing the new symbols were valued true in the extended theory, it would seem that new concepts would have been added, and the theory would have changed. So if a theory previously lacked the symbol 'relative', and the addition of this symbol resulted in the sentence "Morals are relative" to be valued true, then it would seem that a new concept has been added to the original theory, namely relativity, and the theory would thereby have changed. Something in the new theory is relative, whereas nothing was relative in the original system, since the concept of relativity did not even appear. However, if all atomic sentences containing the new symbol were valued false, these new sentences would not substantially change the initial set of sentences held true that constitute the original theory.[11] So if every atomic sentence containing the symbol 'relative' were valued false, the addition of the symbol would not introduce a new concept, since the putative concept of relativity in that theory would represent a vacuous contrast within the resulting theory, because nothing would be relative. Consequently, I suggest that new symbols for the relativity notions can be added to the languages of sub-theories that lack those terms provided that the resulting overall relative system ensures that atomic sentences with those new symbols are never valued true by the system with regard to the

---

in this case, by suggesting that one of the languages is better than the others. Rather the designation is understood to be arbitrary and therefore merely as a convention for the purposes of this study.

[11] Since the theory is closed under entailment, the theories would still change on the addition of new symbols. New tautological statements including the new symbols would be added to the theory, as well as new statements logically equivalent to statements in the original theory. However, since there would be no new true atomic statements, I suggest that these new statements in the theory do not make a significant difference to the theory. One might say that the facts of the original theory would not be changed if new atomic statements are all false, if one enjoys speaking about facts.

elements of the relativizing domain to which the sub-theories in question are indexed.

This solution with regard to modeling the relativity terms likewise seems to provide a solution for another potential problem with regard to conceptual relativism. The problem concerns the comparison of statements in one sub-theory containing concepts that may be lacking in another sub-theory. In order to evaluate whether a sentence is relative or absolute, it would seem necessary to compare the valuation of that sentence in one sub-theory with its valuation in the other sub-theories. However, if the sentence uses concepts that are alien to some other sub-theory, then it is not clear how this comparison might proceed.

Yet if new symbols can be added to the language of a sub-theory for the relativity terms, and if those new symbols could be designated symbols from the language of some other sub-theory, then why could this not be done for every symbol used in the language of any sub-theory in the entire relative system? So long as the restriction just outlined above is honored, namely that atomic sentences containing symbols not in the original language of the sub-theory are never valued true therein, then it appears that every symbol appearing in any language within the overall relative system could appear within every sub-theory.[12] In this way, the differences between languages and concepts used within particular relativized sub-theories need not pose an obstacle against the formulation of an overall logic of relative systems.

However, before proceeding to the formulation of the proposed relative systems, two additional theses must be considered: objective equity and incommensurability.

---

[12] It might be thought that this strategy effectually invalidates conceptual relativism, since permitting a superset of symbols may suggest that no language or theory really lacks any given concept. I do not think that this conclusion is justified, though. Rather, this strategy merely suggests that having or lacking a concept is not the same as having or lacking a symbol in a language. This seems to be the point of Whorf's investigation into covert features of a language and calibration between languages as will be discussed in section 6.2, whereby a concept may be inherent in a language even if the language lacks an explicit term for it. I would suggest, however, that there is no difference between lacking a concept and having a new symbol in the language that results in non-tautological sentences containing it never being evaluated as true, at least on this strategy.

Chapter 5

Thesis of Objective Equity

Objective equity represents a claim of radical indexing according to the proposed definition of relativism offered in this study. Each relativized sub-theory is indexed to some member of the relativizing domain. However, if one of the relativized sub-theories is better than the others, then the indexing in question would seem to be a shallow sort of indexing, rather than a radical one, since it seems in that case that the best theory ought to be indexed to every member of the relativizing domain, effectively undermining the claim of relativism.[1] Indexing to sub-theories that are less than best seems to represent an indexing of errors rather than truths. The notion of equity in this thesis therefore captures the common claim with regard to relativism that none of the relativized sub-theories is better than any other.[2]

The notion of objectivity is invoked here since every relativized sub-theory might be claimed to be the best in a subjective sense, namely from the perspective of the element of the relativizing domain to which it is indexed. In a case of moral relativism indexed to cultures, for example, each culture is likely to claim that its own theory of morals is better than any other theory. Yet these claims are themselves relativized and merely reiterate the very relativity that is in question. A claim that one sub-theory is better than

---

[1] Or in a case in which some theories were better than others, even if there were not a single best theory, it would seem that the worse theories should be abandoned for one of the better ones.

[2] Geoffrey Harrison briefly discusses this thesis to distinguish between moral and non-moral uses of the phrase "as good as" (Harrison, 1976, p. 132). Here I intend to discuss only non-moral uses of the phrase.

the others or that equity obtains among all the sub-theories must somehow transcend the particular perspectives represented by the relativized indexing, and this transcendence seems to be precisely what objectivity expresses. Relativism requires the objective equity of all relativized sub-theories.

The invocation of objectivity here may seem strange, since relativism is commonly taken to be opposed to objectivity. Indeed, one way to demonstrate objective equity would be to demonstrate that objectivity is impossible with regard to the subject matter in question.[3] Thus, if there can be no objectivity with regard to morality, then equity among the relativized sub-theories of morals would be represented precisely by this lack of objectivity. However, I suggest that there may be other ways to establish equity between relativized sub-theories that in fact require an operative notion of objectivity, thereby suggesting that relativism might be compatible with objectivity according to some conception of objectivity.[4] One way might be for all relativized sub-theories to succeed equally well with regard to objectivity. Likewise, all sub-theories might fail equally. Furthermore, objectivity itself might permit relativization, such that all relativized sub-theories might prove to be objectively best, but only according to a relativized notion of objectivity.

These last three proposals might seem to be immediately precluded by the very notion of objectivity. For all relativized sub-theories to succeed equally well with regard to objectivity requires a conception of objectivity that countenances pluralism; yet it might be thought that the hallmark of objectivity is the rejection of such pluralism in favor of one true account. Consider the following characterization of objectivity:

> ...it is possible for an inquiry to be objective if, and only if, a / it is possible for its descriptions and explanation of a subject-matter to reveal the actual nature

---

[3] Philip E. Devine takes the core of the relativist argument to include a difference in fundamental standards between frameworks (Devine, 1984, pp. 408–409). While this may indeed demonstrate objective equity, I will later claim that objective equity can be established on the basis of shared standards.

[4] Though, of course, relativism is not compatible with all conceptions of objectivity. Compare with Michael Lynch's efforts with regard to pluralism and objectivity: "Finding a solution to the problem of how to reconcile pluralist philosophies with an objective notion of truth remains as the most pressing and difficult of the problems associated with such views" (Lynch, 1998, pp. 1–2).

of that subject-matter, where 'actual nature' means 'the qualities and relations of a subject-matter as they exist independently of an inquirer's thoughts and desires regarding them,' and b / it is not possible for two inquirers holding rival theories about some subject-matter and having complete knowledge of each other's theories (including the grounds for holding them) both to be justified in adhering to their theories. The second condition is necessary to exclude from being considered as objectivists those relativists who deny that it can be justified to adopt and sustain belief in one theory to the exclusion of others on non-pragmatic grounds. (Cunningham, 1973, p. 4)

Yet the author's inclusion of the second condition specifically to block relativism seems to be an *ad hoc* maneuver. If relativism is indeed opposed to objectivity, that opposition should be apparent simply from a clear understanding of the nature of objectivity and relativism without being obliged to characterize objectivity precisely in terms of a supposed opposition. If the subject matter in question happens to be pluralistic in nature, then revealing the actual nature of that subject matter would seem to require acknowledging that two inquirers might be equally justified in holding different theories. This kind of consideration seems to be at the heart of the position termed 'objective relativism' in the early twentieth century, wherein "Theories of objective relations and the interrelatedness of the world lead to relativism" (Robischon, 1958, p. 1127). If relativism does obtain in the world, it is not immediately clear that such relativism could never be understood in an objective manner, though this kind of objective relativism would likely not be a case of global relativism.

These considerations do not prove that relativism is congenial to objectivity, but merely suggest that there is conceptual space within objectivity to support the sort of transcendence of perspective required to demonstrate radical indexing in a claim of objective equity. What is required here is to identify a conception of objectivity sufficient to explicate the meaning of objective equity. Consequently, the examination of objectivity that follows will not aim to provide a definitive account or critique of objectivity, but will simply explore various conceptions of objectivity as a means for delineating what is required to support a claim of objective equity in relativism, even if there are alternative conceptions of objectivity that preclude allowing objectivity to serve any role within relativism. The argument in this chapter is not that relativists must claim that each relativized sub-theory is objectively equal to every other one, according to every conception of objectivity. Rather, the argument is that there seems to be some conception of objectivity that characterizes the equity that prevails among relativized sub-theories in a case of relativism, and that the notion of objectivity is broad enough to accommodate this particular conception.

5.1 Various Conceptions of Objectivity

Inquiring into the nature of objectivity would seem to assume that objectivity is a definite, unified notion, but this does not seem to be the case. Peter Novick calls objectivity "a sprawling collection of assumptions, attitudes, aspirations and antipathies. At best it is what the philosopher W. B. Gallie has called an 'essentially contested concept,' like 'social justice' or 'leading a Christian life,' the exact meaning of which will always be in dispute" (Novick, 1988, p. 1). Likewise, Lorraine Daston claims, "Our usage of the word 'objectivity' ... is hopelessly but revealingly confused. It refers at once to metaphysics, to methods, and to morals" (Daston, 1992, p. 597). Indeed, Sandra Harding has noted that the notion of objectivity is applied to a variety of referents, including individuals or groups of individuals, knowledge claims, methods, and knowledge-seeking communities (Harding, 1995, p. 332). Robert Nozick considers objectivity of both facts and beliefs (Nozick, 2001, p. 75), and Crispin Wright focuses on the objectivity of statements, further identifying three species of the objectivity of statements: objectivity of truth, of meaning, and of judgment (Wright, 1986, pp. 5–6). While one constant in the notion of objectivity seems to be its opposition to the notion of 'subjectivity', it should be noted that the meaning of the terms 'objectivity' and 'subjectivity' were inverted from their earlier scholastic usage as a result of Kant's appropriation of the terms (Daston & Galison, 2007, pp. 29–31), further adding to the confusion concerning this concept.

Daston and Peter Galison have traced the emergence of objectivity as an epistemic norm in a study of the representation of

5.1. VARIOUS CONCEPTIONS OF OBJECTIVITY

knowledge in a variety of scientific atlases (Daston & Galison, 1992, 2007). According to their study, objectivity emerged in part as a reaction to the norm of truth-to-nature in which ideal or characteristic images were presented to display the regularity of natural types opposed to the variance and multiplicity of individuals. The questionable artistic and interpretive license involved in creating these idealizations prompted scientists to seek a more mechanical means of presenting images that would not be subject to manipulations or distortions, and mechanical objectivity, best embodied in the use of photography, emerged as a norm that restrained the imaginative excesses of artists and scientists. However, objectivity itself eventually was partly supplanted as the leading epistemic norm by the norm of trained judgment, in which the necessity for interpretation was recognized even in the clearest cases of mechanical objectivity. Yet Daston and Galison are careful to note:

> ...mechanical objectivity did not drive out truth-to-nature, but nor did it leave truth-to-nature unchanged. Epistemic virtues do not replace one another like a succession of kings. Rather they accumulate into a repertoire of possible forms of knowing. Within this slowly expanding repertoire, each element modifies the others: mechanical objectivity defined itself in contradistinction to truth-to-nature; truth-to-nature in the age of mechanical objectivity was articulated defensively, with reference to alternatives and to critics. Epistemic virtues emerge and evolve in specific historical contexts, but they do not necessarily become extinct under new conditions, as long as each continues to address some urgent challenge to acquiring and securing knowledge. (Daston & Galison, 2007, pp. 111–113).

The implication of these considerations seems to be that further epistemic virtues may emerge in the future, which will in turn modify the current conception of objectivity as well as the other epistemic virtues. The search for the meaning and nature of objectivity thus seems to amount to aiming at a moving target.

Yet the multiplicity of applications and conceptions of objectivity and its potentially changing nature need not pose a problem for this study, since what is required is simply some conception of objectivity that is applicable to the equity that obtains among relativized sub-theories, not a definitive universal conception of objectivity, as already noted. Consequently, the availability of a variety of conceptions and applications seems rather to be an asset rather than a liability, since this variety would seem to increase the chances that some applicable conception of objectivity may already be available. In this section, therefore, I consider some available characterizations of objectivity that might apply to relativism.

Thomas Nagel has provided a particularly notable characterization of objectivity in his use of the slogan "view from nowhere" (T. Nagel, 1986), which seems to capture much of the intent behind objectivity. Yet Nagel does not assert that objectivity is such a view from nowhere, but poses the slogan as a problem for objectivity: "how to combine the perspective of a particular person inside the world with an objective view of that same world, the person and his viewpoint included" (p. 3). Accordingly, Nagel's application of objectivity is to beliefs and attitudes: "Objectivity is a method of understanding. It is beliefs and attitudes that are objective in the primary sense. Only derivatively do we call objective the truths that can be derived this way" (p. 4). While Nagel's project is to combine subjective and objective viewpoints, he does not proceed by placing subjectivity and objectivity in opposition, which would seem merely to perpetuate the problem without advancing toward a solution, but rather develops dual conceptions of objectivity applicable to the physical and the mental realms as a means of facilitating the combination of both viewpoints. The specifics of his attempt at such reconciliation are not especially important for this study, only his conceptions of objectivity.

Nagel describes physical objectivity as a progression:

> The development goes in stages, each of which gives a more objective picture than the one before. The first step is to see that our perceptions are caused by the action of things on us, through their effects on our bodies, which are themselves part of the physical world. The next step is to realize that since the same physical properties that cause perceptions in us through our bodies also produce different effects on other physical things and can exist without causing any perceptions

> at all, their true nature must be detachable from their perceptual appearance and need not resemble it. The third step is to try to form a conception of that true nature independent of its appearance either to us or to other types of perceivers. This means not only not thinking of the physical world from our own particular point of view, but not thinking of it from a more general human perceptual point of view either: not thinking of how it looks, feels, smells, tastes, or sounds. These secondary qualities then drop out of our picture of the external world, and the underlying primary qualities such as shape, size, weight, and motion are thought of structurally. (p. 14)

Nagel thus seems to equate physical objectivity with the search for primary qualities. Note that Nagel's third step involves independence from perceivers, which seems to capture a common thread in many accounts of the nature of objectivity. What relates primarily to the perceiver is subjective, whereas what relates to what is perceived independently of any particular perceiver is objective, even if that objectivity itself is a method of understanding in which a perceiver is required as one who understands the object of perception and understanding.

This recognition of the place of subjects in the natural order, particularly with regard to the act of understanding, leads Nagel to posit mental objectivity in addition to physical objectivity. While physical objectivity is ultimately correlated with primary qualities, Nagel does not narrowly characterize mental objectivity in terms of secondary qualities. Rather, mental objectivity is the product of the same effort to understand an object independently of any particular perceiver, but in this case the object is one's own mental life and the mental lives of others, which certainly includes the perception of secondary qualities, but is not necessarily restricted to such perceptions: "if we are parts of the world as it is in itself, then we ought to be able to include ourselves — our minds as well as our bodies — in a conception that is not tied exclusively to our own point of view" (p. 17). Note that this conception of mental objectivity seems structurally similar to the attempt to characterize relativism, since someone describing relativism, like the author of this study, is purporting to describe all perspectives from outside any particular perspective, while including the perspective from which the description is made within that description, which raises the question of incoherence. Nagel acknowledges that mental objectivity "will necessarily be incomplete", but does not see this as a problem, "because there is no reason to assume that the world as it is in itself must be objectively comprehensible" (p. 18). Whether a comparable response can be made in the case of relativism remains to be seen.

Nicholas Rescher takes issue with the characterization of objectivity in terms of a view from nowhere, and considers the analogy with scenery painting: "...what is at issue with objectivity is not point-of-view-lessness but what might be characterized as photographic accuracy — trying to represent pretty much what any normal observer would recognize as a depiction of that scene from that point of view" (Rescher, 1997, p. 6). For Rescher, "Objectivity, then, is a matter of universality (or at least generality) of recognition access, unrestricted availability to the community of standard respondents — in the cognitive case *rational thinkers*, in the photographic case *normal observers*. Such objectivity calls for seeking to eliminate the distorting influence of personal or parochial eccentricities" (p. 7). This account of objectivity seems to accord well with Daston and Galison's account of the emergence mechanical objectivity, though Rescher is not strictly concerned with the conveyance of knowledge but judgment in general, and he ties such objectivity of judgment closely with rationality: "Reason is (circumstantially) universal, and it is objectivity's coordination with rationality that links it to universality" (p. 8).

This demand for universality may seem to lead to a totalitarian regime of uniformity of thought and action, but Rescher takes pains to explain how the universality of objectivity and rationality are compatible with diversity and pluralism. Ultimately, he explains this compatibility in terms of a functional hierarchy: "At the top there are uniform general principles that are inherent in the very nature of the project at issue. But at the lower levels of concrete implementation there is room for variation brought about by the variability of circumstance." So the rationality of diverse particular cases is granted if it is "'covered' by a universal principle of rationality that holds good generally and for everyone" (p. 19). In Rescher's example, ordering steak at a restaurant could be considered rational by virtue of a universal general principle to select the

5.1. VARIOUS CONCEPTIONS OF OBJECTIVITY

tastiest item on the menu, where different people may order different items according to what they find tastiest. He therefore claims that this high level of universal objectivity is compatible with lower level pluralism and relativism (p. 20).

Rescher tends to describe the path to objectivity in terms of abstraction: "An objective judgment is one that abstracts from personal idiosyncrasies or group parochialisms" (p. 7); yet abstraction alone seems to leave room for a relativized conception of objectivity, which would seem to put pressure on the role of universality in Rescher's account. The issue here is that abstraction retains the traces of the starting perspective from which idiosyncrasies are abstracted. An abstraction cannot add content, so to speak, only subtract content, so the result of abstraction will contain only so much content as the original perspective contained. Objectivity about a given subject matter, though, would seem to require all the relevant information about the subject matter, not just information available from some particular starting point. Consequently, any abstraction of idiosyncrasies should likely be taken only after all the relevant perspectives have been explored and possibly even synthesized together to provide a basis for subsequent abstraction. However, Rescher's primary concern with objectivity of judgment assimilated to rationality seems to relate precisely to a kind of situated objectivity, namely a concern with what one should rationally do in a particular situation, where the situation in question represents a perspective whose starting point cannot be abstracted away. The relevant perspectives in this case are not situational perspectives but rather are the perspectives of all rational agents, which provides Rescher with the kind of objective universality he seeks: "One potentially effective means of achieving objectivity is 'to put oneself in another's place' and to proceed by taking into view some paradigmatically reasonable person and asking what they would do if confronted by a situation of the sort that one is facing oneself" (p. 7).

Rescher notes at one point that "Physicists see objectivity as a matter of the invariance of results under changes of an observer-correlative coordinate system" (p. 6). Robert Nozick takes up the notion of invariance and places it at the heart of his account of objectivity. Nozick first outlines three marks of the ordinary notion of objectivity with regard to facts: "accessibility from different angles, intersubjectivity, and independence" (Nozick, 2001, p. 76), representing many of the notions of objectivity already considered, later arguing that these three marks can be explained by a fourth characteristic of objectivity, namely invariance under transformations (p. 85), thus making invariance the primary characteristic of objectivity. The notion of invariance certainly seems to capture the idea of independence from particular perspectives by seeking what remains the same when perspectives shift.

Yet it would appear that nothing is invariant under all transformations, since there will be some transformations that destroy the object in question. Rather than invariance under all transformations, "A property or relationship is objective when it is invariant under the appropriate transformations" (p. 79). The question then becomes which transformations are appropriate or admissible. Nozick argues that the criteria for admissible transformations are not given by some prior definition, but instead the list of admissible transformations is developed as science itself progresses. "The development of our understanding of objective facts is a stepwise process, involving mutually modifying knowledge of new facts and of new admissible transformations" (p. 80). Because of the variance in what transformations are admissible at a certain level of theory, Nozick considers the possibility of a relativized notion of objectivity:

> Should we speak of *objectivity-at-a-level*, and claim that something is absolutely objective if and only if it is objective at all levels? Perhaps nothing is objective at *all* levels, but when the objectivity of x fails when it reaches a certain level, there always will be a y at that other level which is objective at that level. If there were an infinite series of levels, then at every level there could be objectivity, without there being the same objectivity at each level. (p. 83)

Rather than relativizing objectivity, though, Nozick seems ultimately to prefer that objectivity as invariance under transformation comes in degrees, particularly since the three marks of the ordinary notion of objectivity likewise comes in degrees: "There can be more or fewer routes by which a fact is accessible, it can admit of greater or lesser intersubjective agreement, it can be more or less independent of our beliefs and desires.... It seems promising

5.1. VARIOUS CONCEPTIONS OF OBJECTIVITY

to hold that one property is more objective than another when the first is invariant under a wider range of (admissible) transformations than the second is" (p. 87).

Yet feminists epistemologists such as Sandra Harding view the search for invariances and the quest for neutrality as problematic because they seem to distort the subject matter, rather than revealing its essential nature: "Objectivism defends and legitimates the institutions and practices through which the distortions and their often exploitative consequences are generated" (Harding, 1995, p. 337). Characterizing the conceptions of objectivity investigated thus far as weak objectivity, Harding argues for a strong version of objectivity that includes the knower in the account of the known: "The subject of knowledge — the individual and the historically located social community whose unexamined beliefs its members are likely to hold 'unknowingly,' so to speak — must be considered as part of the object of knowledge from the perspective of scientific method" (Harding, 1993, p. 69). Rather than abstracting away from particular perspectives or ignoring variances when perspectives change, strong objectivity seeks to maximize objectivity by including all perspectives and all the views of the subject matter from those perspectives.

Harding presents her conception of strong objectivity as an alternative to a choice between objectivity and relativism, not so much as a third alternative, but as a rejection of the need for a choice between these two, by updating the notion of objectivity to address current social and scientific needs while retaining the merits of the older conception of objectivity (Harding, 1995, p. 332). The need to include every perspective within a strong program of objectivity may seem to result in a relativist system, but strong objectivity in this sense instead tends to destroy relativism in a way particularly relevant to the thesis of objective equity. Strong objectivity seems to generate a new perspective that incorporates all other perspectives. Yet this new perspective is not considered as just one more perspective on par with the others. Instead, the demand for strong objectivity seems to suggest that this new perspective is better than all the others precisely by virtue of being more inclusive, thereby denying the thesis of objective equity. Rather than appearing as just another competitor to the other perspectives, the perspective of strong objectivity seems to impose itself on all the other perspectives with the demand that in addition to the recognition of the perspective's own viewpoints, each perspective must recognize all the other perspectives. Since the perspective of strong objectivity is inclusive of other perspectives, the imposition of this new perspective apparently does not constitute an injustice on existing perspectives, but precisely represents the demands of justice with regard to all perspectives.[5] Yet strong objectivity seems to run the same risk of incoherence that relativism does by the normative imposition of all perspectives upon each separate perspective, though it is not immediately clear that the problem is related to self-refutation in the case of strong objectivity as with relativism. Since it seems that no concrete example of strong objectivity has been presented at the time of writing this study, it is not even clear what form such an example would take.

Finally, an earlier challenge to objectivity comes from Friedrich Nietzsche, who objects to the ascetic kind of renunciation involved in the abstraction from and restraint of personal idiosyncrasies typically embodied in traditional conceptions of objectivity.[6] This criticism follows from Nietzsche's perspectivism:

> There is *only* perspective seeing, *only* a perspective 'knowing'; the *more* affects we allow to speak about a thing, the *more* eyes, various eyes we are able to use for the same thing, the more complete will be our 'concept' of the thing, our 'objectivity'. But to eliminate the will completely and turn off all the emotions without exception, assuming we could: well? Would that not mean to *castrate* the intellect? (Nietzsche, 1994, p. 92)

Like Harding, Nietzsche seeks not to reject the notion of objectivity, but to amend it. Nietzsche points ahead to a future conception of objectivity: "*having in our power* our 'pros' and 'cons': so as to be able to engage and disengage them so that we can use the *difference* in perspectives and affective interpretations for knowledge" (p. 92). Of course, Nietzsche's reference to castration suggests that his concerns are not precisely the same as feminist epis-

---

[5] Contrast this position with Lyotard's notion of a differend as discussed in section 3.7. In Lyotard's terms, Harding seems to be arguing for a kind of meta-narrative according to a new genre of discourse that does not thereby create a differend.

[6] Daston and Galison likewise note the moral connotations of objectivity (Daston & Galison, 1992, p. 82).

5.1. VARIOUS CONCEPTIONS OF OBJECTIVITY 137

temologists. Whereas strong objectivity is designed to include all perspectives to eliminate the abuses of any one perspective, Nietzsche's future objectivity allows equally for the disengagement of perspectives in the service of knowledge.

Such future objectivity seems to consist in a mastery over all perspectives such that one can shift perspective at will to use each of them according to their strengths. While the notion of power over all perspectives is not particularly congenial to specifically feminist interpretations, Nietzsche's future objectivity does seem to capture something about the traditional conception of objectivity that Harding's account captures in a different way, namely that under this sort of objectivity, one is not trapped in any particular subjective perspective, doomed to see the world in one and only one way, since the future objective inquirer may adopt a variety of perspectives in search of knowledge. Of course, Nietzsche must deny that this shows that there is something outside of perspectives that can shift perspectives, which would result in a variety of realist metaphysics rather than the kind of perspectivism he espouses.

It is not immediately clear how these varying conceptions of objectivity can be coordinated to provide a conception of objectivity suitable for the purposes of this study. Each conception seems to result from a reaction to different concerns, and the concerns of this study are somewhat different from each of these philosophers. Nor does a synthesis of these conceptions seem feasible, given that some of these conceptions were formulated precisely to criticize others. Consequently, I will simply leave them as background considerations before proposing a conception of objectivity according to which the thesis of objective equity can be understood. What I hope to have shown thus far is that there is sufficient diversity in the conception of objectivity to justify even looking for some conception that could serve to elucidate the claims of relativism.

Yet before proceeding to identify this conception within the question of objectivity in history, I think it is worth considering in some detail the challenge to objectivity from Richard Rorty, whose work has sometimes been understood to have relativistic overtones.

5.2 Richard Rorty

Whereas Harding and Nietzsche advocate an expansion of the conception of objectivity to make it stronger, Richard Rorty advocates a contraction of objectivity to the weaker notion of solidarity with one's own community of inquirers. Such solidarity seems to suggest that knowledge would thereby be relativized to different communities of inquirers. Rorty argues that the image of epistemology as accurate representation of reality is fundamentally misguided, and that rather than seeking a replacement for epistemology that is not misguided in this way, we should "rather try to free ourselves from the notion that philosophy must center around the discovery of a permanent framework for inquiry" (Rorty, 1980, p. 380). As a consequence of the argument for this form of pragmatism, Rorty challenges the traditional notion of objectivity on the grounds that it leads to self-deception.

According to Rorty, the word 'objective' is used in two different ways: (1) "characterizing the view which would be agreed upon as a result of argument undeflected by irrelevant considerations", and (2) "representing things as they really are" (pp. 333–334). "The two are largely coextensive, and for nonphilosophical purposes no trouble arises from running them together" (p. 334). Yet trouble does arise for metaphysical and epistemological questions that aim to establish a link between language and thought, on the one hand, and an independent world, on the other hand. The trouble follows from Rorty's earlier argument that "the notion of 'accurate representation' is simply an automatic and empty compliment which we pay to those beliefs which are successful in helping us do what we want to do" (p. 10). Accordingly, the second usage of objectivity as accurate representation falls empty, and therefore "the application of such honorifics as 'objective' and 'cognitive' is never anything more than an expression of the presence of, or the hope for, agreement among inquirers" (p. 355).

The aspect of self-deception in objectivity arises from Rorty's appeal to philosophers like Heidegger and Sartre. Whereas Heidegger sees "the search for objective knowledge ... as one human project among others", Sartre, "sees the attempt to gain an objective knowledge of the world, and thus of oneself, as an attempt to avoid the responsibility for choosing one's project" (pp. 360–361). According to this line of thought, then, "objectivity should be seen

5.2. RICHARD RORTY

as conformity to the norms of justification (for assertions and for actions) we find around us. Such conformity becomes dubious and self-deceptive only when seen as something more than this — namely, as a way of obtaining access to something which 'grounds' current practices of justification in something else" (p. 361). Avoiding such self-deception therefore requires conceiving objectivity merely as solidarity among inquirers, thus repudiating objectivity's stronger metaphysical pretensions.

With regard to my current project of understanding the thesis of objective equity in relativism, if Rorty is correct, and objectivity should be conceived in terms of solidarity, then it seems that objective equity may be achieved in terms of solidarity among the various inquirers represented within the relativizing domain. Yet these inquirers disagree among themselves, which is why their theories needed to be relativized to elements in the relativizing domain to begin with. Therefore, on the one hand, under Rorty's account, objectivity as solidarity does not obtain across relativized sub-theories, so the kind of equity embodied in the thesis of objective equity would be represented solely by an absence of objectivity in Rorty's sense, not by any positive conception of equity among the relativized sub-theories with regard to objectivity. If solidarity were achieved among perspectives, then the disagreement would end, thereby destroying the need for relativization. On the other hand, and more problematically, the thesis of objective equity is designed to express radical indexing within relativism, but under Rorty's understanding of objectivity as solidarity, objective equity would effectively become mere disagreement among inquirers represented within the relativizing domain. However, this disagreement is already posited in the formal requirements for relativity independently of the thesis of objective equity. Under Rorty's conception of objectivity, objective equity would add nothing to the understanding of relativism and therefore seems to fall empty. Yet the thesis of objective equity was needed in the understanding of relativism to express the notion that none of the relativized sub-theories is better than the others. Consequently, it seems either that Rorty's conception of objectivity is inappropriate for understanding objective equity, or that the solidarity by which Rorty understands objectivity must apply to something other than the relativized sub-theories on which there is evident disagreement in a case of relativism.

Alternatively, this solidarity might be understood in terms of communities of evaluators of the various relativized sub-theories, where those communities are not identical with elements in the relativizing domain, but stand outside as assessors of the overall relativistic system. However, since different communities may express solidarity of judgment in different ways, this alternative seems merely to spawn an instance of higher order relativity against judgments of the original relativistic system, and this higher order relativity would also need an operative conception of objectivity in order to evaluate the question of objective equity at that level. Continuing to understand objectivity in terms of solidarity would either continue to spawn further higher order instances of relativity against different groups of evaluators, or would merely reiterate the disagreement among the same groups of evaluators. Consequently, identifying solidarity in this way would not seem to provide any grounds by which objective equity could be understood either.

It would seem that solidarity would need to be established among groups that are either within the relativizing domain or outside of it, and these two alternatives would seem to be exhaustive. If the groups are within the relativizing domain, then objectivity as solidarity either destroys or reiterates the formal requirements for relativity. If the groups are outside the relativizing domain, then higher order instances of relativity arise that themselves require the application of objectivity as solidarity by which to evaluate the thesis of objective equity. Since neither alternative succeeds in elucidating the conception of objectivity for the purposes of this study, it would seem that solidarity cannot properly be used to understand objective equity with regard to relativism.

Yet beyond the immediate needs of this study, there seems to be an odd tension in Rorty's pragmatic understanding of objectivity that merits comment before proceeding. First, it is not clear that Rorty's line of argument requires the pragmatic rejection of objectivity as representing things as they really are. While Heidegger does not write in the pragmatist tradition, Rorty notes that Heidegger considers "the search for objective knowledge...as one human project among others" (p. 360); yet insofar as it is a human project at all, that human project would seem to have some pragmatic value. A classical pragmatist such as William James would argue that the meaning of the quest for objectivity consists precisely in this pragmatic value as a human project, but would likely

5.2. RICHARD RORTY

not argue that the quest for objectivity should therefore be abandoned, since that would also abandon the pragmatic value of the search.

In accordance with the pragmatist motto to accept no distinction that does not make a difference, Rorty might be thought to be arguing that there is no pragmatic difference between objectivity and solidarity, but this interpretation does not seem to hold. Rorty endorses the Sartrean notion that objectivity constitutes a self-deception when it entails more than mere "conformity to the norms of justification ...we find around us" (p. 361), but if objectivity constitutes a self-deception whereas solidarity does not, then there must be some pragmatic difference between them. Nor could Rorty posit a choice between objectivity and solidarity as two different ways of giving meaning to lives (Rorty, 1989, p. 35) if Rorty did not see a pragmatic difference between them.

So it seems that Rorty must be arguing that whatever pragmatic value objectivity has over and above solidarity is not worthwhile. This value for Rorty seems to consist in "two sorts of metaphysical comfort":

> One is the thought that membership in our biological species carries with it certain "rights," a notion which does not seem to make sense unless the biological similarities entail the possession of something nonbiological, something which links our species to a nonhuman reality and thus gives the species moral dignity.... The second comfort is provided by the thought that our community cannot wholly die. The picture of a common human nature oriented toward correspondence to reality as it is in itself comforts us with the thought that even if our civilization is destroyed, even if all memory of our political or intellectual or artistic community is erased, the race is fated to recapture the virtues and the insights and the achievements which were the glory of that community. (1989, p. 45)

Even if Rorty is correct that these metaphysical comforts are part of the pragmatic value of objectivity beyond solidarity, it is not clear that these metaphysical comforts are thereby worthless, even if they are not strictly true, and even if obviously false, they may have an instrumental value in prompting further inquiry where satisfaction with mere solidarity might have stopped short. It is hard to see a classical pragmatist such as William James arguing for the abandonment of these pragmatic values rather than simply recognizing these values for what they are. Yet Rorty often takes a cavalier attitude toward the pragmatist tradition of which he claims to be a part, dismissing "the bad ('metaphysical') parts of Dewey and James" (Rorty, 1982, p. 214), while essentially banishing Charles Sanders Peirce from pragmatism altogether: "His contribution to pragmatism was merely to have given it a name, and to have stimulated James" (1982, p. 161). So perhaps it is not surprising to find in Rorty's variety of pragmatism an argument against certain pragmatic values that earlier pragmatists may have acknowledged, if not cherished.

A second odd tension in Rorty's understanding of objectivity concerns the applicability of solidarity to a community that takes objectivity to be more than mere solidarity. By criticizing this community and this tradition, Rorty seems to place himself outside that community, namely "the community of the liberal intellectuals of the secular modern West" (1989, p. 44), thereby failing to show the kind of solidarity that he advocates. This situation seems to bear some similarity to a criticism of relativism in which the relativist, by articulating relativism, seems to place himself outside of the very relative system that he describes, but whereas in the case of relativism, this criticism seems to lead to a charge of self-refutation, in the case of Rorty, what seems to be at stake is a potential charge of hypocrisy on Rorty's part by failing to exemplify the solidarity that he recommends in others. Yet such a charge of hypocrisy may not be justified since Rorty might be understood to be demonstrating and advocating solidarity with the pragmatist tradition, rather than with the objectivist tradition. However, given Rorty's dismissive attitudes to certain aspects of the pragmatist tradition as noted above, it is not clear how well this solidarity succeeds or at what price it may be gained. In a cynical mood, I might say that Rorty seems mainly to want everyone else to achieve solidarity with him, rather than to demonstrate solidarity with any pre-existing community of which he claims to be a part. However, I am not certain that this issue surrounding the application of solidarity is an insuperable problem for Rorty, but again it does seem to represent a tension that needs to be resolved, the same tension that needs to be resolved in any instance of ethnocentrism, such as Rorty advocates (1989, p. 44), that nevertheless countenances criticism and innovation. Yet in any case, as already noted, Rorty's conception of objectivity does not seem relevant to an understanding of the thesis of objective equity, which is my main concern here.

5.3 Objectivity in History

The question of objectivity in history seems much more relevant to the purposes of this study, particularly since the question has been debated specifically with regard to the prospect of relativism in historical accounts. One common argument against such objectivity is that history is always written from the perspective of present values and interests, which can frequently be seen fairly clearly from an investigation of older historical accounts in which the biases of the period in which those accounts were written appear to shape the nature of the historical account itself. It might be thought that the subjectivity introduced in older accounts was merely a methodological failing that could be remedied by greater care and attention in current historical practice, but there is reason to doubt that this is possible since contemporary historians lack the kind of perspective toward their own potential biases that they bring to bear on those older accounts. Consequently, even a conscious attempt on the part of a historian to preserve objectivity may inadvertently introduce biases into the account that are not apparent to current historians, but that might be painfully obvious to future historians who have better perspective.

Another common argument holds that historians have no direct access to the events that they aim to describe. The documentary evidence and testimony on which historians base their accounts are themselves merely interpretations of events which historians in turn reinterpret. Without such direct access to events, no verification of a historian's account is possible, and therefore no objectivity is possible. The disagreement of historians over what really happened is taken as evidence for this lack of objectivity, since if there were direct access to events, such disagreement could be much more easily resolved, rather than accepted as an inevitable difference in interpretation.

I do not intend to trace the full debate over objectivity in history,[7] nor to engage with the issue directly. Rather I will merely present several key philosophical responses within this debate. As it turns out, these responses lead directly to an understanding of objective equity with regard to relativism.

Responding to the common arguments against objectivity just outlined, Christopher Blake notes "that among the working canons of historians are standards for determining the accuracy or reliability of sources", and that "they are observed by common consent, and, moreover, there is common recognition, in spite of some residual disagreement over detail, where they have been transgressed" (Blake, 1955, p. 63). Blake continues to claim that by demanding more than such standards for accuracy, the arguments against objectivity in history seem to demand higher standards that could not be met without making history itself impossible to write, "for if history cannot be objective as long as it is necessary to select facts, or possible to state them ambiguously or by different locutions, then it never will be" (p. 64). This demand for higher standards seems to violate the principle of non-vacuous contrast, namely "the general requirement that no predicate apply either to everything or to nothing in its universe of discourse, since such a rule of use would be tantamount to no rule at all" (p. 64). Consequently, it seems that the question of objectivity in history would become senseless if the demand for objectivity would preclude writing any history at all.

The problem as Blake sees it lies in the demand for the kind of objectivity in history that exists in the sciences. "But history is not a science, and therefore as a paradigm of objectivity for the philosophy of history science just will not do" (p. 68). Instead, history seems to have its own paradigm of objectivity that works perfectly well for it: "being objective entails reporting accurately, together with some vaguer notion of neutrality in the idioms used and in the choice and arrangement of what is said — so that we might wish to say of the whole 'No reasonable person would argue with that' " (p. 66). Therefore the question of objectivity in history on this conception of objectivity can be answered by acknowledging that some history meets this paradigm of objectivity and some does not (p. 67).

---

[7] For a detailed history of the debate concerning objectivity in the American historical profession, covering these two common patterns of argument, see (Novick, 1988).

5.3. OBJECTIVITY IN HISTORY

Responding to Blake's arguments, John Passmore evaluates the following eight proposed criteria of objectivity in history, dismissing "out of hand all proposed criteria of objectivity which would make it vacuous" (Passmore, 1958, p. 98):

> Criterion I (The Cartesian or mathematico-deductive): An objective inquiry either (a) deduces its conclusions from self-evident axioms or (b) unfolds them from essences or definitions. (p. 98)
>
> Criterion Two (Mach's criterion): An objective inquiry is one which begins from data which are literally such, i.e. which nakedly confront us. (p. 99)
>
> Criterion Three: An objective inquiry is a direct examination of the world which does not rely upon testimony. (p. 100)
>
> [Criterion Four:] a science proceeds objectively only if its statements contain no expressions except those which "mean the same" for all observers. (p. 102)
>
> Criterion Five: An inquiry is objective only if it keeps to atomic facts. (p. 102)
>
> Criterion Six: An inquiry is objective only if it does not select from within its material. (p. 103)
>
> Criterion Seven: A branch of inquiry is objective only if it contains a method of deciding between conflicting hypotheses. (p. 106)
>
> Criterion Eight: In objective inquiries, conclusions are reached which are universally acceptable. (p. 108)

Each of the criteria is proposed in reaction to the failings of previous criteria; however, Passmore argues that each criterion has difficulties. Whereas earlier criteria such as the first and the second cannot be met by history at all, the situation is different with regard to the later criteria. Passmore demonstrates considerable sympathy for the seventh criterion, involving a method for evaluating hypotheses: "Like the rest of us, he [the historian] has various ways of testing his hypotheses, or his reconstructions, none of them committing him to a 'criterion of truth' " (p. 107). However, a problem arises, as with Blake's argument, when the kind of objectivity found in the sciences is demanded for history, such as a demand for universal acceptability as embodied in Criterion Eight, which history does not meet, given the evident disagreement among historians. Yet Passmore notes that even in the sciences, absolutely perfect agreement does not occur, given the existence of "an insignificant band of flat-earthers, a much larger group which refuses to accept the evolutionary theory of human origins" (p. 109). Passmore's conclusion here is similar to Blake's: "if we press the criterion of objectivity too hard, it applies to no form of inquiry; slacken it slightly and history edges its way in with the rest" (p. 109). The presence of "regular ways of settling issues, by the use of which men of whatever party can be brought to see what actually happened" (p. 109) seems to be a perfectly serviceable conception of objectivity within history when sufficiently slackened as Passmore suggests.

To the argument against objectivity in history on the grounds that all history is written from the perspective of present biases and interests, Passmore responds with a kind of aspectualism. First, he notes that historical events are not typically atomic: "although we talk happily enough about '*the* French Revolution,' or '*the* English Civil War,' obviously these descriptive phrases refer to extremely complex and diversified states of affairs" (p. 110). Consequently, an explanation can be given for each generation's tendency to rewrite its history texts: "men come to be interested in quite new aspects of past events; we look differently at the French Revolution now we have experienced the Russian Revolution, with a new interest in the way in which it passed into a dictatorship" (p. 111). Thus it seems that Passmore would accept that each generation's account of history could be quite different, yet equally objective, according to a reasonable and achievable standard of objectivity pertaining to aspects of events.

Arguing from a background in hermeneutics, Foucauldian genealogy, and deconstructionism, Mark Bevir notes that philosophers writing in these traditions "reject the possibility of access to a given past for rather different reasons — the historicity of our being, the influence of power on discourse, the absence of any stable meanings — but they all agree that we cannot grasp the past as a presence, and that this threatens the very possibility of objective historical knowledge" (Bevir, 1994, p. 329). Yet Bevir argues for an account of historical objectivity on different grounds, "on criteria of comparison, not on our having access to a given past" (p. 329). Rather than reject objectivity because there is no means for ensuring that the truth of historical interpretations can be made certain,

5.3. OBJECTIVITY IN HISTORY

Bevir proposes that "an objective interpretation is one we select in a process of comparison with other interpretations using rational criteria" (p. 332).

Bevir notes that in evaluating various historical interpretations historians "engage in a human practice which has a number of rules defining a standard of intellectual honesty" (p. 335), then proceeds to outline these rules:

> The first rule is: objective behavior requires a willingness to take criticism seriously.... The second rule is: objective behavior implies a preference for established standards of evidence and reason backed by a preference for challenges to these standards which themselves rest on impersonal and consistent criteria of evidence and reason.... The third rule is: objective behavior implies a preference for positive speculative theories, that is, speculative theories postulating exciting new predictions, not speculative theories merely blocking off criticisms of our existing interpretations. (p. 335)

These rules inherent in historical practice therefore dictate a number of criteria for the selection of historical interpretations:

> First, because we should respect established standards of evidence and reason, we will prefer webs of interpretations that are accurate, comprehensive, and consistent.... Second, because we should favor positive speculative theories to those merely blocking criticism, we will prefer webs of interpretations that are progressive, fruitful, and open. (p. 336)

Consequently, objectivity in history consists in following standards of accuracy, comprehensiveness, consistency, progressiveness, fruitfulness, and openness.

On Bevir's account of objectivity, multiple acceptable interpretations are still possible: "Sometimes there might be no way of deciding between two or more interpretations, but this will not always be the case, and even when it is the case, we still will be able to decide between these two or more interpretations and innumerable inferior interpretations" (p. 332). If "objectivity is principally a product of our intellectual honesty in dealing with criticism" (p. 335), and there is no way to decide between two rival interpretations on the grounds of the standards that Bevir outlines, then it seems that both interpretations should be counted equally honest and therefore equally objective.

Whether these three accounts present a viable conception of objectivity in history is not my main concern. However, I do note that each of these accounts emphasizes shared standards among historians, and each suggests that objectivity can found in these shared standards, since it appears that demands for stronger or at least different forms of objectivity cannot be met by history. Further, the accounts of Passmore and Bevir both seem to accommodate claims of equal objectivity among rival historical interpretations, just as I have suggested that equity may be established among competing perspectives in relativism according to a conception of objectivity.

5.4 Objective Equity in Relativism

Whereas Rescher argues that consensus is neither sufficient nor necessary for objectivity, since consensus concerns what people actually think, whereas objectivity concerns what the ought to think (Rescher, 1997, p. 48), consensus with regard to the standards of choice between theories seems to be a plausible candidate for understanding objectivity in the thesis of objective equity with regard to relativism.[8] The main issue here is not objectivity as

---

[8] Yet consensus may be too strong here, since it seems to rely upon agreement with regard to standards actually employed by a given group, whereas I suspect that there may be room for normativity with regard to standards. Perhaps a group explicitly endorses a certain set of standards. It still seems possible to suggest that they should properly endorse a different set of standards. While it may seem that such normativity would rely upon having a set of standards for choosing standards, and thus risks incoherence, it is not clear that normativity is always grounded in standards of evaluation. I think that normativity itself would need to be understood better before this question could be resolved. So the kind of shared standards discussed in this section might be considered in terms of standards that ought to be held by particular groups. While this appeal to normativity of standards might suggest that there should be an absolute set of standards for theory evaluation, I think this begs the question against relativism. Again, until normativity is understood better, I am not certain that there could not be a difference between the standards that different groups actually endorse and those that they *ought* to endorse.

a property of particular statements within a theory, but objectivity in the judgment that one theory is better than another or that they are equally acceptable. Since I invoked the notion of objectivity in this study to prevent the preference of one theory over another from merely reflecting one particular perspective that might not be shared by advocates of a rejected theory, the demand for shared standards of evaluation seems to provide a kind of shared perspective[9] that constitutes a sufficient notion of objectivity for explicating the thesis of objective equity. Again, this notion of objectivity may not be sufficient to understand objectivity as a property of statements, but that is not my concern here.

It does not seem necessary to argue here for which particular standards must be shared in order to meet the thesis of objective equity, since it would be sufficient only that some set of standards be shared. The particular standards would be dependent upon what form of relativism is under consideration, and which relativizing domain is identified. In a case of cultural relativism, for example, the standards would need to be shared among all cultures within the relativizing domain. It seems that the standards involved need not all be considered to be rational standards either, so long as those standards are shared, since the point here is simply that if one relativized sub-theory is deemed to be better than another, the judgment needs to be made according to the standards for theory evaluation shared by adherents of the worse theories themselves. If the standards are shared, whether rational or non-rational, then adherents of the rejected theory cannot complain that alien standards have been imposed on them. Likewise, it seems irrelevant whether the shared standards embody objective values, according to some other conception of objectivity, since the nature of the values and standards are not operative in the thesis

---

[9] Since I am primarily using the term 'perspective' merely to indicate a relativized sub-theory that is indexed to some member of the relativizing domain, I should clarify the sense in which I understand the kind of perspective I mean here. I do not mean a shared perspective with regard to the original relativizing domain, which would effectively eliminate the original relativistic system, but a shared perspective simply with regard to the restricted topic of standards of judgment. Since those standards may be applied differently, as will be argued later, the original perspectives remain distinct, but there is still something common between them providing the kind of transcendence that objectivity seems to entail. As John Weckert points out, "an appeal to *shared* criteria is very different from an appeal to *absolute* criteria" (Weckert, 1984, p. 38).

of objective equity, only the general pattern of shared standards. Again, this may seem to present a very weak conception of objectivity, but what is needed here is only a conception sufficient to understand the thesis of objective equity in relativism, not a conception necessary to understand all forms of objectivity.

It does seem necessary, however, for all the standards to be shared among elements in the relativizing domain and not merely for some subset of standards to be shared. Each of the standards used by a particular group seems to contribute in some way to a preference of one theory over another, where such a preference occurs. Since the rejection of even one of the standards might in some cases lead to a preference of a different theory, such a rejection would constitute a different perspective on theory choice, not a shared one. Objective equity suggests a kind of common perspective from which to judge theories, so it seems that all standards must be shared. If it happens that not all standards are shared among elements in the relativizing domain or even none at all, then the thesis of objective equity would be met by default. Since no shared evaluation could be made in this case, all the relativized sub-theories would be equal with regard to this lack of shared evaluation.

Since standards for theory evaluation must be held by some agent or group of agents capable of applying those standards, it seems necessary that the relativizing domain comprises agents or groups of agents, or at least that agents can be relevantly associated with the elements in the domain.[10] For example, if an instance of relativism is proposed in which sub-theories are relativized to presuppositions, standards can be associated with the presuppositions by correlating them with agents who adopt those presuppositions. By comparison, it would not be clear how to associate standards or agents with a form of relativism in which the relativizing domain consisted of prime numbers.

Consequently, I propose that *the thesis of objective equity is met either: (a) when all relativized sub-theories evaluate equally well according to standards of evaluation that are shared completely among agents relevantly associated with elements in the relativizing domain, or (b) when no such shared standards can be identified.*[11]

---

[10] This point is likewise discussed above in section 4.1 with regard to the formal requirements for relativity.

[11] I can imagine a third possible way by which objective equity might be

5.4. OBJECTIVE EQUITY IN RELATIVISM

If standards are shared, it might be wondered how two different theories could possibly evaluate equally well according to those standards, particularly if the standards are rational standards, and the agents applying those standards are rational agents. Should not rationality dictate that one and only one theory be judged best according to rational standards that ought to be shared among all rational agents? Without inquiring into the nature of rationality, I argue that it is possible that two different theories may indeed meet the thesis of objective equity by evaluating equally well according to shared standards, given a multiplicity of standards that might be applied. The issue here is that where multiple standards are recognized, they need to be balanced against each other. Hartry Field makes this point:

> We want our belief systems to be reasonably reliable, but not unless they are reasonably powerful as well. But now notice that there is a trade-off between reliability and power: by being more cautious in our judgments, we can increase reliability at the expense of power. Moreover, different investigators are likely to disagree as to precisely how the reliability/power trade-off should be made: if one investigator adopts a bolder evidential system in which some slightly speculative claim of contemporary physics is justified on current evidence, whereas the other adopts a more cautious evidential system according to which there is not yet sufficient evidence to justify it, it seems pointless to insist that one of their attitudes is right and the other wrong. (Field, 1982, p. 565)

---

demonstrated: Suppose that standards for theory evaluation were not shared, but differed by perspective. Suppose further that all relativized sub-theories compared equally well according to each relativized set of standards. Then it would seem that all theories would be equitable according each set of standards, though not equitable according to the same set of shared standards, as in a kind of argument by cases. Given that it is probably much more difficult for objective equity to be established on the basis of being evaluated equally well according to shared standards, rather than on the basis of the absence of shared standards, it seems even more unlikely that relativized sub-theories would be evaluated equally well according to multiple sets of standards that are not shared. Therefore, I think the two alternatives given in the criteria for objective equity are practically sufficient, even if not logically exhaustive.

Here, even with just two standards that might be shared, the trade-off between these two might justify two different theories. The presence of more than two standards would require yet more complicated trade-offs. While Field makes the point that justification is therefore relative to evidentiary systems, I would suggest here that this trade-off indicates how two different theories can meet a set of shared standards equally. The equity involved here is gained by acknowledging the role of each of the standards in the evaluation of theories, for example, reliability and explanatory power, whereas if there were a theory that was both less reliable and less powerful than another theory, the first theory would clearly be rejected according to these standards.

Thomas Kuhn makes a similar point with regard to the comparison of theories across different paradigms. Such theories can be compared against a common set of standards, such as accuracy, consistency, scope, simplicity, and fruitfulness (Kuhn, 1977, pp. 321–322), even though the theories may be incommensurable, and it seems that Kuhn acknowledges that theories across paradigms might compare equally well on such standards, given the need to balance standards against each other. Apparently for Kuhn, what constitutes an advance in science is not having better theories according to these standards, since these standards get applied differently between paradigms, but more particularly how well competing paradigms resolve anomalies.[12]

In addition to the need to balance multiple standards of evaluation, specific individual standards may lead to a judgment of equity with regard to different theories. Here I am thinking of Quine and Joseph Ullian's list of "five virtues that a hypothesis may enjoy in varying degrees" (Quine & Ullian, 1978, p. 66): conservatism (p. 66), modesty (p. 68), simplicity (p. 69), generality (p. 73), and refutability (p. 79). Of course, Quine and Ullian are discussing hypotheses, not theories, but theories are built from accepted hypotheses, so these five virtues might equally be considered to be operative within the kind of shared standards that I am considering. Of interest in this context is the first virtue, conservatism:

> In order to explain the happenings that we are invent-

---

[12] Jack Meiland presents a similar understanding of Kuhn, likewise recognizing a conception of objectivity dependent upon shared standards (Meiland, 1974). Thomas Kuhn will be discussed in greater detail in section 6.3 below.

5.4. OBJECTIVE EQUITY IN RELATIVISM

> ing it to explain, the hypothesis may have to conflict with some of our previous beliefs; but the fewer the better. Acceptance of a hypothesis is of course like acceptance of any belief in that it demands rejection of whatever conflicts with it. The less rejection of prior beliefs required, the more plausible the hypothesis — other things being equal. (pp. 66–67)

What is notable here is that conservatism is relative to prior beliefs. If theories from different perspectives begin with different prior beliefs, the incorporation of new hypotheses into those theories may preserve those differences on the grounds of conservatism. Therefore different hypotheses may be equally conservative, and the nature of conservatism would permit such equality among different resultant theories, given a difference in starting perspectives. Of course pragmatism and realism may posit that these difference will ultimately converge at an ideal end of inquiry, but my point here is simply that the nature of some standards may allow for equity among different theories.[13]

Since standards of judgment seem to be applied mainly with regard to some evidence, there seems to be a further question concerning the scope of the evidence used in theory evaluation, namely whether there might be evidence that is recognized solely from one perspective and not from other perspectives. If the shared standards are taken to apply only to evidence recognized within a perspective, then it seems that each relativized sub-theory would equally meet these standards, since it may be supposed that the sub-theories are indexed to the corresponding element of the relativizing domain precisely because that sub-theory meets the evidence recognized by the perspective associated with that element, and because evidence contrary to the relativized sub-theory

---

[13] Quine considers a case of irresolvable rivalry between two theories that evaluate equally well according to a set of standards (Quine, 1992, pp. 98–101), and considers two possible attitudes towards such a situation: "One possible attitude to adopt toward the two theories is a *sectarian* one, as I have called it: treat the rival theory as in the preceding case, by rejecting all the contexts of its alien terms.... The opposing attitude is the *ecumenical* one, which would count both theories true" (p. 99). Quine does not think there is much to be gained in adopting either attitude. However, in relativism, both attitudes seem to be adopted simultaneously to some extent, since the rival theories are relativized to preserve sectarianism, while the thesis of objective equity seems to view that sectarianism in an overall ecumenical light.

is simply rejected. However, if shared standards are taken to apply to evidence from outside a given perspective, then some sub-theories may meet these standards better than others, or it may be that none of the sub-theories may meet even their own standards when those standards are not shared. For example, suppose in a case of cultural relativism that one culture takes a certain phenomenon to constitute evidence that another culture rejects, either because the categories recognized by the second culture preclude the recognition of the phenomenon altogether, or because the second culture takes the phenomenon to be a mere illusion, or because of some other reason. The question of whether that phenomenon counts as evidence that needs to be incorporated within the sub-theory indexed to the second culture may affect whether the second culture's theory is judged to be objectively equal to the theory of the first culture. In such a case, I would argue that the decision whether to count evidence that is sensitive to perspective itself represents a standard that might be adopted in theory evaluation, and that the exposition of the thesis of objective equity in general should not dictate how evidence should be treated in any specific instance of relativity. Normally I doubt that the question would even arise, but if it does and one culture adopts standards that require consideration of evidence from other cultures, then unless all other cultures likewise adopt those standards, there will not be a set of shared standards.[14]

Suppose now that there is a case in which two or more relativized sub-theories evaluate better than the others according to the shared standards, but evaluate equally well with regard to each other. Is the thesis of objective equity met in this case? I would answer that it is not met, since not all of the sub-theories evaluate equally well. That two or more sub-theories do evaluate equally well may suggest an instance of pluralism where there is more than

---

[14] The use of standards to characterize objective equity and the role of evidence leads me to wonder about some forms of epistemic relativism that claim that knowledge is relative precisely to standards of evaluation. Insofar as these standards of evaluation figure into the thesis objective equity in *any* instance of relativism, it is not clear to me that there is anything special about epistemic relativism distinct from relativism in general. Further, if epistemic relativism is characterized in terms of abstract standards of evaluation, standards that need not be endorsed by any actual group, such a claim of epistemic relativism seems to follow trivially out of the definition of relativism offered here by virtue of the thesis of objective equity.

5.4. OBJECTIVE EQUITY IN RELATIVISM

one acceptable theory, but such pluralism is not thereby indexed to the entire original relativizing domain as a pluralistic relativized sub-theory and would therefore not count as relativism. There may indeed be some other relativizing domain that indexes only the relativized sub-theories that meet the shared standards equally well, in which case the thesis of objective equity would be met. However, objective equity is always evaluated with regard to a given relativizing domain as specified by the formal requirements for relativity.

Thus I think that there is a conception of objectivity in the form of shared standards according to which relativism and objectivity need not be opposed. Indeed a failure of objectivity, where shared standards cannot be identified, may provide the grounds for an instance of relativism. However, relativism may still be supported where objectivity is recognized, in which competing perspectives evaluate equally well according to shared standards across all perspectives, whether because the multiplicity of standards require them to be balanced against each other, or whether because the nature of specific standards, such as conservatism, permit competing theories to evaluate equally well.

Chapter 6

Thesis of Incommensurability

Incommensurability represents a claim of radical pluralism according to the proposed definition of relativism offered in this study. The plurality of sub-theories in a relativistic system is not intended to be merely apparent, but rather represents a radical difference between the theories indexed to elements of the relativizing domain. Where those sub-theories can be understood simply as contextual differences arising from variations within a common account, the thesis of incommensurability would thereby effectively be denied, and the relativity in such a case would represent a form of contextualism rather than relativism.

In the preliminary investigations in chapter 2 that noted a need for the thesis of incommensurability in an instance of relativism, I described commensurability as providing a path from one relativized sub-theory to another, and cited the Lorentz transformations in the special theory of relativity as a paradigm case of commensurability in relativity. This chapter seeks to determine more precisely what is required to demonstrate the thesis of incommensurability. Since the notion of incommensurability has figured prominently in the recent literature on relativism, I will examine accounts of this notion by certain key thinkers, in order to canvass various conceptions of incommensurability that may be relevant to relativism. Yet as I have cautioned earlier, the conception of incommensurability that ultimately figures within this study of relativism may be significantly different from the conception of earlier thinkers. I have outlined a very specific purpose for invoking incommensurability within an account of relativistic systems, and it is not clear that the purposes for which other thinkers have invoked incommensurability with regard to their various accounts will coincide with the purposes of this study.

The following review of the notion of incommensurability will therefore seek to evaluate the suitability of various prior conceptions of the notion as means to clarify the thesis of incommensurability as used within this study. Given the different reasons for invoking incommensurability, it is not surprising that some of the conceptions do not help to explicate the role that incommensurability serves within the proposed definition of relativism here. The following review will therefore also attempt to distinguish the use of incommensurability in the proposed definition of relativism of this study from earlier uses of the notion, particularly in cases in which there is a clear difference in the reasons for which incommensurability is invoked.

6.1 Ancient Greek Mathematics

The notion of incommensurability seems to have originated with the Pythagoreans. In the commentary to his translation of Euclid's *Elements*, Thomas Heath notes that "the Pythagoreans were the first to address themselves to the investigation of incommensurability, having discovered it by means of their observation of numbers" (Euclid, 1956, p. 1), likely with regard to the diagonal of a square. Their early work was further developed by Theaetetus (p. 3), whose interest in incommensurable numbers was already noted in the discussion of Plato's treatment of Protagoras in section 3.2. In Euclid's presentation in Book X of the *Elements*, incommensurability is defined as follows: "Those magnitudes are said to be commensurable which are measured by the same measure, and those incommensurable which cannot have any common measure" (p. 10, Def. 1).

Since incommensurability is here defined with regard to magnitudes, it is not immediately clear how this sort of incommensurability applies to the question of relativism, where what is measured in general are not magnitudes, but theories or statements. What would it mean for there to be no common measure of two

6.1. ANCIENT GREEK MATHEMATICS

theories? Perhaps it is not profitable to look for an answer from ancient Greek mathematicians, since incommensurability of magnitudes was their sole concern. However, there are two features of Euclid's treatment of incommensurability that are worthy of note in this context.

First, every proposition in which Euclid proves magnitudes to be incommensurable are either *reductio ad absurdum* proofs or depend on prior propositions proved by *reductio*.[1] Indeed, Heath's reconstruction of the Pythagorean's proof of the incommensurability of the side of a square with the diagonal is likewise a *reductio* proof (p. 2). Whereas in a proof of the commensurability of two magnitudes, it suffices to identify some third magnitude that measures the original two magnitudes, as in Proposition 6, there does not seem to be any other way to prove incommensurability except to show that the assumption of commensurability leads to absurdity.

Second, Heath claims that Proposition 2 "states the test for incommensurable magnitudes" (p. 18), namely "If, when the less of two unequal magnitudes is continually subtracted in turn from the greater, that which is left never measures the one before it, the magnitudes will be incommensurable" (p. 17). The difference between the two magnitudes is used to measure the greater magnitude until a remainder results. Then that remainder is used to measure the lesser of the two magnitudes until another remainder results, and so forth. Heath notes, "In practice, of course, it is often unnecessary to carry the process far in order to see that it will never stop, and consequently that the magnitudes are incommensurable" (p. 18). Euclid's proof of this proposition is a *reductio*, as already noted, supposing first that there is some magnitude that results from this process that provides the common measure between the two original magnitudes, then arguing to an absurdity. Whether this test for incommensurability of magnitudes has any analogue with regard to incommensurability of theories remains to be seen. Yet the availability of some comparably clear test for incommensurability would certainly be desirable in the case of relativism, even if in practice the test need not be carried out to the

---

[1] Ignoring the construction propositions, the following are *reductio* proofs: Propositions 2, 8, 9 (fourth part), 13, and 16. Proposition 11 relies on Proposition 8. Propositions 14, 22 and 84 rely on Proposition 11. Proposition 18 relies on Proposition 16.

end to demonstrate any given instance of incommensurability.

6.2 Benjamin Whorf

On the basis of his researches into non-Indo-European languages such as Aztec and Hopi, Benjamin Whorf proposed "a new principle of relativity, which holds that all observers are not led by the same physical evidence to the same picture of the universe, unless their linguistic backgrounds are similar, or can in some way be calibrated" (Whorf, 1956, p. 214).[2] For example, after noting that Hopi has no word or grammatical structure to express time (p. 57), Whorf claims that there is a metaphysical difference between Hopi speakers and English speakers.

> In this Hopi view, time disappears and space is altered, so that it is no longer the homogeneous and instantaneous timeless space of our supposed intuition or of classical Newtonian mechanics. At the same time, new concepts and abstractions flow into the picture, taking up the task of describing the universe without reference to such time or space — abstractions for which our language lacks adequate terms. (p. 58)

Within Whorf's linguistic relativity, it seems that similarity and calibration of linguistic backgrounds represent a kind of commensurability through which the relativity of pictures of the universe to linguistic backgrounds collapses. Incommensurability in this case therefore consists in the dissimilarity of languages that cannot be calibrated.

What is notable in this account is that apparently Whorf did not consider mere dissimilarity of languages sufficient to provide the basis for the linguistic relativity that he proposes. Perhaps this is because any two languages, insofar as they are different, are

---

[2] Were I interested in discussing linguistic relativism in any great detail, I would also certainly need to discuss the work of Edward Sapir, who is given credit with Whorf for the so-called Sapir-Whorf hypothesis. For example, see (Sapir, 1963a) and (Sapir, 1963b). However, since my concern here is not to investigate all the various forms of relativism, but rather to examine what sort of incommensurability properly applies to relativism, I ignore Sapir's contributions to linguistic relativism and focus instead on Whorf and his notion of calibration.

thereby dissimilar in some respect, certainly with regard to their different vocabularies. The question is which kinds of dissimilarity are relevant to the relativism that Whorf proposes. It seems therefore that calibration rather than mere dissimilarity is the key notion for understanding the kind of incommensurability found in Whorf.

Unfortunately, Whorf is not explicit about what constitutes calibration with regard to linguistic backgrounds. In many of his examples of differences in expression between two languages that appear to indicate a difference in world-views, Whorf seems merely to highlight the dissimilarity without demonstrating the impossibility of calibration. For example, at one point Whorf diagrammatically presents an example of the way that "Languages dissect nature differently" (p. 208), in this case a difference in the way cleaning a gun with a ramrod is expressed in English and Shawnee. In each case, three linguistic or conceptual elements are involved, but whereas in English the elements are "clean", "with" and "ramrod", in Shawnee the elements are "dry space", "interior of hole" and "by motion of tool, instrument". There is clearly a difference in these two cases, but it is not perfectly clear that these two cases cannot be calibrated in some way, and Whorf does not offer a demonstration of the impossibility of calibration here.

However, in his discussion of implicit Hopi metaphysics, Whorf does seem offers some suggestion of what calibration might be in one case:

> After long and careful study and analysis, the Hopi language is seen to contain no words, grammatical forms, constructions or expressions that refer directly to what we call "time," or to past, present, or future, or to enduring or lasting, or to motion as kinematic rather than dynamic (i.e. as a continuous translation in space and time rather than as an exhibition of dynamic effort in a certain process), or that even refer to space in such a way as to exclude that element of extension or existence that we call "time," and so by implication leave a residue that could be referred to as "time." Hence, the Hopi language contains no reference to "time," either explicit or implicit. (pp. 57–58)

Whereas the lack of explicit references, whether to words, expressions, verb tenses or otherwise, seems to demonstrate a clear case of dissimilarity, it is the lack of implicit references that seems to demonstrate that Hopi cannot be calibrated with English with regard to temporality.

In this case, Whorf appears to provide something like a demonstration of the impossibility of calibration, provided that one accepts certain results of his study and analysis of the Hopi language. The demonstration relies on the notion of the possibility of a residue that is strongly reminiscent of the method Euclid uses in Book X Proposition 2, though the proofs are clearly different. Whorf assumes that the notion of extension is completely exhausted conceptually by spatiality and temporality. Both English and Shawnee apparently contain a notion of extension, which are further assumed to be the same notion of extension. If therefore, Hopi "refer[red] to space in such a way as to exclude that element of extension or existence that we call 'time' " (p. 57), then the residue or remainder of the notion of extension in Hopi could be recognized as corresponding to the English notion of time, even though Hopi does not refer to this remainder explicitly. However, according to Whorf's study and analysis, the Hopi language does not refer to space in this exclusive way, so therefore there is no remainder of the notion of extension that could be correlated to the English notion of time, which would otherwise have provided some means for calibrating the two languages. Interestingly enough, even if his second assumption concerning the shared notion of extension between the two languages were shown to be false, this challenge to his assumption would serve only to help support Whorf's thesis of linguistic relativity rather than undermine it, since the lack of a shared notion of extension would itself suggest incommensurability at some wider conceptual category.

One potential problem with this kind of demonstration is precisely what constitutes a remainder between two concepts. If this notion could be defined adequately, then there might be some way to apply a method such as in Euclid's Proposition 2 of Book X, by obtaining a conceptual remainder between two conceptual schemes and applying that remainder to one of the schemes to find a further remainder. However, since it is not even clear what a conceptual remainder would mean with regard to just two concepts, such as extension and space, it seems much less clear what such a conceptual remainder would mean with regard to an entire conceptual scheme.

However, this issue does not seem to be a problem for Whorf's specific demonstration, since it does not seem to depend critically on the actual meaningfulness of the notion of a conceptual remainder, but rather on the mere possibility of such a remainder according to some definite meaning. The key consideration in the demonstration is that Hopi does not treat space in an exclusive way such that there even could be a conceptual remainder if the notion of a conceptual remainder were meaningful. Since extension seems not to be differentiated spatially and temporally in Hopi, the issue of conceptual remainder between extension and space cannot even arise. Consequently, it seems that Whorf's demonstration is designed to show the failure of one method that might be imagined to prove an implicit reference to time in Hopi, if indeed the proposed method were coherent, which may itself be questioned.

Whether Whorf's demonstration is effective with regard to his thesis of linguistic relativity or not, it is not immediately clear how his demonstration might be extended to provide a general method for demonstrating the impossibility of calibration. Within relativism, incommensurability needs to apply between the relativized sub-theories as a whole. While in Whorf's demonstration, the key role of time in world-pictures arising within the English language may indicate that a rival world-picture that lacks this concept cannot be calibrated with one that contains it, it is not clear that every relativized sub-theory must have some key concept or feature whose absence clearly indicates incommensurability.

Whorf's ideas have been subjected to severe criticism, notably by Donald Davidson, who argues against the intelligibility of the notion of conceptual schemes that seems to feature strongly in Whorf's account. Equating Whorf's notion of calibration with translatability, Davidson ridicules Whorf for his apparent inconsistency. "Whorf, wanting to demonstrate that Hopi incorporates a metaphysics so alien to ours that Hopi and English cannot, as he puts it, 'be calibrated,' uses English to convey the contents of sample Hopi sentences" (Davidson, 1973, p. 6). Indeed, if Whorf had intended calibration to mean the same as translatability, then it would be absurd of him to provide translations between two languages that he claims cannot be calibrated. Yet because it would be absurd, interpretive charity would seem to require that Whorf be interpreted to mean by 'calibration' something different from translatability. In his review of a collection of Whorf's writings,

Hugo Bedau notes that "Everyone has supposed that Whorf meant to use translation as the method of calibrating two linguistic backgrounds"; yet immediately recognizes "But either these opinions are mistaken and misleading, or Whorf's practices differ from his preachings" (Bedau, 1957, p. 290). It is unfortunate that Davidson does not apply as much interpretive charity as Bedau does.[3] I have suggested that Whorf provides a demonstration of the failure of calibration in his attempts to locate the notion of time within the Hopi use of the concept of extension in general. This demonstration did not depend specifically upon a given understanding of translatability but upon the presence of concepts and their use within a language. Since Whorf was able to provide translations between Hopi and English, it would seem that such translations were possible precisely because the process of translation between languages requires the translator to provide the necessary concepts that are missing in the original language in order to provide clear and fluid expressions within the target language, in cases where those two languages cannot be calibrated. Consequently, it is not clear that Davidson's criticisms hit their mark in this case.

Nor is it clear that Davidson's other major criticism of Whorf succeeds on interpretive grounds. Davidson argues that empiricism suffers from a third dogma in the form of an objectionable scheme-content dualism, and he illustrates this dualism with a quotation from Whorf claiming, "language produces an organization of experience. We are inclined to think of language simply as a technique of expression, and not to realize that language first of all is a classification and arrangement of the stream of sensory experience which results in a certain world-order" (Davidson, 1973, pp. 11–12; Whorf, 1956, p. 55). Davidson seems to be justified for taking this statement by Whorf as some evidence for the endorsement of a scheme-content dualism, according to which there is a pre-existing unorganized experiential content that is organized by a subsequent scheme in the form of a language. However, the remainder of Whorf's writings and arguments do not appear to de-

---

[3] Or indeed it is unfortunate that Davidson seems not to have read Bedau's review or at least not very carefully enough to recognize some grounds for doubting the interpretation of calibration as translatability. This failure of charity on Davidson's part seems particularly egregious coming from the great champion of charity in philosophy. So I have no compunction in casting Davidson's ridicule back squarely onto him.

pend upon this metaphysical picture at all. It seems that the notion of organizing experience may be ambiguous with regard to a commitment to any metaphysical picture.[4] Instead of positing experience as a dubious amorphous entity prior to a language that organizes it, organizing experience by means of language may be understood in the same way that one speaks of organizing a new department in a company or university. The department does not exist prior to its organization in an unorganized form. Rather, the department exists precisely as a particular organization that arises concurrently with the act of organization. In Whorf's case, the organizing language and the organized experience would thereby seem to be two aspects of the same process. While Whorf's explicit description seems more in accordance with an interpretation in terms of a scheme-content dualism, nevertheless, since his overall arguments do not depend critically upon this metaphysical picture, interpretive charity would again suggest that a less objectionable interpretation be adopted, such as the one that I have offered.[5] Whorf's explicit remarks suggesting a scheme-content dualism might therefore be excused as careless exposition, rather than occasioning the basis for a criticism of empiricism as Davidson takes them.[6]

6.3 Thomas Kuhn

In his book *The Structure of Scientific Revolutions*, Thomas Kuhn argued that science proceeds not by means of continuous accumulations of knowledge, moving progressively closer to a true formulation of the real world, but rather by discontinuous jumps in

---

[4] Simon Blackburn makes this same point (Blackburn, 2005, p. 204).

[5] Specifically with regard to Whorf's writings, I think a far better idea of how Whorf understood the relation between language and experience appears within an article entitled "The Relation of Habitual Thought and Behavior to Language" (Whorf, 1956, pp. 134–159). Therein Whorf discusses an incident from his professional work as a fire investigator for an insurance company where the labeling of gasoline drums as "empty" led to careless behavior with regard to smoking in their vicinity. Again, there is no appeal to any dubious metaphysics here, but rather a behavioral understanding of experience in which the role of language can clearly be identified.

[6] Given that Davidson seems to miss the mark twice, I suggest that Davidson's article and the subsequent literature discussing it be classified as tempests in a teapot, and a broken teapot at that.

scientific theory and practice. These discontinuous scientific revolutions are known as paradigm shifts, but Kuhn soon realized that the multiple ways in which he used the word 'paradigm' caused some confusion, later clarifying his two intended uses of the term. The first use follows from the use of the term meaning an exemplar, which in scientific practice "are concrete problem solutions, accepted by the group as, in a quite usual sense, paradigmatic" (Kuhn, 1977, p. 298). So, for example, an equation such as $f = ma$ serves as a paradigm for scientists to solve certain problems of motion, where the solution consists largely in understanding how to apply the equation to a particular circumstance. "For the problem of free fall, $f = ma$ becomes $mg = md^2s/dt^2$. For the simple pendulum, it becomes $mg\sin\theta = -md^2s/dt^2$" (p. 299). The second sense of the term 'paradigm' is an extension of this first sense to include a wide range of shared commitments within a scientific community, including paradigms as exemplars, as well as symbolic generalizations of theoretic statements and heuristic or ontological models of those theoretic statements. Kuhn proposes to use the term 'disciplinary matrix' as a substitute for this sense of 'paradigm'. Therefore, in Kuhn's argument, scientific revolutions consist of shifts in paradigms as disciplinary matrices, which include paradigms as exemplars as parts of those matrices.

Once paradigms as disciplinary matrices achieve a consensus among scientists within a field of study, Kuhn claims that a period of what he calls "normal science" (Kuhn, 1996, p. 11) begins, which is characterized by a primary concern with solving the problems identified as acceptable within the paradigm (pp. 36–39). However, normal science is threatened by the appearance of anomalies, which appear "with the recognition that nature has somehow violated the paradigm-induced expectations that govern normal science" (pp. 52–53). The solution to these anomalies may require the development of new theories and therefore new paradigms introduced into the scientific community, and the consensus of scientists with regard to a new paradigm constitutes a scientific revolution.

Kuhn argues for the discontinuity of paradigms as disciplinary matrices by claiming that they are incommensurable in three respects. "In the first place, the proponents of competing paradigms will often disagree about the list of problems that any candidate for paradigm must solve" (p. 148), so paradigms are incommensurable with regard to the standards used to evaluate what constitutes an acceptable problem to be solved. The second sense in which paradigms are incommensurable is with regard to the meanings of terms and concepts within paradigms. As an example of this incommensurable shift in meaning, Kuhn notes that the concept of space changes with Einstein's general theory of relativity, since prior to the introduction of that theory "space could not be 'curved' — it was not that sort of thing" (p. 149). A second example of shift in meaning concerns the Copernican claim that the earth moved, since prior to Copernicus, "Part of what they meant by 'earth' was fixed position" (p. 149). The third sense in which paradigms are incommensurable is what Kuhn calls "practicing in different worlds" (p. 150) with regard to those working under competing paradigms. "Both are looking at the same world, and what they look at has not changed. But in some areas they see different things, and they see them in different relations one to the other" (p. 150). Unfortunately, Kuhn both considers this third kind of incommensurability the "most fundamental aspect" and claims that he is "unable to explicate further" (p. 150). His later clarification of the two senses of paradigms, though, suggests that what he intends to discuss here are paradigms in the narrower sense as exemplars, that seeing things in different ways means that different exemplars are applied to the same situation, and that the different kinds of objects within these different world result precisely from the application of different exemplars. Kuhn seems to be suggesting that there is no clear distinction between seeing different objects and seeing objects in different ways. If, with regard to two different worlds, "One contains constrained bodies that fall slowly, the other pendulums that repeat their motion again and again" (p. 150), the difference in ontology is tied closely to a difference in the application of an exemplar to solve a problem. In applying a different exemplar, it seems as though a different object were involved, one that was capable of entering into the solution in a way that another object subject to another exemplar would not. This third sense of incommensurability seems most important for Kuhn's argument with regard to the discontinuity of scientific revolutions. "Like a gestalt switch, it must occur all at once (though not necessarily in an instant) or not at all" (p. 150).

Yet Kuhn's conception of incommensurability has changed since his original formulation. The main reason for this change seems to have been his concern with the methodology under which he developed his account of scientific revolutions, namely the historian's attempt to understand older scientific theories according to the concepts prevalent when the theories were formulated, rather than according to the most recent developments of those concepts. "[T]he historian's discovery of the past repeatedly involves the sudden recognition of new patterns or gestalts. It follows that the historian, at least, does experience revolutions" (Kuhn, 2000, p. 56). However, "Whether scientists, moving through time in a direction opposite to the historian's, also experience revolutions is left open by what I have so far said" (p. 57). Though historical accounts of particular scientific discoveries suggest that some scientists do indeed experience the same kinds of gestalt shifts as the historian does, Kuhn later stopped emphasizing the role of such gestalt shifts in his characterization of incommensurability. "If I were now rewriting *The Structure of Scientific Revolutions*, I would emphasize language change more and the normal/revolutionary distinction less" (p. 57).

Indeed, in Kuhn's subsequent change of emphasis, non-linguistic factors previously identified in the incommensurability of paradigms are no longer explicitly discussed. "[Feyerabend] restricted incommensurability to language; I spoke also of differences in 'methods, problem-field, and standards of solution' (*Structure*, 2d ed., p. 103), something I would no longer do except to the considerable extent that the latter differences are necessary consequences of the language-learning process" (2000, p. 34ftn.). Thus if there is incommensurability in standards or exemplars, it seems for Kuhn that such non-linguistic incommensurability would result precisely from incommensurability in linguistic factors. According to Kuhn's revised conception of incommensurability, "The claim that two theories are incommensurable is then the claim that there is no language, neutral or otherwise, into which both theories, conceived as sets of sentences, can be translated without residue or loss" (p. 36). Note that Kuhn here discusses incommensurability of theories, not incommensurability of paradigms as disciplinary matrices, apparently indicating either that Kuhn considers the shared commitments of a scientific community to be embodied fully within theory or that he considers shared commitments not embodied within theory to be insignificant for his purposes. Kuhn calls this revised notion of incommensurability "local incommensurability", because "Only for a small subgroup of (usually interdefined) terms and for sentences containing them do problems of untranslatability arise" (p. 36). With regard to the "residue or loss", involved in the incommensurability of theories, Kuhn clarifies this in terms of taxonomic categories. "Taxonomy must, in short, be preserved to provide both shared categories and shared relationships between them" (p. 53).

Kuhn's shift in emphasis progresses still later in an increasing emphasis on these taxonomic categories and a decreasing emphasis on translation, at least in terms of translations between languages, in favor of a different conception of translatability. "But it is important also to recognize that I was wrong to speak of translation. What I described, I now realize, was language learning, a process that need not, and ordinarily does not, make full translation possible" (2000, p. 238). Accordingly, his further revised characterization of incommensurability is as follows: "Incommensurability thus becomes a sort of untranslatability, localized to one or another area in which two lexical taxonomies differ" (p. 93). Thus incommensurability is now primarily understood in terms of taxonomic categories, which require further explication:

> Terms of this sort [taxonomic categories] have two essential properties. First, as already indicated, they are marked or labeled as kind terms by virtue or lexical characteristics like taking the indefinite article. Being a kind term is thus part of what the word means, part of what one must have in the head to use the word properly. Second — a limitation I sometimes refer to as the no-overlap principle — no two kind terms, no two terms with the kind label, may overlap in their referents unless they are related as species to genus. There are no dogs that are also cats, no gold rings that are also silver rings, and so on: that's what makes dogs, cats, silver and gold each a kind. Therefore, if the members of a language community encounter a dog that's also a cat (or, more realistically, a creature like the duck-billed platypus), they cannot just enrich the set of category terms but must instead redesign a part of the taxonomy. (p. 92)

Thus it may seem that Kuhn's final view of incommensurability amounts to a kind of conceptual relativism, and Kuhn himself equates systems of taxonomic categories with conceptual schemes (p. 94). Yet Kuhn has consistently denied the charge of relativism in his account of scientific revolutions, for a reason that accords well with my proposed definition of relativism: "Later scientific theories are better than earlier ones for solving puzzles in the often quite different environments to which they are applied. That is not a relativist's position, and it displays the sense in which I am a convinced believer in scientific progress" (Kuhn, 1996, p. 206). Kuhn thus denies the thesis of objective equity by identifying some theories as better than others, though it is not clear whether Kuhn thinks that the process of succeeding scientific revolutions will ever converge on a single final adequate paradigm in any given field, or whether the process of scientific revolutions will continue indefinitely for as long as there are practicing scientists. It is true that Kuhn displays some anti-realist tendencies by denying that there is a "theory-independent way to reconstruct phrases like 'really there': the notion of a match between the ontology of a theory and its 'real' counterpart in nature now seems to me illusive in principle" (p. 206). However, this tendency toward anti-realism does not thereby entail relativism, and if Kuhn can in fact consistently deny the thesis of objective equity on the basis of his account of scientific practice, then he should not count as a relativist.

Yet the aim in discussing Kuhn in this chapter is not primarily to determine whether his account qualifies as relativism, but to investigate his notion of incommensurability to see to what extent it can serve the role that the thesis of incommensurability serves in the proposed definition of relativism in this study. However, since Kuhn initially offers three senses of incommensurability, then proceeds to adjust his understanding of incommensurability over successive presentations, it is not clear whether any definitive understanding of incommensurability can be gathered from Kuhn's accounts. It would seem that Kuhn had a particular role that he needed incommensurability to serve, and that he himself was searching for an adequate conception, just as I am searching here. In a sense, the role that incommensurability is intended to serve in Kuhn's account seems somewhat similar to the role that it serves in the proposed account of relativism. Kuhn intends to argue that scientific progress is discontinuous, and therefore that certain revolutionary scientific theories are radically different than

6.3. THOMAS KUHN

their preceding theories, just as in relativism the various relativized sub-theories must be radically different from each other. So if Kuhn had indeed made any progress toward finding an adequate conception of incommensurability, his progress might prove helpful with regard to this study.

Like Whorf, Kuhn becomes the target of the ridicule of Donald Davidson in the latter's criticism of the idea of conceptual schemes. "Kuhn is brilliant at saying what things were like before the revolution using —what else? — our post-revolutionary idiom" (Davidson, 1973, p. 6). As already noted in the last section, Davidson understands incommensurability solely in terms of translatability, and I have noted above that Kuhn had at one point understood incommensurability in the same way. Yet I also noted that Kuhn later refined this understanding to decrease the emphasis on translation in Davidson's sense and to increase the emphasis on taxonomic categories. In this sense, it seems to me that Kuhn ultimately moved closer to the kind of incommensurability embodied in Whorf's understanding of calibration between languages, as exemplified in Whorf's demonstration of how the notion of time cannot even be inferred from a residue of usage in the Hopi conception of extension. Indeed, the principle of no-overlap that Kuhn articulates in his discussions of taxonomical comparison seems inherent in Whorf's demonstration. Assuming no overlap between species of extension, if Hopi used the conception of extension in certain ways exclusively to refer to spatial extension, then the residue of their usage of the genus *extension* could be calibrated to the English use of the notion of time.

Consequently, it seems to me that perhaps the most useful conception of incommensurability that Kuhn provides with regard to the aims of this study is his last conception in terms of taxonomy, developed in response to criticisms of his earlier conceptions. It is notable that this late conception of incommensurability is directed toward a method of correlating concepts between theories, similar to the way that Whorf sought to correlate concepts between languages.

6.4 Paul Feyerabend

Although Paul Feyerabend's concerns significantly overlap with those of Thomas Kuhn, as Feyerabend describes the difference in their approaches, "His approach was historical, while mine was abstract" (Feyerabend, 1993, p. 212). Specifically, Feyerabend is concerned with philosophical accounts of reduction and explanation in science, accounts which he argues are not only inadequate when considered as descriptions of actual scientific practice, but also counterproductive when considered as normative guidelines for scientific practice.

In the account of reduction formulated by Ernest Nagel and the account of explanation formulated by Carl Hempel and Paul Oppenheim, Feyerabend identifies the same two problematic assumptions: (1) that one theory is deduced from another, and (2) that the meanings of common terms do not vary between the two theories (Feyerabend, 1981, pp. 47–49). With regard to reduction, these assumptions mean that one theory is reduced to another by a process of a deduction using bridge principles correlating the two theories, where the meanings of terms appearing within both theories do not change in the course of the reductive deduction. With regard to explanation, one theory is explained by another theory by deducing the more restrictive theory from the more general theory, with the addition of statements identifying the conditions under which it is held that the more restrictive theory applies, where likewise the meanings of terms appearing within both theories do not change in the course of the explanatory deduction. Furthermore, these two accounts suggest a model for the progression of theories in the history of science, in which the success of an earlier scientific theory is explained by reducing that theory to a special case of a later theory, thus justifying the progress to the later theory. Feyerabend holds that the two assumptions underlying this model are mistaken.

Feyerabend argues against the assumption of deducibility using two examples. First, the proposed reductive explanation of Galilean physics to Newtonian physics cannot precisely be achieved by deduction, but only as an approximation, which Feyerabend rejects as being "too vague and general to be regarded as the statement of an alternative theory" (p. 59). Second, the account of motion in celestial mechanics prior to Newton cannot be reduced to Newtonian celestial mechanics, even though there is no quantitative difference as in the first example. In this second example, though, there is a qualitative difference related to the meanings of terms. Where the pre-Newtonian term 'impetus' seems to correlate empirically with the Newtonian term 'momentum', the two concepts are incompatible. "For whereas the impetus is supposed to be something that pushes the body along, the momentum is the result rather than the cause of its motion" (p. 59). Thus Newtonian physics entails the explicit denial of a force such as impetus.

Likewise, Feyerabend argues against the assumption of meaning invariance with more examples: the change of meaning of the word 'temperature' in the development of thermodynamics (pp. 78–81), the change of meaning of the word 'mass' in the transition from Newtonian to relativistic physics (pp. 81–82), even a change in meaning of the words 'up' and 'down' in the transition from pre-Newtonian to Newtonian physics (pp. 85–85).

Having argued against these two assumptions as being unimportant to the description of scientific practice in reduction and explanation, Feyerabend further argues that these assumptions are undesirable as normative prescriptions for productive scientific practice. He claims that the two assumptions yield the following normative principle: "only such theories are admissible (for explanation and prediction) in a given domain which either contain the theories already used in this domain, or are at least consistent with them" (p. 55). The adoption of such a principle "would lead to the elimination of a theory, not because it is inconsistent with the facts, but because it is inconsistent with another, and as yet unrefuted, theory whose confirming instances its [sic] shares" (p. 70). Worse still, if a new theory is rejected solely because it conflicts with an older theory, a potentially better theory might be rejected because of such a conflict.

These considerations lead Feyerabend to formulate a methodological principle reflecting empirical practice. Rather than "comparing a single theory with experience", "the methodological unit to which we refer when discussing questions of test and empirical content consists of a whole set of partly overlapping, factually adequate, but mutually inconsistent theories" (p. 72). The resulting principle is "the principle of proliferation: Invent, and elaborate theories which are inconsistent with the accepted point of view, even if the latter should happen to be highly confirmed and generally accepted" (p. 105). In his later, more polemical discussions, this principle gets subsumed under the general slogan "anything goes": "it will be clear that there is only one principle that can be defended under *all* circumstances and in all stages of human development. It is the principle: *anything goes*" (Feyerabend, 1993, pp. 18–19).[7] Not only does anything go in terms of generating alternative theories to be subjected to testing, but anything goes with regard to arguing for the best theory:

> ...it has emerged that science is full of lacunae and contradictions, that ignorance, pigheadedness, reliance on prejudice, lying, far from impeding the forward march of knowledge may actually aid it and that the traditional virtues of precision, consistency, 'honesty', respect for facts, maximum knowledge under given circumstances, if practiced with determination, may bring it to a standstill. (p. 197)

The slogan "anything goes" has entered the literature of relativism as a criticism at least of certain forms of relativism. However, I note in passing that as used by Feyerabend, this motto does not result in any form of relativism according to my characterization. Not only does Feyerabend acknowledge that some alternative theories prove to be better than others, but more importantly, the proliferation of alternative theories and methods for justification in Feyerabend's account are not relativized to anything. Rather, anything goes for anyone engaged in intellectual pursuits, whether scientific or otherwise, regardless of group, culture, or individuality. Feyerabend rightly characterizes his proposed methodology as "pluralistic" (p. 21) and even "anarchistic" (p. 13), but without relativization it seems to me that there can be no relativism.

Incommensurability enters into Feyerabend's account in the discussion of the concepts of impetus and momentum with regard

---

[7] Interestingly, though, Feyerabend at one point seems to reject this slogan: "As for the slogan 'anything goes', which certain critics have attributed to me and then attacked: the slogan is not mine and it was not meant to summarise the case studies of AM [*Against Method*] and SFS [*Science in a Free Society*]" (Feyerabend, 1987, p. 283). Perhaps this case should count as a cautionary tale in favor of more circumspect presentation in philosophical argumentation to minimize later regret.

6.4. PAUL FEYERABEND

to Galilean and Newtonian mechanics, as reviewed above. There any proposed reduction between the two theories fails because the two concepts were incommensurable. Feyerabend characterizes this incommensurability as follows: "the main concept of the former, the concept of impetus, can neither be defined on the basis of the primitive descriptive terms of the latter, nor related to them via a correct empirical statement" (Feyerabend, 1981, p. 76). As he explains later, "It [incommensurability] occurs only when the conditions of meaningfulness for the descriptive terms of one language (theory, point of view) do not permit the use of the descriptive terms of another language (theory, point of view); mere difference of meanings does not yet lead to incommensurability in my sense" (Feyerabend, 1987, p. 272). In the example concerning impetus and momentum, the attempt to correlate the two terms on the basis of empirical statements fails because the conditions under Newtonian mechanics that permit the use of the term 'momentum' explicitly deny the conditions that would permit the use of the term 'impetus'. So not only do the meanings of the terms differ, but also they are thus incommensurable.

Note first that Feyerabend permits two formal alternatives for understanding commensurability: (1) defining terms of one language from terms in another language, and (2) correlating terms between languages by means of empirical generalizations. The second alternative indicates that commensurability for Feyerabend is more than mere definability of terms. Both of these alternatives must fail to establish incommensurability. Yet both alternatives seem to fail for the same reason, namely that the conditions of use for terms in one theory are denied by the other theory.

Next, note that this reason indicates that incommensurability is more than a simple difference in meaning, as Feyerabend explicitly states. If two terms differ in their meanings, they may still be commensurable, provided the theory in which one term appears permits the usage of the other term.

Last, note that with regard to the alternative for commensurability by cross definition, Feyerabend seems to neglect the possibility that there may be a third set of terms that defines terms from both theories, in accordance with the conception of incommensurability as the denial of some third thing that measures two given things. Such a case would seem to constitute a kind of commensurability relevant to Feyerabend's purposes. However, I do not think that this is ultimately a problem for Feyerabend at all, since it is the demands of reduction and explanation that prompt the definition of terms from one theory on the basis of terms from another theory. If it is necessary to resort to the terms of a third theory to define the terms of the original two theories, then that situation would seem to provide evidence that it is not the two original theories that enter into a reductive or explanatory relation with each other, but rather that it is the third theory that enters into such relations with the original two. Furthermore, the second alternative for commensurability by means of an empirical correlation between the two terms would seem to cover the case in which a third set of terms is needed to define the two terms, since if such a third set of terms is available for cross-definition, then it seems that there must also some empirical correlation available to justify the cross-definition.

In *Against Method*, Feyerabend seems to offer yet another definition of incommensurability: "let us call a discovery, or a statement, or an attitude *incommensurable* with the cosmos (the theory, the framework) if it suspends some of its universal principles" (Feyerabend, 1993, p. 205). It might seem that this is simply a different use of the term 'incommensurability', since his previous characterization of incommensurability was with regard to two theories, while this characterization is with regard to the cosmos and a discovery, statement or attitude. Yet insofar as the cosmos might be considered as a global theory, and discoveries or statements are theory fragments, this definition may seem merely to restate Feyerabend's earlier characterization. However, if the cosmos is taken to be more than a mere theory, then this definition seems to represent a stipulative extension of his earlier characterization, particularly with regard to attitudes that might be incommensurable with the cosmos. This latter interpretation seems to be what Feyerabend has in mind, as his further explication of principles of the cosmos in terms of "grammatical habits" indicates (p. 206). Indeed, he introduces this definition of incommensurability in the context of investigating the supposed irrationality of investigators in a time of transition between two theories, when attitudes and habits would be somewhat unsettled. Yet it seems to represent more to Feyerabend than a mere stipulative extension, but a correction of his previous characterization, since he draws the following conclusion: "It is therefore not feasible to define 'incommensurability' by reference to statements" (p. 206), as part of a response to a criticism by Dudley Shapere. Thus it seems that at this point Feyerabend wishes to extend his prior characterization of incommensurability to apply to practices in terms of actions and attitudes rather than just to theories as sets of statements.[8] However, this extension of usage seems to come at the price of difficulty of demonstration. In Feyerabend's discussion of the incommensurability of impetus and momentum, it was fairly easy to demonstrate that the Newtonian theory that enabled the use of the term 'momentum' explicitly prevented the use of the term 'impetus', precisely because statements within the theories could be produced indicating a conflict in usage. If, however, incommensurability cannot be defined with reference to statements, but rather must be defined with regard to universal principles of the cosmos or to grammatical habits, it is not clear how this kind of incommensurability could be demonstrated. In the example that occasions Feyerabend's later definition, he merely asserts that a fragment from Heraclitus is incommensurable with a certain cosmology, without much supporting argument. I do not see here the same level of demonstration that Feyerabend provides in the earlier example of impetus and momentum.

Consequently, it is not clear how useful Feyerabend's later definition of incommensurability can be. His earlier conception relied on the differing conditions of use for terms between theories, and it is this conception that seemed to permit some means for demonstrating incommensurability. It is tempting to see Feyerabend's original conception of incommensurability operating in accordance with Whorf's demonstrations concerning the notion of time among the Hopi. Whorf seems to be inquiring whether the conditions of the use of the notion of extension in that language community permitted the restricted use of the notion of time as a species of extension, just as Feyerabend would later argue.

---

[8] Interestingly, Kuhn began with a conception of incommensurability that included actions and attitudes, but later restricted it to accord more closely with Feyerabend's original formulations. Feyerabend, on the other hand, seems to have moved in the opposite direction, expanding his conception of incommensurability to include what Kuhn ultimately found problematic.

6.5 Value Incommensurability

Since the work of Kuhn and Feyerabend, the question of incommensurability has been raised with regard to values, namely whether values can be incommensurable, which question naturally depends upon establishing what might be meant by incommensurability with regard to values. The question arises primarily within a critique of utilitarianism, since if the kind of maximization of utility that characterizes utilitarianism is feasible, then it must be possible to place the values inherent in various instances of utility onto some common scale such that a total value of utility might be computed, at least in principle. Thus utilitarianism seems to require commensurability of values, and if some values can be shown to be incommensurable in some pertinent way, then utilitarianism faces a fundamental problem.

In an early article, James Griffin considers and rejects a number of alternative conceptions of what the incommensurability of values might mean, he ultimately settles upon the following characterization:

> ...although many values can, with some plausibility, be measured on a scale of satisfaction of desires, although the values we attach to beauty, convenience, knowledge, perhaps even to human life, may reside entirely in their being desired, and conflict between them may be resolved by determining what course of action most satisfies desires, other values — and values in the sense of valuable states of the world — although they too may be desired, are not fully explained by their being desired, and conflict between them cannot be resolved simply by determining what most satisfies desires. (Griffin, 1977, p. 56)

In a later explication, Griffin confirms that the best characterization of incommensurability of values is in terms of the incomparability of values (Griffin, 1997, p. 35). If not all values can be placed upon the same scale, whether a scale of pleasure or desirability or otherwise, some values therefore cannot be compared at all, since a comparison requires precisely such a common scale. An example he suggests is the inability to place justice and utility on the same comparative scale, since "A state of the world in which welfare is

6.5. VALUE INCOMMENSURABILITY

equally distributed, or so that no one falls below a minimum level, may be of value apart from the amount of welfare" (Griffin, 1977, p. 57).

A later attempt by Joseph Raz to understand the incommensurability of values defines incommensurability as follows: "A and B are incommensurate if it is neither true that one is better than the other nor true that they are of equal value" (Raz, 1986, p. 115). So if justice and utility are incommensurable as Griffin suggests, according to Raz's definition, this means that neither justice nor utility are better than each other, nor are they equal in value. Since Raz likewise takes incommensurability of values to be a kind of incomparability, it seems easy to see how the inability to place values on a common scale as Griffin suggests would lead to the state of incomparability in the definition that Raz proposes. Raz further identifies a sufficient but not necessary condition (p. 121) of incommensurability of values in what he calls the failure of transitivity of value comparisons: "Two valuable options are incommensurable if (1) neither is better than the other, and (2) there is (or could be) another option which is better than one but is not better than the other" (p. 120). The kind of value commensurability that utilitarianism would seem to require holds "that if A is not worse than B and C is better than A it is follows that C is better than B" (p. 121), but this kind of commensurability would thereby fail if Raz's conditions for incommensurability of values were to obtain.

There may be other definitions of value incommensurability,[9] but from the two definitions considered here, it seems clear that the incommensurability of values is quite different from what is required for incommensurability with regard to relativism. First, the notion of incomparability inherent in these definitions seems more relevant to what I have been calling the thesis of objective equity than the thesis of incommensurability, as suggested by Raz's definition, which sounds much like the claim in relativism that any one of the relativized sub-theory is no better than any other. Second, the incommensurability of values is something that might occur within a single relativized sub-theory, whereas incommensurability with regard to relativism is something that occurs between two sub-theories, a point which Griffin makes, though not specif-

---

[9] Compare also Kuhn's discussion of differing judgments of value in "Objectivity, Value Judgment, and Theory Choice" (Kuhn, 1977, pp. 320–339).

ically with regard to relativism (Griffin, 1997, p. 39). For example, one culture might hold values that are incommensurable among each other, whereas another culture's values might be perfectly commensurable internally. The question with regard to this relativistic system is whether the two cultures' theories are commensurable between them. Though the incommensurability of values in the one case and commensurability of values in the other might suggest that the two theories are thereby incommensurable in this particular case, it is not clear that incommensurability with regard to relativism must always be correlated with incommensurability of values, as opposed to concepts, for example. In a case in which two cultures each has commensurate values within their respective cultures, there is still a question whether the theories relativized to the two cultures are commensurable, and this question would seem to address values only insofar as those values can be embodied within statements of the theory.

Since this conception of incommensurability relates more properly to the thesis of objective equity, I will ignore it here. The kind of incommensurability most relevant here seems to concern transformations between theories, rather than comparability of theories.

6.6 Incommensurability with Regard to Relativism

What unites these various accounts of incommensurability seems to be the bare root meaning of the word, namely "no common measure".[10] The field in which the term is applied and the reason for invoking the term seems to determine what should constitute a measure in any particular case. Whereas Theaetetus and Euclid are concerned with incommensurability in a literal sense with regard to the measurement of two lengths, Kuhn is concerned

---

[10] There are other accounts of incommensurability that I have not discussed here, such as Richard Rorty's account based on settling conflicts (Rorty, 1980, p. 316). Likewise, David Wong identifies three conceptions of incommensurability, but the version he ultimately favors seems more relevant to the thesis of objective equity (Wong, 1989). Since I have already discussed one conception of incommensurability that is not strictly relevant, namely value incommensurability, I will not exacerbate the tedium of this study by attempting to review every conception of incommensurability.

6.6. INCOMMENSURABILITY IN RELATIVISM

with the question of continuity between successive scientific traditions, Feyerabend is concerned with the question of deducibility and meaning invariance in accounts of explanation and reduction, and value incommensurabilists are concerned with the question of adding and maximizing utility that involved disparate values.

The reason that I invoked incommensurability with regard to relativism in this study was to distinguish relativism from other forms of relativity such as contextualism. Here incommensurability represents a claim of radical pluralism between the various relativized sub-theories. The claim is not that the relativized sub-theories are literally the same theory in a strict sense,[11] since that would violate the formal requirements for relativity, as I have discussed in chapter 4. Rather, it is recognized that the relativized sub-theories are different, but the question is raised concerning the degree of their difference. Are they so different that they cannot be coordinated in some way? If they can be so coordinated, then it would seem that the difference between the sub-theories is not especially deep, and therefore the system of relativized sub-theories represents a case of relativity or contextualism but not relativism, according to the distinctions I have been making in this study. Nor does commensurability here represent a claim that the perspectives embodied in the different relativized sub-theories can in any way be explained away or even reduced to a single perspective. Rather, the relativization of different theories to elements in a relativizing domain, such as a set of cultures, ensures that those perspectives retain their importance, even if failure of the thesis of incommensurability in any given instance indicates a case of mere relativity rather than a more radical relativism.

Incommensurability with regard to relativism seems to represent the measure of difficulty in shifting perspectives, for example, from one culture to another. If two sub-theories were commensurable, then a shift in perspectives would seem perfectly feasible, and whatever constitutes commensurability between the sub-theories would represent what such a change in perspective would mean and how that change might be effected. It is not clear at

---

[11] Compare with Quine's efforts to distinguish between theories and theory formulations by means of transformations (Quine, 1975). What is at issue with regard to relativism is not an identity relation between relativized sub-theories, but whether those sub-theories can be considered part of a correlated common account of contextual differences.

this point whether incommensurability between two sub-theories would demonstrate that a change in perspective is impossible, but at the very least such incommensurability would indicate that such a shift in perspective would be a radical change, requiring not merely a minor adjustment in language or practices, but the necessity of learning wholly new languages or practices, for example. This sort of radical pluralism is precisely the reason that incommensurability is invoked with regard to relativism.

Although I have warned earlier that the conception of incommensurability that figures strongly in the literature on relativism may not strictly apply with regard to the role that incommensurability was invoked to serve in this study, I have noted that there is some similarity between the role for which Kuhn invoked incommensurability and the corresponding role in this study. Furthermore, I have attempted to correlate certain conceptions of incommensurability as used by Kuhn and Feyerabend with the notion of calibration in Whorf, specifically with regard to what I have identified as a demonstration of an instance of failure of calibration by Whorf. Unfortunately, as already noted, Whorf was not perfectly clear on what he meant by calibration, so I cannot merely rely on his notion of calibration to clarify the meaning of incommensurability with regard to relativism.

Fortunately, though, I identified in section 2.6 what I take as a paradigm[12] case of commensurability with regard to relativity and relativism, namely the Lorentz transformations in the special theory of relativity. Although measurements of space and time are relative to an inertial framework, this does not thereby show that the special theory of relativity counts as a form of relativism, since the measurements can be coordinated or calibrated between frameworks by means of the Lorentz transformations, which thus represent the kind of commensurability that seems important to the question of relativism. Note that the question of translation seems out of place here, if the term 'translation' is understood in the common linguistic sense of providing sentences in different languages that mean the same thing. The commensurability provided by the

---

[12] Clearly I am not using the word 'paradigm' in Kuhn's derivative sense, but in the word's original sense of a typical case or model. Furthermore, I hope that it is perfectly clear that I am not intending this usage to constitute a pun in any way, which would be deplorable. The word 'paradigm' is simply the most appropriate word to use in this instance.

6.6. INCOMMENSURABILITY IN RELATIVISM

Lorentz transformations does not suggest that the simultaneity of two events in one framework provides a linguistic translation for the difference of two seconds between those events in another framework, for example. Simultaneity does not mean difference of two seconds, whether across frameworks or otherwise. Rather, translation in this sense must be understood more generally as a transformation. This suggests that the question of meaning invariance may be tangential to the question of incommensurability. Commensurability might be demonstrated with regard to certain sub-theories containing a difference in meaning of terms within statements that get correlated, and it might also be the case that incommensurability may occur between theories where the meaning of terms between the theories remains invariant.

In general, the Lorentz transformations seem to represent a model for generating one relativized sub-theory from another. Note that the velocity inherent in inertial frameworks enters into the computations of the Lorentz transformations, in accord with my earlier suggestion that commensurability with regard to relativism identifies what it would mean to shift from one perspective to another. With regard to the special theory of relativity, the shift in perspective is precisely a shift in the relative velocity of a framework. Consequently, as an initial proposal, commensurability with regard to relativism seems to be the ability to generate one relativized sub-theory from another sub-theory by means of a transformation according to which the transformation represents a shift in the perspective from one element in the relativizing domain to another.

However, this proposal is too general to be informative, since it is not clear what would qualify as representing a shift in perspective. In particular, any successful transformation might thereby be claimed to represent a shift in perspective precisely because of the success of the transformation. Furthermore, the putative transformation might simply take the form of a brute mapping of statements from one relativized sub-theory to statements in another sub-theory, so that any two sub-theories that can be placed in a one-to-one correspondence would turn out to be commensurable. The result might be that statements concerning justice in one sub-theory get mapped to statements concerning domestic plumbing in another sub-theory, for example. This situation would seem to trivialize the notion of commensurability. Whereas I suggested that the requirements for linguistic translation and meaning invariance were too strong for commensurability with regard to relativism, it seems that the notion of meaning should have some relevance, since it would seem arbitrary to correlate abstract ethical notions with plumbing techniques as part of a claim of commensurability. Yet what is there about meaning short of translation and meaning invariance that could provide greater clarification to commensurability?

I suggest that the key to this question lies in the form of the Lorentz transformations, in which the transformations needed to generate measurements in one inertial framework from measurements in another proceed along dimensions that are recognized as common among the frameworks, namely three spatial dimensions and one temporal dimension. The presence of such common dimensions seems to provide a framework whereby justice might be prevented from being correlated with plumbing, as in my previous example, and thereby to provide a stronger requirement for transformation than mere correlation of statements. While not requiring full linguistic translation or meaning invariance, these dimensions thus seems to provide some element of meaning correlation that was missing from the initial proposal for commensurability. Whereas in the Lorentz transformations the dimensions are physical dimensions, in a case of conceptual relativism the dimensions might be higher order concepts within which certain concepts that fall under these conceptual dimensions could be correlated, either by identification of one concept with another or by distributing the application of those concepts by making finer distinctions within the concepts. This seems precisely the kind of approach that Whorf was taking in his attempt to calibrate English notions of time with the Hopi language. There he identifies the higher order concept of *extension* common to both languages under which both time and space could be subsumed and attempts to identify the notion of time within the range of the Hopi usage of extension not covered by explicitly spatial usage. The failure to identify this notion constitutes a failure of calibration for Whorf and therefore incommensurability in this sense.

Thus I propose that *commensurability with regard to relativism consists in the ability to transform one relativized sub-theory into another by means of a substitution or correlation of elements of the sub-theories along common dimensions recognized within each*

6.6. INCOMMENSURABILITY IN RELATIVISM

sub-theory. Incommensurability would therefore be a failure of such commensurability, either because common dimensions cannot be found among the sub-theories, or because the elements of the sub-theories, whether concepts or entities or values, cannot be redistributed along those dimensions in such a way as to permit a successful transformation. This conception of incommensurability bears some superficial similarity to value incommensurability, insofar as the inability to identify a common scale or dimension would provide grounds for incommensurability, but also grants that incommensurability might obtain even where such a common dimension can be identified, so long as elements placed along that dimension cannot be correlated in such a way as to permit the transformation of one sub-theory into another.[13]

As a somewhat fanciful example, suppose that the moral theories of two cultures differ only in that they treat cats and dogs in opposite ways. So one culture treats cats the way the other culture treats dogs. In this case, it would seem that two dimensions can be identified according to which a transformation could take place. First there is a dimension of creatures into which cats and dogs would appear, and second there is a dimension of ethical terms governing the treatment of such creatures. The way to transform these two moral theories into each other is to substitute the term 'cat' for the term 'dog' when used within those ethical predicates, and to substitute 'dog' for 'cat' in those same predicates. The ability to transform these two theories constitutes commensurability between them. Note that this kind of substitution does not represent a global substitution of one term for the other, merely calling cats by the term 'dogs', since the substitution is restricted to ethical predicates, though a global substitution would appear also to count as an instance of commensurability, if possible. In this example, though, descriptions of the characteristics of cat's ears and dog's teeth would remain the same, still predicated of cats and dogs respectively as before, so long as those descriptions do not appear

---

[13] Gregory Landini suggested to me an analogue of commensurability in the field of topology, whose concern is to map topological spaces onto each other without either loss of continuity or introducing new continuity. I think this is a very good analogue, expressing the kind of aim involved in finding commensurability. However, from the theoretical point of view adopted in this study, it is not clear to me how to adapt the mathematics of topology for the purposes of understanding relativism. Such an adaptation would certainly be welcome.

within ethical predicates. There may indeed be problems developing this example consistently, but it is intended merely to illustrate the kind of transformation that commensurability would require.

This example and the Lorentz transformations within the special theory of relativity represent commensurability in the sense required by relativism. I have suggested that Whorf's demonstration of the failure of calibration between the Hopi and English languages with regard to the concepts of space and time likewise constitutes an example of incommensurability. Of course his demonstration would count as a successful instance of incommensurability only if his arguments were correct, and I am not competent to judge those arguments. I would not want here to affirm or to deny any actual instance of commensurability or incommensurability other than the Lorentz transformations, which I have taken to be a paradigm of commensurability. The aim of this study is not to argue for or against specific instances of relativism, but merely to investigate the structural requirements that must be demonstrated in any successful claim of relativism. It may turn out to be the case that no claim of incommensurability turns out to be successful, in which case there would be no successful demonstration of relativism. However, it is beyond the scope of this study to evaluate any such specific claims.

Yet in general, it should be observed that it may be the case that sets of higher order concepts representing transformative dimensions could always be devised between any two apparently disparate theories, even those between different domains of discourse such as justice and domestic plumbing. However, the mere presence of such dimensions does not guarantee commensurability. Rather, it is the ability of the two theories to be transformed into each other across those dimensions that counts critically in demonstrating commensurability. If indeed two theories could be transformed into each other by means of dimensions correlating justice and plumbing, then I might be prepared to accept that such a correlation would constitute commensurability, representing a fairly peculiar shift in perspective between the two theories. If, however, no way of substituting elements across various dimensions can be found to transform one theory to another, then the two theories would be incommensurable in the sense required by this study. Such a demonstration of incommensurable based on impossibility of transformation would likely need to proceed by means of *reductio ad absurdum*, by supposing that a transformation were available, then demonstrating that this suppositions results in an absurd consequence, comparable to Euclid's demonstrations of incommensurability between two magnitudes.

There are a few remaining questions that need to be answered with regard to the scope of application of this conception of incommensurability with regard to relativism. First, would a partial transformation of one sub-theory from another count as commensurability, namely a transformation of some statements of a sub-theory but not others? I think this case should not count as commensurability, since the statements that could not be transformed would constitute precisely the kind of remainder that characterizes incommensurability. Since the purpose of commensurability is to identify what would be entailed in a change of perspective between theories, such a remainder would indicate that a full shift of perspective was not perfectly accountable within the transformation. Perhaps the degree of partial transformation might be used to measure how radical a change of perspective is represented by the given case of incommensurability, but it seems that a full transformation is required for commensurability.

Second, are common dimensions required among all relativized sub-theories, or can dimensions be determined between sub-theories on a pair-wise basis? The Lorentz transformations provided dimensions that applied across all inertial frameworks, but it is not clear that such global dimensions are required in all cases of commensurability with regard to relativism. Since this sort of commensurability is intended to describe a shift in perspective, it seems that such shifts could properly be described using dimensions identified between two perspectives at a time, since a shift from one perspective to another might involve considerations quite different from a shift to some third perspective. Perhaps the degree to which a single set of dimensions can describe all shifts of perspective might be used to measure the degree of commensurability, but it does not seem necessary to require a single set of dimensions to demonstrate commensurability itself. However, it seems that global dimensions applicable to all relativized sub-theories would constitute the basis for the clearest sort of commensurability, and in any assertion of commensurability where dimensions are not global, it would seem to be incumbent upon the overall theory that asserts this commensurability to account for why those no global dimensions are available or required.

Last, if commensurability can be determined pair-wise among relativized sub-theories, does partial commensurability among sub-theories still indicate a denial of the thesis of incommensurability with regard to relativism? Suppose that some pairs of relativized sub-theories are commensurable, whereas other pairs are not. If a set of sub-theories can be identified that are all commensurable among each other, it might seem that this set of sub-theories would represent a case of relativity rather than relativism, given their commensurability. However, if there are elements in the relativizing domain whose relativized sub-theories are not commensurable with other sub-theories, then a situation of partial commensurability would still seem to constitute a case of incommensurability across the entire relativistic system. In order to identify a case of relativity among the set of mutually commensurable sub-theories, it would be necessary to identify some relativizing domain that covers the commensurable sub-theories but excludes the incommensurable ones in order for the formal requirements for relativity to hold. But with regard to the entire relative system, it would appear that any incommensurability between relativized sub-theories should be grounds for the incommensurability of the entire system, since any incommensurable sub-theory pair would seem to represent precisely the kind of remainder that should not occur in a demonstration of commensurability.

This conception of incommensurability thus seems to serve the structural role required for radical pluralism of relativism within this study. Again, I certainly do not claim that it serves every role for which the notion of incommensurability has been invoked, but it may prove fruitful to re-evaluate those other invocations of incommensurability in terms of the conception offered here. However, such a re-evaluation falls outside the scope of this study.

Chapter 7

Proposed Logics of Relative Systems

The notions of relativism and relativity introduce two terms into the philosophical vocabulary: 'relative' and 'absolute'. The logic of relative systems must provide the semantics for these two terms, which I will call *relativity operators*. The preceding chapters were all preparatory for the development of the logic of relative systems by investigating the nature of relativism and the components of any claim of relativism. I argued in section 3.1 that each of the three theses explored in detail in the last three chapters must be asserted in any claim of relativism in order to distinguish relativism from other formally similar doctrines. However, the three theses do not seem to contribute equally to the logic of relative systems.

The thesis of incommensurability was the key factor in distinguishing between relativism as a radical form of pluralism and less radical forms such as contextualism and relativity in general. However, since the logic of relative systems aims to model the relativity operators, and since those terms also figure in contextualism and relativity as well as relativism, it seems that the thesis of incommensurability does not play a key role in modeling those operators. It is for this reason that I speak in this study of the logic of *relative* systems, rather than the logic of *relativistic* systems, since the two relativity operators are not unique to relativism. The claim of incommensurability does not obviously lend itself to a semantic model, such as the models outlined below, but it might be expressed within a relativistic logic by means of one or more axiom schemas in a sufficiently strong language that was capable of discussing competing theories. Yet since it is the role of the relativity operators not incommensurability that have been historically important in discussions of self-refutation, I will allow incommensurability to drop out of the logic of relative systems, though it may have an optional role to play, as I will explain.[1]

The thesis of objective equity seems primarily to justify modeling a system of logic using the relativity terms rather than omitting them altogether, since the claim of radical indexing embodied in the thesis precludes omitting any competing relativized sub-theory on the grounds that it is objectively inferior to any others. If any one sub-theory were objectively to be preferred, then the appropriate logic of such a system would merely be a formalization of that single sub-theory alone, in which the need to model the relativity operators would seem to vanish. Therefore, it seems that objective equity lies fundamentally in the background of the logic of relative systems, though it will likewise have a role to play in the philosophical interpretation of the semantics of the relativity operators.

The formal requirements for relativity, however, are essential to the logic of relative systems, as would be expected. The key elements of the formal requirements, namely the relativizing domain, the relativized sub-theories, and the indexing relation between them, must be modeled in the semantics of relative systems in order to demonstrate the logical behavior of the relativity operators. These key elements suggest the Kripke semantics of the modal logic of possibility and necessity, in which the elements in the relativizing domain are correlated with possible worlds.[2] A

---

[1] Of course just because incommensurability drops out of the logic of relative system, it does not follow that it has been futile to discuss incommensurability in this study. The thesis of incommensurability is still needed to understand relativism as opposed to relativity in general. Furthermore, identifying its specific role in relativism in general provided the grounds for excluding it in the logic of relative systems, thus saving unnecessary formalization and tedium.

[2] At one point I had considered a pseudo-Kantian strategy for the semantics of relativism in which objects enter into the relations assigned to predicates not by themselves, but in conjunction with elements of the relativizing domain, which would provide the needed variance of truth values for statements in the relativized sub-theories indexed to elements of the relativizing domain. Therefore, rather than a relation such as $\{<a,b>, <a,c>, <b,b>,...\}$ assigned to a particular two-place predicate, where a, b, and c are elements of the domain of interpretation, a relation would be assigned such as $\{<<a,p_1>, <b,p_1>>, <<a,p_1>,$

number of logical systems have already been proposed for relativism.³ In the following discussion, I will investigate one of these proposals in detail, formulated by Steven D. Hales, arguing that it follows the semantics of possibility and necessity too closely, and I will use this criticism as a basis for developing more advanced features according to which a wider range of relative claims might be expressed within a logical system. It should be mentioned in advance that whereas I criticize Hales very strongly in the following, I owe a great debt to his initial analysis, which facilitated the formulation of the five relative systems presented in this study, as the following reflections should make clear.

7.1   Steven D. Hales' System RL

Steven D. Hales argues for what he calls "a consistent relativism" (Hales, 1997, p. 33, 2006)⁴ on an exact analogy with modal logic, in which the term 'relative' behaves the same way as 'possible' does,

---

$< c, p_1 >>, << b, p_1 >, < b, p_2 >>, \ldots\}$, where p_1 and p_2 are elements of the relativizing domain. The interesting aspect of this form of semantics is that for two-place predicates and higher, it supports truths that straddle perspectives and therefore that seem to be inaccessible from within a single perspective. For example, since $<< b, p_1 >, < b, p_2 >>$ is part of the sample relation shown above, b is reflexive in the relation, but this reflexivity is not apparent from the perspective either of p_1 or p_2 on the basis of this element of the relation, since this element spans perspectives. However interesting this strategy may be, I could not see how it would lead to a significantly different semantics for the relative terms as developed within this chapter, besides this feature of straddling perspectives, and it seemed to rely on the kind of substantive metaphysical claims that I intended to avoid in this study, so I abandoned it.

³ One notable system has been formulated by Thomas Bennigson (Bennigson, 1999), who likewise uses his formulation of the logic of relativism to evaluate the claim that relativism is self-refuting. I am sympathetic with his argument, but I do not think that he considers the full range of self-refutation arguments against relativism, as I will aim to address in chapter 8.2. Bennigson's system is much like RL1 presented below. See also the logical analysis of relativism by Robert Lockie (Lockie, 2003). Also of interest, Gert-Jan Lokhorst has analyzed the logic of logical relativism in terms of metalogical definitions based upon doxastic logic, rather than using axiom schemas or semantical structures (Lokhorst, 1998). Of course this approach models logical relativism within a particular non-relativistic logic, so his account would only appear to offer one perspective on logical relativism. I would want also to see logical relativism modeled within some alternative logic, to appreciate the relativity of logical relativism.

⁴ Hales' 2006 book substantially reprints the bulk of his 1997 article, including the formal appendix where RL is articulated. I will cite mainly from the later book.

and 'absolute' behaves the same as 'necessary', where perspectives take the place of possible worlds in a system that he calls RL. Therefore what is relative is true in some perspective, and what is absolute is true in all perspectives. After demonstrating that relativism is in fact self-refuting under this system, Hales argues for a consistent relativism by revising the conception of global relativism against which the charge of self-refutation arises. Rather than holding that "everything is relative", the consistent relativist should hold that "everything true is relatively true" (Hales, 2006, p. 103), a weaker claim that avoids self-refutation. Hales uses this conception of relativism as part of a later argument supporting the claim that "*philosophical* propositions are merely relatively true, true relative to a doxastic perspective defined at least in part by a non-inferential belief-acquiring method" (Hales, 2004, p. 271), where the belief-acquiring methods include philosophical intuitions, Christian revelation, and the ritual use of hallucinogenic drugs (Hales, 2006, p. 4).[5] Rather than describe Hales' system RL in its entirety, I will discuss the pertinent details of the system as I critique them.

First, Hales argues for the cogency of the idea of perspectives, partly on intuitive grounds (Hales, 2006, p. 109), but also in terms of shared guilt with possible worlds semantics: "Perspectives themselves I propose we treat in the same manner as possible worlds, namely, as abstract intensional objects. They are ways of knowing" (p. 113). If possible worlds are acceptable in modal logic, then perspectives should likewise be acceptable. It seems that Hales carries forward the notion of perspectives from his earlier book on perspectivism in Nietzsche (Hales & Welshon, 2000). His characterization of perspectives as ways of knowing clearly pertains to the thesis in his book concerning the relativism of philosophical propositions, but it is not clear that it is generalizable to every form of relativism that might be modeled.

Alternatively, I have spoken in section 4.1 in terms of a relativizing domain, where elements of the domain must be capable of forming perspectives. Any proposed instance of relativism must be able to identify a definite relativizing domain, in order to specify the y term in the formula "x is relative to y". As used within this

---

[5] Hales' 2004 article is a preliminary exposition of the philosophical argument of his later 2006 book. While it is tempting to comment upon the broader argument in the book, I will restrict my attention to the logic of RL here.

7.1. STEVEN D. HALES' SYSTEM RL

study, the term 'perspective' refers merely to the holding of a theory by some agent, and corresponds to the indexing of relativized sub-theories to elements of the relativizing domain. Rather than sharing the guilt of possible worlds semantics, it seems to me that the logic of relative systems incorporating a well-defined relativizing domain can stand firmly on independent grounds with regard to the status of perspectives within the system, without getting involved in any corresponding controversies over the nature of possible worlds in the modality of possibility and necessity.

Furthermore, it is not clear that perspectives can always be equated with ways of knowing, as Hales claims. Where the relativizing domain consists of inertial frameworks, for example, as in the special theory of relativity, those frameworks do not seem specifically to represent ways of knowing themselves, but are rather contextual elements that figure into a common scientific way of knowing, but that result in different spatial and temporal measurements. Here it seems that incommensurability may play an interpretive role, in that where incommensurability holds, unlike the case of the special theory of relativity, the radical plurality of sub-theories may indeed suggest that different ways of knowing are involved. Yet the logic of relative systems in general may likewise include commensurable theories, where this suggestion seems less plausible.

Second, just as in the modal logic of possible worlds, Hales' system RL supports accessibility relations between perspectives to provide greater flexibility in the kinds of relativity modeled. Rather than simply being considered true in some perspective, a relative statement is true in some perspective accessible to the perspective in which it is evaluated. So if a statement is true only in a perspective that is not accessible to a given perspective, that statement will not be considered relative in that second perspective. Hales calls this accessibility relation between perspectives the "commensurability" relation (Hales, 2006, pp. 106–109), and promptly deflates the notion: "there is no reason to be concerned with any kind of 'analysis' of commensurability. The reason is that there *is* no deep fact about commensurability. The relation is invented to service the needs of the logic" (p. 108). So Hales seems to be claiming not only that no analysis of commensurability in particular is needed, but also that no analysis is required of how to understand accessibility relations in general within a relative system.

However, simply calling the accessibility relation between perspectives by the term 'commensurability' does not entitle Hales to claim that there is no deep fact about commensurability in general, if indeed that is his intent. Hales has not provided any detailed investigation of incommensurability and its role in relativism, so he has not demonstrated that the role of commensurability serves the same role as accessibility relations between perspectives. In fact, he notes the apparent strangeness of equating commensurability and accessibility: "relativists have traditionally talked about different perspectives being *incommensurable* to each other" (p. 107). This strangeness suggests to me that commensurability and accessibility are serving quite different functions in relativism, and that Hales is only confusing the matter by using the term 'commensurability' to discuss accessibility between perspectives. In this study, I have argued that incommensurability is a required thesis in any claim of relativism to establish a case of radical pluralism, but it is not necessary with regard to relativity in general. The role of accessibility conditions, by contrast, is to provide some flexibility in the judgments of relativity between perspectives. So I think that Hales is either jumping to conclusions about incommensurability or providing a stipulative characterization of commensurability that only further confuses the question of incommensurability with regard to relativism.

Moreover, even on accepting commensurability merely as a stipulative name for accessibility relations between perspectives, it is not clear that there is no deep fact about these accessibility relations. Again, Hales uses a strategy of shared guilt between possible worlds semantics and relativism here, such that since there is no deep fact about the accessibility relations between possible worlds (Hales, 2006, p. 108), one should not expect there to be any deep fact about the commensurability relations between perspectives.[6] Yet here again, I would suggest that the logic of relativism may stand on firmer ground in this regard than possible worlds semantics. Later I will argue that there are in fact several candidates for deeper analyses of the accessibility relations between elements

---

[6] It is not clear to me on what ground Hales claims there to be no deep fact about accessibility relations in modal logics of possibility. If there is no deep analysis of these relations currently available, I think one could and perhaps should demand that there ought to be such an analysis in order to understand the nature of possibility and necessity adequately.

of the relativizing domain that form perspectives. Consequently, I will not follow Hales in using the term 'commensurability' to refer to the accessibility relations between elements of the relativizing domain.

Third, in his demonstration that relativism is self-refuting, Hales relies on what he calls Principle P:

Principle P: REL(ABS(α)) $\supset$ ABS(α)

where REL() stands for 'relative' and ABS() for 'absolute', and α is some statement.[7] According to Principle P, whatever is relatively absolute is absolute. This principle Hales notes is the correlate of an S5 principle under modal logic (p. 101), and he demonstrates that this principle is delivered by symmetrical and transitive accessibility relations between perspectives (pp. 145–146).

Both Max Kölbel and Tomoji Shogenji have challenged the use of this principle and its resultant S5-style semantics (Kölbel, 1999; Shogenji, 1997), noting that the principle is too strong for any relativist to accept. I tend to agree with these criticisms on grounds of charity, that if acceptance of the principle makes the position self-refuting, it would be uncharitable for that principle to be attributed to that position, particularly if it could just as easily be omitted. Hales provides one and only one reason for claiming that relativists should accept Principle P, namely, "Honest relativists worry about the self-refutation problem, and any adequate account of relativism should be able to not only defuse the puzzle, but also explain its power" (Hales, 2006, p. 103). I have considerable sympathy with this reason. Yet as Kölbel points out, there is a feasible explanation without accepting Principle P: "The relativist can just say that the self-refutation problem has been so powerful because many have mistakenly and unjustifiedly assumed Principle P" (Kölbel, 1999, pp. 93–94, ftn. 92), and he offers an additional pragmatic conception of the power of the self-refutation argument according to

---

[7] Hales uses the symbols ♦ and ■ for 'relative' and 'absolute', respectively, again on strict analogy with the modal logic symbols ◊ and □. Since I intend to cast doubt on this strict analogy, I will not follow him with the use of these symbols. In casting about for a substitute, I had briefly considered using the astrological symbols ♎ and ♉ respectively for 'relative' and 'absolute', given the purported characteristics of the Libra and Taurus signs under astrology. Although I find it particularly amusing to incorporate elements of one disreputable doctrine within the logic of another disreputable doctrine, the typography would not be especially clear and convenient for broader use.

which relativism seems to violate "the communicative function of assertion", namely "conveying information" (p. 102). Furthermore, it seems to me that it might be possible to show that under a relative system, there is a perspective that does accept this principle, though not a relativistic perspective. According to that perspective, relativism may be self-refuting, but it may not be self-refuting from all perspectives, in particular, not from a relativist perspective. If this could be shown, it would likewise explain the power of the self-refutation argument by drawing on the resources of the perspectives that form a key part of system RL without accepting Principle P from within a relativistic perspective.

Since Hales claims that there are no deep facts about the accessibility relations between perspectives, he cannot provide an argument on those grounds to establish the acceptance of Principle P within the logic of relativism. For example, if he could show that a relativist must accept accessibility relations that are symmetrical and transitive on the basis of an analysis of those relations, then he would seem to be able to argue that Principle P is thereby justified according to the kind of accessibility relations demanded by the relativist's own argument. Without any analysis of accessibility relations, Hales would seem to have no grounds for imposing Principle P on relativists. I have already indicated that I think several candidate relations are available for an analysis of the accessibility relations between elements of the relativizing domain, and the specific analyses will dictate the characteristics of those relations and therefore the kinds of principles that relative systems under those accessibility relations should accept. It is not clear to me that the kinds of accessibility relations that would justify Principle P would always be required in an instance of relativism, if ever.

However, the primary point I would like to make here extends beyond Principle P to the rules of inference in RL. Again, Hales characterizes Principle P as an 'S5-like principle' (Hales, 2006, p. 101), but S5 is a normal modal logic, namely one that includes the Rule of Necessitation:

Rule of Necessitation: If $\vdash \alpha$ then $\vdash \Box \alpha$

(If a statement is a theorem, then the necessary form of the statement is also a theorem.) Consider then the analogue in RL, which I will call the Rule of Absolution:

7.1. STEVEN D. HALES' SYSTEM RL

Rule of Absolution: If $\vdash \alpha$ then $\vdash \text{ABS}(\alpha)$

(If a statement is a theorem, then the absolute form of the statement is also a theorem.)

RL as outlined by Hales does not specify any proof theory providing rules of inference, and I think the omission of a discussion on this point neglects a potentially important aspect of the logic of relativism. It is not clear why any logic of relative systems, particularly one that intends to model inferences within a relativistic perspective, would endorse the Rule of Absolution, since it is hard to see why any relativist would immediately draw an inference that any statement that was a theorem was thereby absolute. Yet rejecting the Rule of Absolution would make the logic of relative systems a non-normal logic, with a significantly different semantics than S5 or S4. More likely it might be thought that a relativist perspective would accept a Rule of Relativization:

Rule of Relativization: If $\vdash \alpha$ then $\vdash \text{REL}(\alpha)$

Yet accepting a Rule of Relativization would likewise seem to cause problems for a global relativist, since if every sentence that was a theorem were relative everywhere, then such relative statements would seem to be absolutely relative.

With regard to non-normal modal logics, Kripke commented that "(in our opinion), they are intuitively somewhat unnatural; but nevertheless they have an elegant model theory" (Kripke, 1965, p. 206). Yet I would suggest that what may seem intuitively unnatural with regard to the modality of possibility and necessity may seem much more natural with regard to the modality of relativity and absoluteness. So it seems that the logic of relative systems might breathe new philosophical life into a series of fairly questionable modal systems. As will be argued later, non-normal systems will be of especial importance with regard to the evaluation of the charge of self-refutation.

Fourth, in correlating relativity and absoluteness with possibility and necessity, Hales makes the relativity operators duals of each other, so they can be defined in terms of each other. Just as in modal logic where

$$\Diamond \alpha \equiv \neg \Box \neg \alpha$$

(possibly true is not necessarily not true), so in system RL

$$\text{REL}(\alpha) \equiv \neg\text{ABS}(\neg\alpha)$$

(relatively true is not absolutely not true). "This accords well with our intuitions," Hales abruptly claims (Hales, 2006, p. 145). This characterization of the relativity operators seems to help support his reformulation of global relativism as "everything true is relatively true" (p. 103), since even if everything is absolute, everything true could still be relatively true if the ABS() operator were the dual of REL().

However, I do not agree that 'relative' and 'absolute' behave as duals in the way that Hales claims. It seems to me rather that the two terms are contradictories. What is relative is not absolute. What is absolute is not relative. Hales might claim that this disagreement merely indicates a difference in philosophical intuitions, but I find it hard to reconcile Hales' analysis with common usage of the relativity operators in English. In working through the formal requirements for relativity in section 4.2, I argued that there must be multiple, different relativized sub-theories. Suppose that this requirement were not met, and that each perspective held the same theory. According to the semantics that Hales delineates for RL, every statement held true in this theory could qualify as being relative even though each relativized sub-theory was identical, with no difference in the statements held true. In fact, even if there were only a single perspective holding a single theory, every true statement would turn out to be relative so long as that perspective was accessible to itself. I claim that in such cases, it would be a mistake to apply the term 'relative'. I think it would only confuse the discussion of relativism to use the relativity operators in the way that Hales suggests.

Rather than being true in some perspective, something relative would seem to require that it is true in some perspective and not true in another perspective, which is simply the consequence of having multiple different relativized sub-theories in an overall system. Therefore, the model for relativity in modal logic is not possibility, but rather seems to be that of contingency. Likewise, being absolute does not always imply the truth of a statement, since something can be absolutely false. Therefore, I suggest that for a statement to be absolute, it must either be true in all perspectives or false in all perspectives. Understanding the relativity operators in this way would preserve them as contradictories.[8]

Yet I am not convinced that even these characterizations of the relativity operators are adequate. For the purposes of this study, theories are sets of statements closed under entailment, but I have allowed the notion of entailment to vary with each relativized sub-theory. Suppose that there are two dialethic sub-theories, which allow for true contradictions, each indexed to different members of a relativizing domain. Let one theory contain the following statements: $\{\alpha, \beta, \neg\beta\}$, and the other contain the following: $\{\neg\alpha, \beta, \neg\beta\}$. Since the two sub-theories differ with regard to α, they count as different sub-theories, even though they agree with regard to β in allowing a contradiction here. Where relativity is defined in terms of truth and falsity, REL(α) holds, as expected, but REL(β) also holds, since β is true in one perspective and false in another, even though both sub-theories agree with regard to both β and $\neg\beta$. I find it difficult to accept an instance of relativity between perspectives with regard to a statement where they agree concerning the valuation of that statement. Consequently, rather than define the semantics of the relativity operators based on truth and falsity,[9] I would suggest that they be defined more generally in terms of the valuation of statements according to perspectives. A statement is relative if there are two perspectives that value the statement differently, and a statement is absolute if every perspective values the state-

---

[8] Thomas Bennigson also analyses relativity and absoluteness this way (Bennigson, 1999, p. 219), but he relies on a prior notion of possibility in his analysis, which I find problematic, particularly when the two modalities of possibility and relativity are modeled together as Hales does, as will be discussed below. Interestingly, Bennigson cites Hales, but offers no criticism of his system RL. Likewise, Robert Lockie takes the two relativity terms as contradictories (Lockie, 2003, pp. 325–326).

[9] Crispin Wright expresses some doubts concerning relativism specifically about truth: "relativism about truth is always relativism about something else" (Wright, 2008, p. 165). Certainly relativism about truth seems different than relativism about morals. It is typically not asserted that there are different theories about truth and that each theory is appropriate according to some relativizing domain, like there are different theories about morals. Rather, the central question seems to be whether truth can be relativized at all, and this seems to equivalent to the question of the coherence of relativism in general. Peter Davson-Galle argues that there are problems for relativism under both the correspondence and coherence theories of truth (Davson-Galle, 1998), but it seems to me that if relativism does obtain anywhere, then a new theory of truth would be required, and the nature of this new theory is what the question of relative truth properly concerns.

ment the same way. So where two dialethic perspectives both value a statement true and false, the valuations of the perspectives are considered to be the same, and therefore not subject to relativity. Contrariwise, if one perspective values a statement true and false, and another perspective values it true, the difference in valuation would permit a judgment of relativity in such a case, even though the statement is true according to both perspectives. This way of modeling provides greater flexibility for incorporating a variety of non-classical logical systems within an overall relative system. The semantics associated with these suggestions will be formalized in the systems proposed below.

Last, and perhaps most interestingly, Hales models the modalities of both possibility and relativity concurrently within system RL. Consequently, he includes both a set of possible worlds and a set of perspectives, and two different accessibility relations, one between possible worlds and one between perspectives. What is curious is that Hales relativizes the accessibility relations between possible worlds to perspectives, which "permits the claim that necessity is perspectival" (p. 143), once again drawing on his earlier work on Nietzsche (Hales, 1997, pp. 47, n. 11). What I find puzzling is that Hales does not permit the accessibility relations between perspectives to be relativized to possible worlds as well, thereby effectively making perspectives ontologically primary by this omission. However, with multiple modalities, all combinations seem to be viable. Not only can I contemplate statements that are relatively possible, I can also contemplate statements that are possibly relative. Hales' system RL easily permits the valuation of such statements, but by leaving the accessibility relations between perspectives fixed, the possibility modeled within such a system is constrained by the relativity, which Hales seems to consider to be more fundamental. Yet the nature of possibility seems to allow that something may be possibly relative even if actually absolute. Consequently, accessibility relations between perspectives themselves might be different than they actually are, and therefore it would seem that rather than making accessibility relations between perspectives fixed, those relations should also be allowed to vary according to the claims of possibility. The easy and obvious remedy for this situation is to allow the accessibility relations between perspectives to vary according to possible worlds.

This seems to be a trivial point of criticism, bearing more on the modality of possibility than on the modality of relativity, particularly since there is an easy way to address the point. However, I find this issue to be especially interesting because once the consequences of the possibility of modeling multiple kinds of modalities are explored further, there emerge a number of ways by which a fairly simple relative system might be complicated by the addition of increasingly relativistic features. Consequently, I will put criticism of Hales' system behind me for now and will start to develop some of these features.

7.2 Complications

The strategy of this study with regard to the question of self-refutation of relativism is to develop a wide range of proposed relativistic systems, since if one relativistic system might be self-refuting, perhaps there is another system that is not. Based on the critique of Hales' system in the previous section, a fairly simple relativistic logic can be devised on analogy with the modal logic of possibility and necessity. This system is RL1 outlined in section 7.3 below. In order to motivate the need for more complicated systems, I will explore in more detail a suggestion that emerged from the critique Hales' system.

As noted in the previous section, Hales models the modality of possibility and necessity in the same system as the modality of relativity. Yet perhaps there are more modalities than these two that might be modeled together. For example, perhaps there is a modality of teleology concerning what is directed toward the proper ends of certain creatures. It would seem that in this example, there would be something like a relativizing domain containing those creatures, as well as teleology operators expressing whether a given sentence represents an optimal teleological situation. Such a modality would thus seem structurally similar to the modalities of possibility and relativity. Perhaps this particular example is flawed in some way, but if there are indeed more than two modalities with similar structures, it might be wondered how to extend Hales' modeling of two modalities to a more general strategy for modeling an arbitrary number of modalities. The following discussion is fairly dense and abstract, but the ideas developed here will be reiterated and expanded in the following sections and in the presentation of the formal systems at the end of this chapter.

Consider then the question of how to model an arbitrary number of modalities, n. First, there will be n sets of the appropriate correlate of possible worlds or relativizing factors for the kinds of modality, call them M_n. So if the modality numbered i is a modality of possibility, M_i will be a set of possible worlds, and if i indicates a modality of relativity, M_i will be a relativizing domain, and so forth for other kinds of modalities. The valuation of statements will be made according to combinations of elements from each M_i, namely valued according to a particular perspective in a particular possible world, and so forth. Furthermore, there will be n accessibility relations corresponding to those n sets of possible world correlates, call them R_n, such that R_j is a binary relation only between members of M_j. Yet given the multiple intertwined modalities, each R_j will need to be relativized to combinations of members of each M_n except for M_j. Just as Hales allowed that possibility might be subject to relativity, and I suggested that relativity might be subject to possibility, so it would seem that any given kind of modality might be subject to all the other kinds of modality combined. Since R_j represents the accessibility relations associated with the j kind of modality, those accessibility relations are not relativized to the factors represented by that kind of modality, namely M_j, as in Hales' system. So if j represents the modality of possibility, the accessibility relations between possible worlds may be relativized to conceptual schemes, for example, but they are not relativized to possible worlds. More generally, if m_i is an element from some M_i, R_j will be indexed to $< m_1, m_2, \ldots, m_{j-1}, m_{j+1}, \ldots, m_n >$, for all combinations of elements from each M_n, excluding M_j. The idea here is that when evaluating a given modal term, the accessibility relations associated with that modality are held fixed, but are allowed to vary in accordance with other modalities, since those modalities might precisely require a modification of those relations, as with the possibility that something may be relative, when it actually is not.

Given this generalization, two proposals for complicating the logic of relative systems suggest themselves. First, the generalization seems to provide models for multiple, different modalities, but there is no reason why it cannot also model multiple different kinds of the same modality. Just as there are different kinds of necessity, there are different kinds of relativity, such as moral rela-

7.2. COMPLICATIONS

tivism and the special theory of relativity, and it seems plausible to want to model them concurrently. Those different kinds of relativity will have different relativizing domains, and therefore different accessibility relations between those relativizing domains. Consequently, I propose that one strategy for complicating the logic of relative systems will be the inclusion of systems that can model multiple relativities.

Second, it is not immediately clear why the relativization of accessibility relations should always be exempt from relativization to the relativizing domain associated with the corresponding modality, particularly with regard to the modality of relativity. If cultural relativism can be relativized according to possible worlds, why could the accessibility relations for cultural relativism not also be relativized according to cultures rather than remaining fixed with regard to those cultures? With the modal logic of possibility and necessity, it may not make sense for accessibility relations between possible worlds to vary by possible world, but where perspectives in relative systems are concerned, a variance in accessibility relations by perspective seems to be precisely what one would expect in a particularly radical relativistic system. This variance would represent a kind of perspectivism of perspectives, not with regard to other kinds of perspectives as with multiple kinds of modalities, but with regard to the same kind of perspective. For example, perhaps in a case of moral relativism, there may be two different groups holding relativistic moral systems, but different relativistic moral systems, according to which the relative assessments by the first group concerning the second group differ from the relative assessments that the second group makes concerning itself. Thus there could be differences in evaluations of relativity within certain perspectives by other perspectives. So I propose that the logic of relativism may include systems that permit the relativization of accessibility relations according to the relativizing domain associated with that kind of relativism.

In the following two sections, I will attempt to motivate and to explain these two complicating factors in greater detail before proceeding to implement them in formal systems.

7.2.1 Multiple Relativities

At the beginning of this study, the wide variety of kinds of relativism was noted as a problem for understanding relativism in general. The guiding hypothesis of this study is that generic relativism can be understood as a common structural feature of certain doctrines and positions. However, the exercise in generalizing multiple kinds of modalities in the last section suggests that the logic of relative systems in general need not ignore these different varieties of relativities. Each kind of relativity in the logic would still appear as a certain structure within the overall system, but these relativities would seem to be able to coexist. The question to investigate now is how they work together.

Consider the issue of perspectives. Again, for the purposes of this study, a perspective is the non-arbitrary indexing of a theory to a member of the relativizing domain. Yet where multiple kinds of relativity are involved, there will be different relativizing domains,[10] where each member of the relativizing domain is supposed to hold a different theory. In this case not only are there multiple perspectives, but there may also be multiple kinds of perspectives. However, the valuation of statements would need to be indexed to combinations of these different relativizing domains. Just as in Hales' system RL, which models two different modalities concurrently, in which the valuation function is indexed to combinations of possible worlds and perspectives, where the multiple modalities are all relativities, the valuation of statements would need to be indexed to combinations of elements from all relativizing domains. So if M and N are relativizing domains, and m_i and n_j are corresponding elements of those domains, statements would be valuated for each combination of $\{< m_1, n_1 >, < m_1, n_2 >, < m_2, n_1 >, \ldots, < m_i, n_j >, \ldots\}$. These different valuations each result in different relativized sub-theories as required by the formal requirements for relativity outlined in section 4.2, indexed not to a single relativizing domain, but to several of them.

---

[10] There may indeed by different kinds of relativity that utilize the same relativizing domain, for instance, a set of cultures in cultural and moral relativism. However, using the same relativizing domain does not guarantee that the accessibility relations between those domains are the same for different kinds of relativity. See section 7.2.2 on relativized accessibility relations below. For this reason, I treat them as functionally different relativizing domains, though they may be strictly identical in extension.

7.2. COMPLICATIONS

In this case, I think the notion of perspectives needs to be adjusted to support the multiplicity of relativizing domains. It would still make some sense to speak of the perspective from a particular culture, where one of the relativizing domains is a set of cultures. However, in speaking of the relativized sub-theory indexed to that culture, this sub-theory would need to be understood as a rough generalization, other things remaining equal, where the other things in this case include the effects of other relativizing domains, since in a case of multiple relativities, the effect of indexing to combinations from all relativizing domains means that a given element from one relativizing domain may be indexed to several relativized sub-theories. What seems to emerge from these considerations is that perspectives under multiple relativities are precisely these combinations of elements from different relativizing domains, namely that perspectives under multiple relativities are what might be called *compound perspectives* rather than the *general or simple perspectives* that figure in a relativizing domain of a single kind of relativity. Instead of speaking simply of the general perspective of a certain culture, here a compound perspective would be of a certain culture, using a certain conceptual scheme, with certain pragmatic aims, in a certain inertial framework, for example. Consequently, the requirement of the formal requirements for relativity concerning perspectives given in section 4.1 above would need to be amended in an instance of multiple relativities. Not only must elements in a single relativizing domain be capable of forming perspectives, but combinations of elements from different relativizing domains must be capable of forming perspectives, meaning effectively that some other factor must be able to appear in concurrent relations with regard to some element of each relativizing domain. For example, perhaps that other factor is a rational agent that is part of a given culture, in a given inertial framework, and so forth, that endorses a given theory. Perhaps the other factor is merely the bundle of elements from the relativizing domains. Of course the particular relative system would need to clarify precisely what this other factor is and how it relates to each of the relativizing domains to form compound perspectives. Perhaps it may happen that certain combinations of these relativizing domains cannot support a rational agent, for example, and that the conflicting demands of these general perspectives are such that no rational agent could balance these demands and still remain rational. In such a case, then, it seems that the sub-theory for that compound perspective would need to be empty, perhaps modeled by valuing every statement false, since no agent in that compound perspective could hold a theory. However, if all compound perspectives were empty in this way, then it would seem that not all of the relativities could properly be modeled together under a relative system, since the relativized sub-theories would not be different, violating another requirement of the formal requirements for relativity indicated in section 4.2.[11]

Since relativized sub-theories are indexed to compound perspectives, there is a further concern precisely how the general perspectives of each separate relativizing domain combine to contribute to a single sub-theory relativized to that compound perspective, particularly in cases where independent relative systems can be formulated against each separate relativizing factor. For example, suppose there is a system including compound perspectives comprising both cultures and sexes. Suppose further that an additional relative system could be devised whose relativizing domain was simply that of cultures, and another system could be devised whose relativizing domain was simply that of sexes. Assuming each of these systems were adequate, there would seem to be a question concerning the relation between these three systems. Some culture could value a statement true, and some sex could value that statement false. How then would the compound perspective comprising that culture and that sex value the statement in question? Of course if some of the systems in this example were inadequate, the question would not arise, since the inadequate systems could be ignored. However, since it does seem that relative systems are typically proposed independently using single relativizing domains, it may be wondered how those various systems could be combined to form a single system with multiple relativizing domains if those independent systems are each adequate.

Where the different relativizing domains govern different kinds of predicates, this issue would seem to provide little grounds for concern. For example, the special theory of relativity governs predicates relating to measurements of space and time and judgments of simultaneity. Moral relativism does not seem to af-

---

[11] I would not want to say such a case is therefore impossible, but it might suggest that what initially seemed to be an instance of relativism was more properly an instance of anti-realism.

7.2. COMPLICATIONS

fect those measurements and judgments, but governs specifically moral predicates, likewise apparently not affected by differences in inertial frameworks. Consequently, in cases in which the kinds of relativities govern different kinds of predicates, there is no conflict between general perspectives in the forming of a compound perspective.

Yet it is not clear that every combination of kinds of relativities will resolve itself in this way. There may indeed be conflicts in the ways that two general perspectives from different relativizing domains treat the same predicate. It may be that the requirements of a specific form of conceptual relativism conflict with a specific form of moral relativism in the valuation of a specific statement. In this case it is tempting to conclude thereby that where such conflicts occur, the particular combination of general perspectives cannot combine to form a compound perspective, that no rational agent could remain in such a compound perspective and remain rational, as suggested above. However, this may be a premature conclusion, relying on an impoverished conception of rationality. Where two general perspectives conflict in the valuation of a given sentence, the compound perspective may accept both valuations, holding the sentence both true and false as a true contradiction, for example. The compound perspective may thereby be a dialethic perspective, thereby preserving a sense of conflict among general perspectives.[12] Permitting dialethic compound perspectives within a relative system may seem to deflate or undermine my earlier amendment of the requirement concerning forming perspectives, since if compound perspectives can accept dialethic valuations, then it would appear that any combinations of general perspectives should be able to form a compound perspective. However, dialethism is not automatically an option for all instances of conflict, and accepting some true contradictions does not mean that all contradictions are true.[13] Since this study is concerned only with relativism from a general point of view, I merely indicate that any specific proposal for a system that incorporates multiple relativities must demonstrate whether certain conflicting compound perspectives are rationally unsupportable or whether

---

[12] See the classic defense of dialethism in (Priest, 2006b). I leave the defense of the rationality of dialethism to Priest.

[13] (Priest, 2006a, p. 56).

they are dialethic or otherwise paraconsistent perspectives, which can only be demonstrated on the basis of the specific relativizing domains proposed, not from the formal structure alone.

Another issue concerns the relativity operators 'relative' and 'absolute' themselves. Since there are different kinds of relativity modeled concurrently, it may seem that the unqualified relativity operators are ambiguous and that they should properly be disambiguated according to the specific kinds of relativity modeled in the system, such as 'special-theory-relative' or 'moral-absolute'. These additional relativity operators certainly seem useful additions that can easily be assigned semantics as in a system with a single kind of relativity. However, the acknowledgement of these more specific relativity operators does not thereby indicate that the unqualified relativity operators are ambiguous. Rather, they seem to be general terms comparable to 'red' or 'blue' that can further be specified as 'rustic red' or 'Bermuda blue', for example.

Yet here there is the strong possibility that different kinds of relativity may value the general relativity operators differently, that a statement may be relative according to one kind of relativity but absolute according to another, given the different accessibility relations assigned. One possibility for addressing this difference is the dialethic alternative, in which it is both true and false that a statement is relative, or some other paraconsistent alternative.[14] Of course, given that I have claimed that the relativity operators are contradictories, this means that it is also true and false that the statement is absolute. This alternative may be stretching the usage of the term 'absolute', if not violating its usage altogether. A better alternative, I think, is to recognize this apparent conflict as yet another instance of relativity, namely that the judgment of a statement's relativity can be relative to a specific kind of relativity. This recognition would suggest that any statement that is deemed relatively relative according to some kind of relativity

---

[14] My continued reference to dialethism may seem strange, perhaps an instance of sycophancy toward my teacher and advisor. However, dialethism represents another alternative attitude with regard to the problem of irreconcilable disagreement, besides skepticism, anti-realism, and relativism, as discussed at the beginning of this study. Whereas relativism affirms each disagreeing party, but confines the disagreement by means of a relativization, dialethism seems bluntly to affirm each disagreeing party with no concern for confining the disagreement to separate perspectives. Again, this is a rough caricature of the dialethic position, hence the references to Graham Priest's work for more details.

7.2. COMPLICATIONS

should be deemed generally relative, preserving the contradictory relation with the term 'absolute', which as a general term in a case of multiple relativities would be assigned to a statement only when deemed absolutely absolute according to all the various species of absoluteness. Therefore, a statement is generally relative when there is some relativity according to which it is relative and generally absolute when there is no relativity according to which it is relative. This understanding of the relativity operators likewise suggests an alternative characterization of global relativism according to which for every statement there is some relativizing domain according to which it is relative, not simply that every statement is relative according to a single relativizing domain or kind of relativity.

The system RL2 in section 7.4 below models multiple relativities.

7.2.2 Relativized Accessibility Relations

The formal requirements for relativity demand that each element in the relativizing domain be associated with some relativized sub-theory. That sub-theory is a description of what is true from the perspective of that element. If the theory were sufficiently powerful to describe its own logic, it would likely contain descriptions of each competing perspective as well as the accessibility relations that obtain between perspectives. Yet from a different perspective, with a different relativized sub-theory, why should it be expected that the accessibility relations should be the same as those from another perspective? The issue is not merely that some perspectives are accessible from certain perspectives and not from others, but that the total description of accessibility relations between perspectives, including relations regarding inaccessible perspectives may itself differ according to perspectives.[15]

Again, this suggestion seems to make little sense with regard to the modality of necessity and possibility, since the notion of the variance of overall accessibility relations would seem to pertain

---

[15] Thomas Bennigson makes a comparable point: "according to global relativism, what counts as a tenable framework is also framework relative" (Bennigson, 1999, p. 218). However, this consideration prompts Bennigson only to adopt Kripkean modal semantics with fixed accessibility relations, not to consider the possibility that those accessibility relations themselves might be relativized.

mainly to the possibility of differing accessibility relations. However, this possibility of a difference seems merely to represent the difference between one possible world to another, in which the accessibility relations centered at one possible world are different from the relations centered at the other world, which is already given in the overall pattern of accessibility relations. The same might be claimed with regard to accessibility relations in a relative logic. Hales claims with regard to his system RL that the accessibility "relation is invented to service the needs of the logic", and that no analysis of this relation should be expected (Hales, 2006, p. 108). Under this conception of the accessibility relations for relativity, perhaps the relativization of those relations likewise makes no sense, since it would seem to be just a gratuitous complication without adequate motivation. However, as I suggested earlier, not only do I think that an analysis of the accessibility relations for relativity is available, but I think that there are several alternative analyses, thus suggesting that different analyses of these relations held by different perspectives may lead to relativized overall accessibility relations. If two perspectives adopt different conceptions of the nature of the accessibility relations between perspectives, then those accessibility relations themselves may be quite different according to which perspective is applying them.

The function of accessibility relations is to identify those competing perspectives that need to be evaluated when determining the relativity of a statement from a given perspective and which can be ignored. For example, one perspective may consider another perspective sufficiently worthy of consideration and would therefore take that perspective into account when determining whether a statement is relative or not. It may consider a different perspective to be simply incorrect and would thereby ignore that perspective entirely when determining whether a statement is relative. So the accessibility of perspectives indicates the worthiness of consideration of the theories of those perspectives. A concrete analysis of such relations should probably start with the perspectives in question and the criterion they use in evaluating the relativity operators with regard to other perspectives. For perspectives that acknowledge disagreements with other perspectives concerning certain statements, there are likely some standards of appraisal by which they determine which perspectives contribute to a judgment that a statement is relative, and which perspectives are simply wrong with regard to that statement and can be ignored. The accessibility relations are concerned precisely with these standards, so rather than equating accessibility relations with commensurability, as Hales does, it seems that accessibility relations have more in common with the thesis of objective equity, as I will discuss below. Since I am not providing a concrete analysis of any specific instance of relativism in this study, but only an overall general analysis, I can only offer a few suggestions of alternative analyses of accessibility relations that might be held from differing perspectives within any concrete analysis.

One alternative is mere awareness of a different perspective. Perhaps this alternative could be understood in an ontological way by saying that one perspective is accessible to another if the latter's theory includes the element from the relativizing domain associated with the perspective of the former. If the relativizing domain in question is a set of cultures, for example, then the perspective of one culture is accessible to another culture, only if the second culture's theory includes the first culture within its account.[16] This alternative is very broad, making a wide range of other perspectives available to a perspective that accepts this sort of accessibility relation.[17]

---

[16] I do not suggest that this example is perfect, particularly since I would not want to suggest that mere ignorance is a reason for denying accessibility between cultures. The point would have to be not that one culture is simply unaware of another culture living on the other side of the globe, but that the culture's theory precludes the existence of that other culture, possibly because there is no other side of the globe in that culture's theory. The example may not hold together in the end, but as an illustration for the sort of alternative I have in mind, I hope it suffices.

[17] I think it is instructive to consider the set-theoretical characteristics of this awareness relation, in particular the characteristics of reflexivity, symmetry, and transitivity that feature in discussions of the accessibility relations between possible worlds in various systems of modal logic. It seems likely that every perspective would be aware of itself, so that this kind of accessibility relation would be reflexive. However, in the ontological formulation I gave above, the perspective would need to have a concept of self or something similar in order for ontological awareness to qualify as reflexive. So perhaps perspectives lacking a concept of self are not reflexively accessible, or perhaps this may indicate that the ontological formulation of accessibility as awareness was simply too strong. Awareness of one perspective by another does not entail that both perspectives are mutually aware, so this accessibility relation does not seem symmetric. Likewise, awareness of another perspective does not entail awareness of everything that perspective is aware of, so the relation does not seem transitive. The consequence is that Hales'

As another alternative, consider the notion of a real option presented by Bernard Williams, where S is a system of belief in general and $S1$ and $S2$ are different systems of belief:

> $S2$ is a real option for a group if either it is their S or it is possible for them to go over to $S2$; where going over to $S2$ involves, first, that it is possible for them to live within, or hold, $S2$ and retain their hold on reality, and, second, to the extent that rational comparison between $S2$ and their present outlook is possible, they could acknowledge their transition to $S2$ in the light of such a comparison. (Williams, 1981, p. 181)

So perhaps something like Williams' conception of a real option could be the basis for accessibility relations from some perspective, where one perspective is accessible to another if it is a real option for it. Williams' second condition concerning rational comparison strongly suggests the analysis of the thesis of objective equity given in section 5.4 above, in the case in which shared standards of theory appraisal are available and each relativized sub-theory meets those standards equally well. Williams suggests that incommensurable theories may be a limiting case in which only brute conversion to an alien system can take place, subject to the first condition, namely continued sanity (p. 181). This suggestion accords well with the analysis of incommensurability given in section 6.6 above, in which commensurability as a kind of theoretical transformation indicates what it would mean for one to shift perspectives between sub-theories, where incommensurable sub-theories indicate that the shift from one perspective to another would be quite radical, like a kind of conversion experience.

Note however that Williams' conception of relativism, at least in a form that is coherent, is different from the analysis presented in this study. His conception is dependent upon the distinction between a real confrontation, namely a situation in which there are multiple real options available, and a mere notional confrontation in which the options presented are merely available without being real options (p. 180). For Williams, "relativism ... is the view that for one whose S stands in purely notional confrontation with such an S, questions of appraisal of it do not genuinely arise" (p. 183).

Principle P would fail according to this conception of accessibility relations.

7.2. COMPLICATIONS

By contrast, this study suggested that the question of appraisal must always arise in an instance of relativism according to the thesis of objective equity, where either no shared standards of theory evaluation can be identified between perspectives, or that the relativized sub-theories all evaluate equally well under shared standards.

Yet even if this study differs with Williams with regard to his conception of relativism, his notion of real options seems to provide a viable alternative for an analysis of accessibility relations between perspectives, particularly when considered in terms of standards of evaluation, though not necessarily shared standards. If some different perspectives evaluate favorably under standards of evaluation for a given perspective, that perspective may thereby include those perspectives in their evaluation of the relativity operators, while excluding perspectives that fail to meet those standards, even if the perspectives in question do not accept those standards. A more restricted version of this alternative might acknowledge accessibility relations only where shared standards exist and competing perspectives evaluate favorable against them.[18]

Finally, consider the alternative of using commensurability as an accessibility relation. Above, I argued against Hales' conception of commensurability with regard to accessibility relations in general, but where it is allowed that the conception of these accessibility relations can vary by perspective, perhaps there is some perspective that does acknowledge relativity only on the grounds of commensurability.[19] According to this suggestion, one perspective would be accessible to another only when the sub-theories associated with both perspectives are commensurable to each other. In section 6.6, I suggested that commensurability be understood

---

[18] According to this alternative then, every perspective would presumably evaluate favorably according to their own standards, whether shared or not. Consequently, such accessibility relations would count as reflexive. Only when standards are shared, though, would the relations be both symmetric and transitive. So in a case in which there are no shared standards, Hales' Principle P would fail.

[19] It is tempting to suggest that Hales inhabits such a perspective, given his characterization of relative accessibility relations as commensurability, but since he does not have a substantive conception of commensurability, that would be an unfair suggestion. From Hales' perspective, it would seem that accessibility relations have no real meaning at all, not that he has a particular conception of accessibility relations as commensurability according to any substantive conception.

by taking the Lorentz transformations as a paradigm, where two theories are commensurable when they can be transformed into each other across appropriate conceptual dimensions. I also argued that incommensurability is required in an instance of relativism to distinguish it from less radical forms of relativity, such as contextualism. If a given perspective uses commensurability as its accessibility relation, this would seem to indicate that the perspective is thereby not prepared to accept any form of relativism at all, according to the definition proposed in this study, since every incommensurable theory would be inaccessible to that perspective. Rather it seems that every statement that is relative according to such a conception would be merely contextually relative, not radically relative.[20]

I have outlined a number of alternative analyses for accessibility relations, alternatives that might be adopted from within a particular perspective, thereby suggesting a relativization of accessibility relations to perspectives. There may certainly be further alternatives that I have not investigated. Of course a specific kind of relativity may by its nature require a certain kind of accessibility relation, and perhaps may require only one kind of relation, thus eliminating the need for relativized accessibility relations. However, it is not clear that every kind of relativity will require a single conception of accessibility relations, so I have attempted to motivate the need for modeling relative systems with relativized accessibility relations. Consequently, there seems to be some grounds for including relativized accessibility relations as a possible form of modeling relative systems.

System RL3 in section 7.5 below models relativized accessibility relations.

The following relative systems are formulated as sentence logics rather than as predicate logics, solely for the purpose of con-

---

[20] The characteristics of commensurability as an accessibility relation are fairly clear. Every theory is commensurable with itself, so the relation is reflexive. Where a theory is commensurable with another theory, that second theory is also commensurable with it, since the transformation between theories can work in both directions, so the relation is symmetric. If one theory is commensurable with a second theory, and the second theory is commensurable with a third, then the first theory is commensurable with the third, since the transformation from the first theory to the third can be run in stages, with the second theory acting as an intermediary step. Therefore the relation is also transitive. Under this conception of the accessibility relations, Hales' Principle P would hold.

venience and clarity. The extension of these systems to include operators for predication and quantification will not substantially affect the behavior of the two relativity operators,[21] so inclusion of these features would only make the systems more complex without thereby adding much of value with regard to the understanding of the relativity operators and how they function with regard to various self-refutation arguments raised against relativism.

7.3 RL1: Simple Relativity Semantics

RL1 is a system that models a single kind of relativity.

7.3.1 Syntax

The language of RL1 consists of:

- an infinite number of sentence letters: $s_1, s_2, s_3, \ldots$;
- grouping symbols: (,); and
- two relativity operators: REL() and ABS().

The well-formed formulas of RL1 are defined as follows:

- All sentence letters are well-formed formulas.
- If α is a well-formed formula, then so are REL(α) and ABS(α).

7.3.2 Semantics

An interpretation of RL1 is a structure $<M, R, v>$, where

- M is a relativizing domain in the form of a non-empty set of relativizing factors,

---

[21] Section 4.4 above considered a potential obstacle to formulating a predicate logic, given that conceptual relativism asserts that different conceptual schemes will rely on different predicates that may not appear within other conceptual schemes. That section argued that if atomic statements containing foreign predicates were always valued false by a conceptual scheme, that pattern of valuation would be functionally equivalent to the absence of those foreign predicates from the scheme. In any case, this issue concerning predication does not seem to affect the logical behavior of the two relativity operators themselves, but seems merely to provide some grounds for difference in valuation of atomic sentences on which the relativity operators rely.

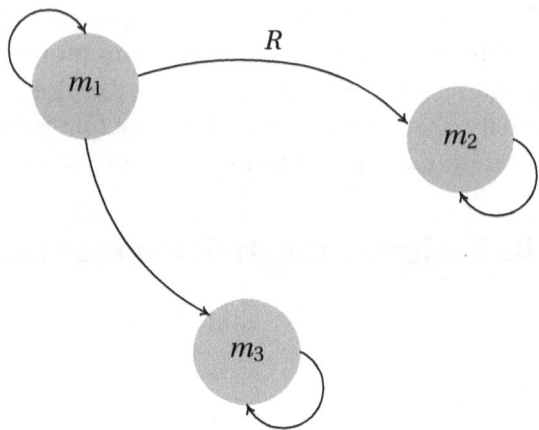

Figure 7.1: Sample RL1 System

- R is a binary relation on M, and

- v is a function that assigns truth values to statements relative to elements in M, with the relativity operators assigned values as follows:

  $v_m(\text{REL}(\alpha)) = 1$ iff $v_{m'}(\alpha) \neq v_{m''}(\alpha)$ for some m' and m'' where mRm' and mRm'', and = 0 otherwise.

  $v_m(\text{ABS}(\alpha)) = 1$ iff $v_{m'}(\alpha) = v_{m''}(\alpha)$ for all m' and m'' where mRm' and mRm'', and = 0 otherwise.

7.3.3 Comments

This system provides fairly simple support for modeling the relativity operators, where the analogy with the semantics for the modality of possibility and necessity is clear. Note however that the semantics for the relativity operators do not correspond directly to the standard modal operators $\Diamond$ and $\Box$, in accordance with the argument in section 7.1. The REL() and ABS() operators are modeled as contradictories here, since if $\text{ABS}(\alpha) = 0$, then there must be some m' and m'' such that mRm' and mRm'' where $v_{m'}(\alpha) \neq v_{m''}(\alpha)$, which is precisely the condition for $\text{REL}(\alpha) = 1$.

7.3. RL1: SIMPLE RELATIVITY SEMANTICS 217

Notably absent from this system are the usual logical connectives ($\neg, \wedge, \vee, \supset, \equiv$), which may seem to be an unacceptable omission. However, the reason for this omission is that although the relativized sub-theories in an instance of relativity must be closed under entailment, the conception of entailment may vary according to each sub-theory. Since the semantics of the logical operators would therefore effectively be relativized to the relativizing domain, there is no system-wide behavior of these operators to be modeled. Considered independently from the overall relative system, particular perspectives may have their own semantics for logical operators, but since these semantics may not be common for all perspectives, these logical features drop out of the overall system. Consequently, statements containing these logical operators are valued as propositional parameters, rather than analyzing them further into atomic statements and connectives.

As noted earlier, RL1 and the following systems are formulated as sentence logics without predication or quantification, and it was claimed earlier that the addition of these features would not affect the behavior of the two relativity operators. Yet if the usual logical connectors are excluded from these systems because the semantics for these symbols may vary according to each relativized sub-theory, then it would seem that the semantics for the quantification operators should likewise vary according to those sub-theories. If there is variation in the semantics for quantification, then it seems that there would indeed be some obstacle in extending these relative systems to include predication and quantification, contrary to my previous claim. If the possibility of adding quantification is precluded from these systems, then there may be further concerns about the expressibility of the thesis of global relativism within the systems, for example, in the form of the statement '$(\forall \alpha)\text{REL}(\alpha)$'.

Yet I think these concerns may be circumvented if any difference in semantics for quantification and predication between relativized sub-theories is implemented according to the pattern of a non-normal modal logic, as will be done with the relativity operators in system RL5 below. According to a non-normal system of predication, elements of the relativizing domain would be divided into normal and non-normal quantificational classes, where the valuations of sentences according to the normal elements would follow the standard semantics for predication and quantification, and the non-normal elements would assign values to the quantificational symbols arbitrarily in accordance with their deviant conception of quantification. Of course, if the quantificational symbols could be modeled this way, then it would seem that the remaining logical operators could be modeled in the same way. Unfortunately, this implementation would result in an extremely complex formal system, even for the simplest relative system, RL1. Furthermore, the implementation of non-normal semantics for the usual connectives and quantifiers would affect only the valuation of the base statements to which the relativity operators are applied. So for the purposes of modeling the relativity operators, statements containing these connectives and quantifiers could effectively be treated merely as propositional parameters, thereby avoiding needless complexity.

In this way, the thesis of global relativism could thereby be expressed in an extended system of RL1 that includes predication and quantification. Within the formulation of RL1 as a sentence logic as presented here, however, the thesis of global relativism would be expressed merely as one of the sentence letters, such as s_r, which would be valued true or false in various perspectives. While the representation of the thesis of global relativism as a mere sentence letter seems to leave the logical behavior of the instance of the relativity operator REL() unanalyzed within s_r, possibly raising concerns about equivocation in the statement of relativism, I suggest that this representation be understood merely as an expedient that stands in place of a full implementation of non-normal quantification.

Given the absence of logical connectors and quantifiers from RL1 as presented, no axioms including those symbols are included in the system. Even if RL1 were extended to include a non-normal implementation of these symbols, the deviance in the semantics of these symbols suggests that no axioms would be acceptable universally across all perspectives. While it is tempting to think that modeling the two relativity operators as contradictories should warrant the inclusion of an axiom expressing that relationship, such an axiom would need to rely on some logical connector, most probably the bi-conditional, and a difference in the conception of that connector would preclude universal acceptability of such an axiom.

With regard to proof theory, consider the two proposed rules of inference discussed earlier in section 7.1, namely the Rules of Absolution and Relativization:

Rule of Absolution: If $\vdash \alpha$ then $\vdash \text{ABS}(\alpha)$

Rule of Relativization: If $\vdash \alpha$ then $\vdash \text{REL}(\alpha)$

Since there are no axioms in RL1, these rules hold vacuously. Consequently, nothing can be proved on the basis of these rules. Nor do any other rules of inference seem appropriate here. Even if the system were extended to include the usual logical connectors and quantifiers, the potential deviance in the conception of the connectors would cast doubt on the universality across perspectives of any rules of inference based on these connectors. For this reason, no proof theory will be provided for RL1 or any of the other systems presented below.[22]

7.4 RL2: Multiple Relativities

RL2 is a system that models several kinds of relativity, with multiple relativizing domains and multiple corresponding accessibility relations.

7.4.1 Syntax

The language of RL2 consists of:

- an infinite number of sentence letters: $s_1, s_2, s_3, \ldots$

- grouping symbols: $(,)$;

- a finite number n of specific relativity operators: $\text{REL}_1(), \text{REL}_2(), \ldots, \text{REL}_n()$; $\text{ABS}_1(), \text{ABS}_2(), \ldots, \text{ABS}_n()$; and

- two general relativity operators: $\text{REL}()$ and $\text{ABS}()$.

The well-formed formulas of RL2 are defined as follows:

---

[22] Therefore, the logic of relative systems does not seem to a system of logic at all in a traditional sense, since nothing can be proved using the logic. Rather, relative systems consist solely of systems of semantics on which arguments can be based in some metalanguage.

- All sentence letters are well-formed formulas.

- If α is a well-formed formula, then so are $\text{REL}(\alpha)$, $\text{ABS}(\alpha)$, $\text{REL}_i(\alpha)$, and $\text{ABS}_i(\alpha)$ for every $0 < i \leq n$.

7.4.2 Semantics

An interpretation of RL2 is a structure $< \mathfrak{M}, \mathfrak{R}, v >$, where

- $\mathfrak{M} = < M_1, M_2, \ldots, M_n >$, where

  each M_i is a relativizing domain in the form of a non-empty set of relativizing factors,

- $\mathfrak{R} = < R_1, R_2, \ldots, R_n >$, where

  each R_i is a binary relation on M_i, and

- v is a function that assigns truth values to statements relative to combinations of elements from each M_i, such as $v_{m_1, m_2, \ldots, m_n}(s_1) = 1$ or 0, each $m_i \in M_i$. The relativity operators are assigned values as follows:

$v_{m_1, m_2, \ldots, m_i, \ldots, m_n}(\text{REL}_i(\alpha)) = 1$ iff

- $v_{m_1, m_2, \ldots, m'_i, \ldots, m_n}(\alpha) \neq v_{m_1, m_2, \ldots, m''_i, \ldots, m_n}(\alpha)$ for some m'_i and m''_i, where $m_i R_i m'_i$ and $m_i R_i m''_i$,

and $= 0$ otherwise.

$v_{m_1, m_2, \ldots, m_i, \ldots, m_n}(\text{ABS}_i(\alpha)) = 1$ iff

- $v_{m_1, m_2, \ldots, m'_i, \ldots, m_n}(\alpha) = v_{m_1, m_2, \ldots, m''_i, \ldots, m_n}(\alpha)$ for all m'_i and m''_i, where $m_i R_i m'_i$ and $m_i R_i m''_i$,

and $= 0$ otherwise.

$v_{m_1, m_2, \ldots, m_n}(\text{REL}(\alpha)) = 1$ iff $v_{m_1, m_2, \ldots, m_n}(\text{REL}_i(\alpha)) = 1$ for some i and $= 0$ otherwise.

$v_{m_1, m_2, \ldots, m_n}(\text{ABS}(\alpha)) = 1$ iff $v_{m_1, m_2, \ldots, m_n}(\text{ABS}_i(\alpha)) = 1$ for all i and $= 0$ otherwise.

7.4. RL2: MULTIPLE RELATIVITIES

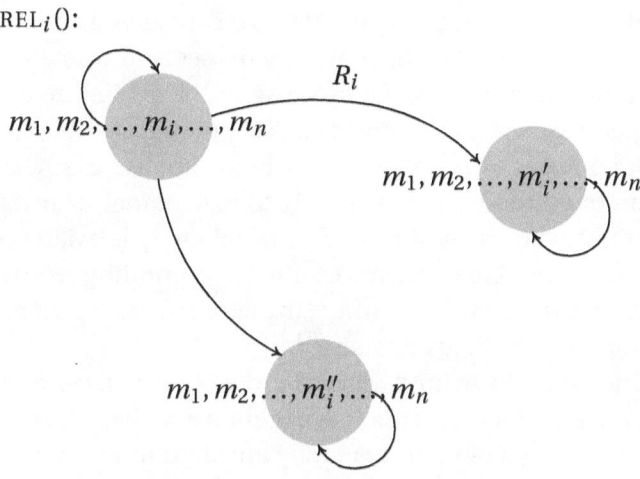

Figure 7.2: Sample RL2 System

7.4.3 Comments

This system concurrently models multiple varieties of relativity, such as moral relativism, conceptual relativism, and the special theory of relativity, for example, as discussed in section 7.2.1. Each kind of relativity is indexed numerically, with separate relativizing domains and separate corresponding accessibility relations. Even where the relativizing domains are the same for two different kinds of relativity, for instance, where two different domains of discourse are both relative to cultures, it may be that the accessibility relations still differ for some reason. Perhaps standards of theory evaluation are shared with regard to one domain of discourse, but are not shared with regard to another, for example. However this situation may arise, relativizing domains and accessibility relations are kept separate in this system.

The evaluation of a particular kind of relativity is always made with regard to a *compound perspective*, namely a perspective that is constructed from elements from each relativizing domain. So if there are three relativizing domains, one containing cultures, the second conceptual schemes, and the third inertial frameworks, a compound perspective would be that of a particular culture using a particular conceptual scheme within a particular inertial framework. When evaluating cultural relativism from a compound perspective, according to this example, the valuations of cultures accessible to the evaluating culture are considered, but only those valuations where the conceptual schemes and frameworks of inertial motion are the same as those of the evaluating compound perspective. Alternate conceptual schemes accessible to the compound perspective's conceptual scheme are irrelevant to the evaluation of cultural relativism, only to conceptual relativism. More generally, when a particular kind of relativity is evaluated, valuations of accessible elements of the corresponding relativizing domain are considered only where the elements of the other relativizing domains are held constant.[23]

The rationale behind the semantics of the two general relativity operators is that a statement is generally relative if it is specifically relative in any way, and generally absolute if it is specifically absolute in every way and therefore relative in no way. This system therefore enables the formulation of a claim of global relativism in which everything is relative in the sense that every statement is relative according to some kind of relativity, though not necessarily that every statement is relative according the same kind of relativity.

RL1 is clearly a special case of RL2, in which there is only a single kind of relativity.[24]

---

[23] Note that the accessibility relations for a given kind of modality have not been relativized in this system, whereas in Hales' system RL and in my discussion of a generalization of modeling multiple kinds of modality, these relations for one kind of modality are relativized according to the perspectives of the other kinds of modality. Were I to formulate a system of multiple kinds of modality as Hales has done, I would certainly provide support for expressing the relativization of possibility and the possibility of relativization. However, in modeling multiple kinds of the same modality, the need for the relativization of accessibility relations seems much less clear. A shift in inertial frameworks in the special theory of relativity would not seem to require any modification of the accessibility relations in moral relativity, for example. There may indeed be some forms of relativism, possibly conceptual relativism, that may motivate the need for such further relativization. The resulting system, however, would be exceedingly complex, and given the complexity of combining RL2 and RL3 into RL4 below, I am reluctant to complicate matters here unnecessarily. The relativization of accessibility relations will appear in RL3, but only within a single kind of relativity, and this relativization is motivated by different considerations.

[24] There is a further question whether RL2 can be reduced to RL1, at least with regard to the general relativity operators, since compound perspectives can be taken to form elements of a single relativizing domain. The key question is whether there is a transformation of the multiple accessibility relations in an RL2

7.5 RL3: Relativized Accessibility Relations

RL3 is a system that models a single kind of relativity, in which the accessibility relations are themselves relativized.

7.5.1 Syntax

As in RL1.

7.5.2 Semantics

An interpretation of RL3 is a structure $< M, \mathfrak{R}, v >$, where

- M is a relativizing domain in the form of a non-empty set of relativizing factors,

- $\mathfrak{R} = < R_{m_1}, R_{m_2}, \ldots, R_{m_n} >$, where

  · each $m_i \in M$,

  · each R_{m_i} is a binary relation on M, and

- v is a function that assigns truth values to statements relative to ordered pairs of elements in M, such as $v_{m_1,m_2}(s_1) = 1$ or 0 with the relativity operators assigned values as follows:

$v_{m_1,m_2}(\text{REL}(\alpha)) = 1$ iff $v_{m_1,m_2'}(\alpha) \neq v_{m_1,m_2''}(\alpha)$ for some m_2' and m_2'', where $m_2 R_1 m_2'$ and $m_2 R_1 m_2''$, and $= 0$ otherwise.

$v_{m_1,m_2}(\text{ABS}(\alpha)) = 1$ iff $v_{m_1,m_2'}(\alpha) = v_{m_1,m_2''}(\alpha)$ for all m_2' and m_2'', where $m_2 R_1 m_2'$ and $m_2 R_1 m_2''$, and $= 0$ otherwise.

---

system into a single accessibility relation in an RL1 system that preserves the valuations of the two general relativity operators. I suspect that there are RL2 models where such a transformation is not available, particularly with regard to reflexive elements among compound perspectives, since the valuation of some specific relativity operators may rely critically on the inclusion of such reflexive elements in the relation, while others may rely critically on the exclusion of such elements from the relation. A proof would need to substantiate this suspicion, but I have not formulated such a proof. Still, since there clearly seems to be a need to model multiple kinds of relativity separate from the general relativity operators, even if a reduction of RL2 to RL1 for the general relativity operators were possible on these grounds, that would not eliminate the theoretical interest in RL2 systems.

224 CHAPTER 7. PROPOSED LOGICS OF RELATIVE SYSTEMS

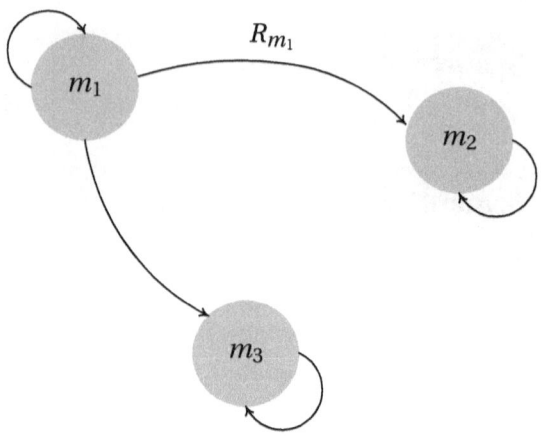

Figure 7.3: Sample RL3 System from the perspective of m_1

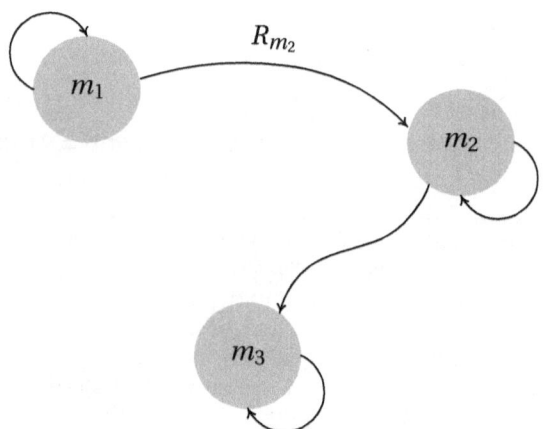

Figure 7.4: Sample RL3 System from the perspective of m_2

7.5.3 Comments

The valuation relative to ordered pairs $< m, m' >$ of elements in the relativizing domain should be understood as the valuation of the statement for m' relative to m's perspective. In this example, call m the *evaluating perspective* and m' the *evaluated perspective*. Where $m = m'$, the valuation is for a perspective from its own perspective. To make the relativization of accessibility relations in RL3 distinct from RL1, the valuations of statements in perspectives must likewise be relativized to perspectives. If valuations had been relativized simply to a single element of the relativizing domain, then the semantics for the relativity operators would have referenced only $mR_m m'$ for valuations according to m, with the consequence that the only elements of the relativized accessibility relations that were relevant to the semantics were elements where the first term was the element of the relativizing domain to which the relations were relativized, namely m. In such a case, these relativized relations could easily be reduced to a single accessibility relation in an RL1 system without any variation in the valuations of the relativity operators.

This system permits the relativization of judgments of relativity itself to perspectives, as discussed in section 7.2.2 above. The semantics permit the valuation of a statement to be relative for a perspective from its own perspective, but absolute for that perspective from another perspective. RL3 therefore represents a more radical kind of perspectivism than either RL1 or RL2. Since valuations are made for a perspective from a perspective, this system seems particularly well suited to model what has come to be known as assessor contextualism as opposed to agent contextualism, where judgments in agent contextualism are made relative to the agent's context, and judgments in assessor contextualism are made relative to an assessor's context.[25] Not only are the valuations of atomic statements made relative to an assessor's context here, but the valuations of the relativity operators are likewise relativized by means of the relativized accessibility relations. This relativization can be given some sense by noting that the conception of which competing theories are taken to be worthy of consideration and which are simply rejected as wrong can vary according to perspectives. A few concrete suggestions of such varying conceptions were presented

---

[25] See, for example, (Lyons, 1976), (MacFarlane, 2003) and (MacFarlane, 2005).

in section 7.2.2 above.

Here again, it seems that RL1 can be understood as a special case of RL3, where the relativized accessibility relations are all identical, and where the valuation of statements for m from the perspective of m' are identical to the valuations of statements for m from m's own perspective.

7.6 RL4: Multiple Relativities and Relativized Accessibility Relations

Systems RL2 and RL3 introduced two different complicating factors to produce more advanced systems than RL1. Yet both of these complicating factors might likewise be modeled concurrently within a single relative system. RL4 therefore models both several different kinds of relativities and the relativization of accessibility relations.

7.6.1 Syntax

As in RL2.

7.6.2 Semantics

An interpretation of RL4 is a structure $<\mathfrak{M}, \mathfrak{R}, \nu>$, where

- $\mathfrak{M} = <M_1, M_2, \ldots, M_n>$, where

  · each M_1 is a relativizing domain in the form of a non-empty set of relativizing factors,

- $\mathfrak{R} =< \begin{matrix} <R_{1,p_1}, & R_{1,p_2}, & \ldots, & R_{1,p_q}> \\ <R_{2,p_1}, & R_{2,p_2}, & \ldots, & R_{2,p_q}> \\ <\ldots, & \ldots, & \ldots, & \ldots> \\ <R_{n,p_1}, & R_{n,p_2}, & \ldots, & R_{n,p_q}> \end{matrix} >$, where

  · each R_{i,p_j} is a binary relation on M_i,

  · each p_j is a combination of elements from each M_i, such as $p_1 = <m_1, m_2, \ldots, m_n>$,

  · $<p_1, p_2, \ldots, p_q>$ is an enumeration of all compound perspectives, and

7.6. RL4: BOTH COMPLICATIONS

- v is a function that assigns truth values to statements relative to ordered pairs of p_j, such as $v_{p_1,p_2}(s_1) = 1$ or 0, with the relativity operators assigned values as follows:

$v_{p_1,p_2}(\text{REL}_i(\alpha)) = 1$ iff $v_{p_1,p_2'}(\alpha) \neq v_{p_1,p_2''}(\alpha)$ for some p_2' and p_2'', where

- $m_j \in p_2, p_2', p_2''$ for all $j \neq i$, and
- $m_i R_{i,p_1} m_i'$ and $m_i R_{i,p_1} m_i''$ where $m_i \in p_2$, $m_i' \in p_2'$, and $m_i'' \in p_2''$;

and = 0 otherwise.

$v_{p_1,p_2}(\text{ABS}_i(\alpha)) = 1$ iff $v_{p_1,p_2'}(\alpha) = v_{p_1,p_2''}(\alpha)$ for all p_2' and p_2'', where

- $m_j \in p_2, p_2', p_2''$ for all $j \neq i$, and
- $m_i R_{i,p_1} m_i'$ and $m_i R_{i,p_1} m_i''$ where $m_i \in p_2$, $m_i' \in p_2'$, and $m_i'' \in p_2''$;

and = 0 otherwise.

$v_{p_1,p_2}(\text{REL}(\alpha)) = 1$ iff $v_{p_1,p_2}(\text{REL}_i(\alpha)) = 1$ for some i, and = 0 otherwise.

$v_{p_1,p_2}(\text{ABS}(\alpha)) = 1$ iff $v_{p_1,p_2}(\text{ABS}_i(\alpha)) = 1$ for all i, and = 0 otherwise.

7.6.3 Comments

The use of p_j as a symbol for a compound perspective $< m_1, m_2, \ldots, m_n >$ is simply an attempt to increase the readability of this very complex semantic system, where the cross-relativizations can be difficult to follow. As in RL3, valuations are always made to ordered pairs of perspectives, but as in RL2, these perspectives are compound perspectives compounded out of one element from each relativizing domain associated with a specific kind of relativity. Call the first compound perspective in this ordered pair an *evaluating context* and the second an *evaluated context*. So a particular kind of relativity or absoluteness for a statement is evaluated for an evaluated context from the perspective of an evaluating context.

228 CHAPTER 7. PROPOSED LOGICS OF RELATIVE SYSTEMS

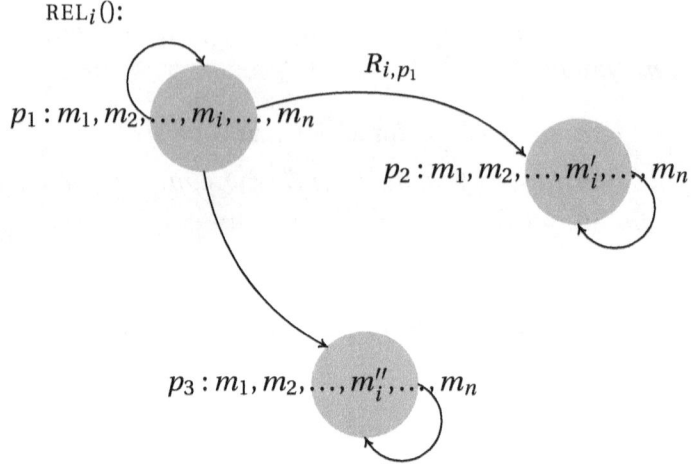

Figure 7.5: Sample RL4 System from the perspective of p_1

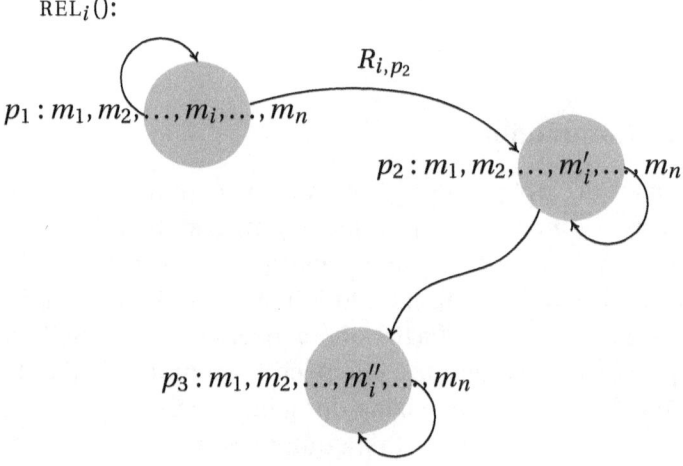

Figure 7.6: Sample RL4 System from the perspective of p_2

A specific kind of relativity ($\text{REL}_i()$) is evaluated true in this way when there are two evaluated contexts (p_2' and p_2'') that give different valuations when evaluated according to the evaluating context (p_1), with the following conditions: (1) the two evaluated contexts and the initial evaluated context (p_2) must all share elements (m_j) from every other relativizing domain besides the domain associated with the specific kind of relativity being evaluated, and (2) the elements (m_i' and m_i'') of the two evaluated contexts from the relativizing domain associated with the specific kind of relativity being evaluated must both be accessible from the element (m_i) of that relativizing domain belonging to the initial evaluated context, according to the accessibility relation (R_{i,p_1}) for that kind of relativity according to the evaluating context. Similarly for a specific kind of absoluteness. The general relativity operators follow straightforwardly according to the pattern in RL2, but relativized to combinations of evaluating and evaluated contexts.

RL1, RL2 and RL3 all form special cases of RL4. If n is 1, then there is only a single kind of modality, and RL4 reduces to RL3. If each compound perspective values sentences for other perspectives the same way that each perspective values itself, and the accessibility relations are all identical, then the relativization of accessibility relations becomes trivial, and RL4 effectively reduces to RL2. If both of these situations obtain, then RL4 effectively reduces to RL1. Given the complexity of this system, however, it seems preferable for expository purposes to articulate the three earlier systems prior to the presentation of this system.[26]

7.7 RL5: Non-Normal Relativity

The discussion of rules of inference in section 7.1 raised the question of normal and non-normal modal logics as the basis for relative systems. However, systems RL1 through RL4 above are all normal modal systems. RL5 is a system that embodies a non-normal modal logic, while modeling a single kind of relativity with a single non-relativized accessibility relation.

---

[26] And indeed for the purposes of development, not merely exposition.

7.7.1 Syntax

As in RL1

7.7.2 Semantics

An interpretation of RL5 is a structure $< M, N, R, V >$, where

- M is a relativizing domain in the form of a non-empty set of relativizing factors,
- N is a subset of M,
- R is a binary relation on M, and
- v is a function that assigns truth values to statements relative to elements in M, with the relativity operators assigned values as follows:

If $m \in N$, then:

$v_m(\text{REL}(\alpha)) = 1$ iff $v_{m'}(\alpha) \neq v_{m''}(\alpha)$ for some m' and m'', where mRm' and mRm''; and $= 0$ otherwise.

$v_m(\text{ABS}(\alpha)) = 1$ iff $v_{m'}(\alpha) = v_{m''}(\alpha)$ for all m' and m'', where mRm' and mRm''; and $= 0$ otherwise.

If $m \notin N$, then:

$v_m(\text{REL}(\alpha))$ is arbitrary.

$v_m(\text{ABS}(\alpha))$ is arbitrary.

7.7.3 Comments

Following the pattern of non-normal modal logics, this system divides the perspectives contained within M into two classes: normal perspectives where $m \in N$, and non-normal perspectives where $m \notin N$. The semantics for the relativity operators are the same as in RL1 for normal perspectives, but for non-normal perspectives, REL(α) and ABS(α) are valued arbitrarily. Consequently, RL5 would be the relative analogue of the modal system S0.5. [27]

---

[27] For a discussion of S0.5, see for example (Priest, 2008, pp. 69–71).

7.7. RL5: NON-NORMAL RELATIVITY

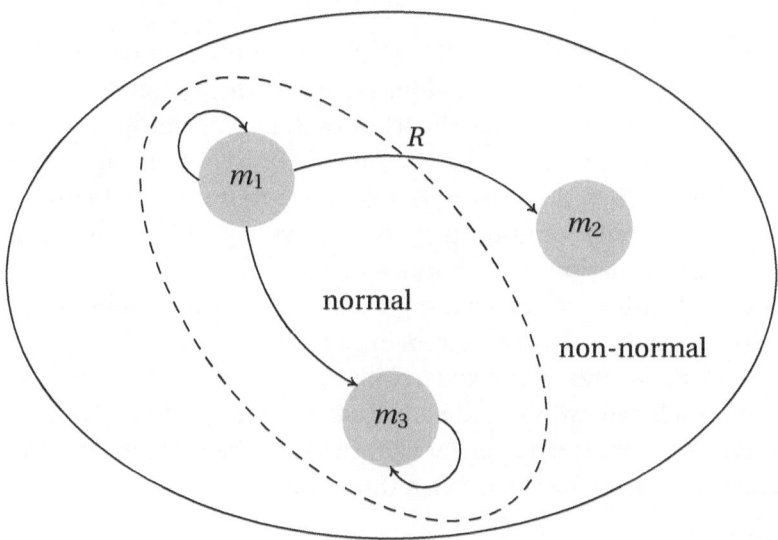

Figure 7.7: Sample RL5 System

This system is motivated by the discussion in section 7.1 above concerning the proposed Rule of Absolution, formulated on analogy with the Rule of Necessitation in modal logics of possibility and necessity, where modal systems accepting the Rule of Necessitation are known as normal modal logics. It was noted earlier that the Rule of Absolution is not a rule that is likely to be adopted within a thoroughly relativistic perspective, so it would seem that any self-refutation argument that employed a logic presupposing the Rule of Absolution would beg the question against relativism. Although none of the systems RL1 through RL4 specify any proof theory for the reasons discussed in section 7.3.3, the semantics for those four earlier systems are analogous to the semantics for normal modal logics. RL5 is therefore formulated explicitly to provide the semantics of a non-normal relative system.

RL1 is clearly a special case of RL5, where $N = M$. The same kinds of complications as in RL2 through RL4, namely multiple relativities and relativized accessibility relations, might likewise be incorporated into non-normal relative systems, thus yielding three further systems, RL6, RL7, and RL8. Consequently, it would seem that system RL8, featuring multiple relativities, relativized accessibility relations, and non-normal semantics, should properly be considered the logic of relative system, since every other system would form a special case of RL8. However, for the purposes of this study, it will be clearer to consider systems RL1 through RL5 separately, to focus first on the effects of each complicating factor in isolation, then in combination in the case of RL4. Since the non-normal features of RL5 appear as exceptions to the normal semantics that hold only for non-normal perspectives, it does not seem that the combination of such non-normal features with the other two complicating factors would pose any significant issues above the consideration of those factors in isolation.

With these five proposed relative systems formulated, the charge of self-refutation against relativism can be evaluated on formal grounds. The next chapter is devoted to the formulation and evaluation of this charge of self-refutation.

Chapter 8

Relativism and Self-Refutation

It is not surprising that Socrates uses a self-refutation argument against the relativism of Protagoras, since self-refutation is Socrates' stock in trade. Rather than deploy arguments of his own against his opponents, concluding that the opponent's position is false, Socrates characteristically employs a method of question and answer to bring out the consequences of his opponent's own views by his opponent's own admission, ultimately obliging the opponent himself to conclude that his position is incorrect. This is a particular kind of self-refutation that has been called *ad hominem*, as will be discussed below.

Yet before exploring the nature of self-refutation and its deployment against relativism, it is worthwhile noting why the self-refutation argument is so important with regard to relativism. As Jack Meiland explains, when any criticism is leveled against a relativist, the response from the relativist will likely be that the criticism may be decisive for the critic, but not for the relativist, since the consequences of relativism that the critic finds so objectionable are perfectly acceptable to the relativist.

> This reply — that the consequences are acceptable *to him* [the relativist] — is *not* an *ad hoc* rejoinder. It is *not* a stubborn maintaining of a position in the face of rational arguments, as it has seemed to some philosophers. It is *not* a refusal to argue, as it would be if given by a non-relativist. Instead, it is just the kind of

thing that the relativist's own position licenses him — indeed, forces him — to say. For this reply relativizes the idea of acceptability to persons, just as a relativist should do. (Meiland, 1979, p. 52) [original emphasis]

However, if relativism could be shown to be false for the relativist, with consequences that are unacceptable to the relativist, then this relativistic response would be unavailable. If relativism is false even for the relativist, according to the very principles of relativism, then it surely cannot be maintained as a doctrine, and therefore, a self-refutation argument would seem to be the most effective means of arguing against relativism, to prevent the relativist from turning the anti-relativist's argument back onto him.

Various relative systems were formalized in the previous chapter, partly in order to understand how relative systems in general work, but partly also to provide a framework for evaluating the charges of self-refutation against relativism. The strategy of this chapter will be first to establish what precisely counts as self-refutation with regard to relativism and the extent to which logical analysis can decide the question of self-refutation, then to examine the standard charges of self-refutation that have been leveled against relativism to determine which of them can be evaluated by means of the five proposed relative systems. After performing an evaluation of those charges, I will finally comment briefly on the various forms of self-refutation charges that are not well suited for logical analysis.

8.1 Nature of Self-Refutation

As Myles Burnyeat points out, "Any refutation, of course, establishes the contradictory of what it refutes, but *peritrepein* [the ancient Greek term used for self-refutation] tends particularly to be used of the special case where the thesis to be refuted itself serves as a premise for its own refutation, where starting out with 'p' we deduce 'not-p' and so conclude that the original premise was false" (Burnyeat, 1976a, p. 48). This section aims to understand how this pattern of self-refutation is supposed to work specifically with regard to relativism.

John Passmore identifies three separate varieties of self-refutation: absolute, pragmatic, and *ad hominem*, each of which

8.1. NATURE OF SELF-REFUTATION

depends upon a kind of contradiction. "Formally, the proposition *p* is absolutely self-refuting, if to assert *p* is equivalent to asserting *both p and not-p*" (Passmore, 1961, p. 60). In absolute self-refutation, the contradiction occurs essentially as a logical consequence of the starting proposition. The contradiction within pragmatic self-refutation, however, occurs as a consequence of the act by which the proposition has been presented, namely "somebody has put forward a thesis while at the same time apparently engaging in a procedure which, according to his thesis, is impossible, e.g. he appears to speak the words 'I cannot speak' " (p. 80). In the case of *ad hominem* self-refutation, "somebody has admitted something to be the case which, if it were the case, would be inconsistent with what he says, or thinks, to be the case" (p. 80). Whereas Passmore notes that charges of pragmatic and *ad hominem* self-refutation can oftentimes be evaded by reinterpreting the act or admission in such a way that no contradiction ensues, with regard to absolute self-refutation, "No evasion is possible. For to try to reply, for example, that 'there are no truths except the truth that there are not truths' would be to leave oneself open to precisely this same objection; that proposition is being put forward as possibly true, and yet it cannot be true if the only truth is that there are no truths" (p. 80).

Henry Johnstone, however, challenges the distinctions that Passmore makes with regard to self-refutation, presenting three reasons that a distinction between absolute and non-absolute forms of self-refutation cannot be maintained:

> In the first place, I do not believe that absolute refutations can be reduced to the assertion of *both p* and *not-p*; or, alternatively, if they can, so can the refutations that Passmore regards as not being absolute. In the second place, I do not believe that the conclusions of absolute self-refutations are immune to evasion in the way Passmore thinks they are. In the third place, Passmore's distinction cannot be made on the supposition that absolute self-refutations are valid and other self-refutations invalid; for if certain other arguments cited as valid by Passmore are in fact valid, these non-absolute self-refutations must also be valid. (Johnstone, 1964, p. 472)

In fact, in a later article, Johnstone argues that "all valid philosophical arguments are *ad hominem*" (Johnstone, 1989, p. 248). So if a distinction between absolute and non-absolute self-refutation cannot be maintained, and all valid arguments are *ad hominem*, then it would seem that all valid self-refutation arguments are *ad hominen*.

Whereas Johnstone's concerns are with Passmore's taxonomy of self-refutation, my concern is with the pattern of contradiction that forms the crux of each form of self-refutation. The main concern is to what degree contradiction can provide the grounds for self-refutation when used against certain claims. Consider for example a form of paraconsistency such as dialethism, which holds that there are true contradictions. How could the demonstration of a contradiction count against the claim of dialethism when the claim itself supports contradictions? If the contradiction in question is to refute dialethism, neither the simple presence of a contradiction nor even the involvement of the claim of dialethism in the contradiction seem sufficient. Rather it would seem that a self-refutation would follow in such a case only if the doctrine of dialethism could not countenance a particular kind of contradiction against itself, but it is not immediately clear what sort of contradictions dialethism could not countenance.

Similarly, relativism by its very nature entails contradictions, as Aristotle notes (Aristotle, 1984, p. 1591, 1007b18–1008a2), since the formal requirements for relativity demand that there be multiple, different relativized sub-theories as noted in section 4.2, with the consequence that there are at least some contradictory statements between relativized sub-theories. However, unlike dialethism, relativism generally seeks to defuse the contradictions by confining each of the contradictory statements separately to different perspectives, such that within a particular perspective there may be no contradictions, as Aristotle also noted (Aristotle, 1984, pp. 1678–1679, 1062b12–24). So the mere presence of a contradiction within relativism would seem insufficient to count as self-refutation, even if directed against the doctrine of relativism, if the contradictory statements were held in different perspectives. Nor would a contradiction within a single perspective necessarily count as self-refutation, since I have allowed that different perspectives may have different conceptions of logical consequence, including paraconsistent and even dialethic conceptions where such contradic-

8.1. NATURE OF SELF-REFUTATION

tions may be countenanced. Rather, it would seem that self-refutation would follow from a contradiction in a case of relativism if that contradiction occurred within a specifically relativistic perspective in such a way that the doctrine of relativism itself did not allow. Yet even this does not seem to be sufficient, since there may be multiple relativistic perspectives available according to a particular claim of relativism. If there is a contradiction that counts as self-refutation for one relativistic perspective, but no such contradiction for another relativistic perspective, then it would seem that the charge of self-refutation is itself only relative, which rather than counting as a refutation of relativism, would seem to be specifically required by a thoroughly relativistic claim. Consequently, it would seem that unacceptable contradictions would need to be demonstrated in every relativistic perspective in order to support a charge of absolute self-refutation rather than merely relative self-refutation.

Expanding upon Passmore's analysis, John Mackie offers a formal analysis of various forms of self-refutation that may arise with regard to any logical operator that takes a proposition as a parameter and returns a proposition. Some examples of Mackie's operators include "I am saying that", "I am writing that", and "It can be proved that" (Mackie, 1964, p. 193). When such an operator is applied to a universal negation using that operator, such as "I say that I am not saying anything" (p. 194), this application results in pragmatic self-refutation, which Mackie demonstrates by means of a formal proof.

Mackie's analysis divides absolute self-refutation into two categories based upon the nature of the specific operators involved. An operator may be what Mackie calls "truth-entailing" (p. 194), meaning that the truth of the application of the operator to a proposition entails the truth of the proposition itself. His examples of truth-entailing operators are "It is true that", "I know that", and "It can be proved that" (p. 194). So if it can be proved that p, then p. An operator may also be what Mackie calls "prefixable" (p. 195), meaning that the truth of a proposition entails the truth of the operator applied to that proposition. His examples of prefixable operators are "It is true that", and "It is possible that" (p. 196). So if p, then it is true that p. For both truth-entailing and prefixable operators, Mackie provides formal proofs demonstrating their self-refutation.

Lastly, Mackie considers operators that are weakly prefixable in the sense that they can be shown to enable self-refutation charges in conjunction with a further operator indicating coherent assertion. As an example of weak prefixability, he suggests that "'I know nothing' cannot be coherently asserted" (p. 196), thereby making the operator "I know" weakly prefixable. Mackie calls such forms of self-refutation "operationally self-refuting" (p. 197). Apparently *ad hominem* self-refutation is not congenial to the kind of logical analysis that Mackie undertakes with regard to the other forms of self-refutation, so he does not address that form of self-refutation.

While criticisms have been raised against Mackie's application of his analysis to a number of specific operators,[1] with regard to the relativity operators it appears that Mackie is begging the question against relativism.[2] He disposes of relativism very briefly: "Since anything that simply is the case is an absolute and not merely relative truth, 'It is an absolute truth that' is strictly prefixable, and 'There are no absolute truths' is absolutely self-refuting" (Mackie, 1964, p. 200). Yet just as a relativist would reject the Rule of Absolution, as noted in section 7.1 above, a relativist would most certainly reject the suggestion that anything that simply is the case is not relative, since the assertion of anything simply being the case is always evaluated relative to a certain perspective. Whether the claim is absolute or not would depend upon the other perspectives, not merely the nature of the relativity term 'absolute'.

Furthermore, and perhaps more importantly for the purposes of this study, Mackie seems to beg the question in another way. His analysis is conducted according to the rules of classical logic, so his self-refutation arguments would properly apply only to doctrines that accept classical logic. Such arguments would not necessarily carry any weight with positions that endorsed paraconsistent or intuitionist logic, for example. With regard to relativism, this study has proposed five separate formal systems as candidates for the logic that relativism might endorse. Not only are they not even

---

[1] For example, W. L. Bonney challenges Mackie's argument that "I believe nothing" is operationally self-refuting (Bonney, 1966). Carl Page is concerned that Mackie's analysis is inadequate with regard to a class of operators that he calls "epistemologically responsible" (Page, 1992, pp. 423–426). Luca Castagnoli offers a close examination of Mackie's analysis with regard to the truth operator (Castagnoli, 2007, pp. 13–16).

[2] As noted also in (Weckert, 1984, p. 31) and (Page, 1992, pp. 416–417).

8.1. NATURE OF SELF-REFUTATION

extensions of classical logic, none of them specify any rules of inference. Consequently, not only would Mackie's analysis impose a foreign logic on relativism, but the kind of analysis that he adopts would seem to be impossible under the five proposed systems, since without rules of inference, no syntactical proof could be conducted. It would appear that any self-refutation argument against relativism would need to take place on the semantic side, within some metalanguage.

F. C. White criticizes Mackie's account on the grounds that "his analysis of 'pragmatic' self-refutations in particular leaves obscure what it is that refutes itself and how it does so", likewise claiming that other treatments of the subject "do not provide an account of the crucial feature of self-refuting propositions — namely, that these actually refute themselves" (White, 1989, p. 84 n1). In response, he outlines three characteristics of self-refuting propositions in general: "[1] They are false. [2] They falsify or contribute to falsifying themselves. [3] They falsify themselves through self-reference" (p. 84). White continues, "How many kinds of self-refuting proposition are there? ...There are as many kinds of self-refuting proposition as there are kinds of false proposition in the first place" (p. 86), ultimately suggesting that there are primarily two kinds, logical and empirical. "Logically self-refuting propositions are false propositions which, as a result of referring to themselves, and without the aid of independent premises, constitute the grounds of their own falsity" (p. 87). "Empirically self-refuting propositions ...are propositions which are false, and false because they refer to themselves, but self-falsifying only *qua* asserted in a particular sort of way — in such a way that a proposition describing the manner of their assertion contradicts the content of the assertion itself" (p. 87). So it seems that White's two principal kinds correspond roughly to absolute and pragmatic self-refutation as described by Passmore. Since White's concern is with propositions not persons, *ad hominem* self-refutation does not appear to be an option.

Yet Johnstone challenges White on the grounds that it is self-application rather than self-reference that should constitute the basis for self-refutation, where self-reference would require explicit names in a system for the system itself. His argument is that the generalizations that typically turn out to be self-refuting do not explicitly refer to themselves but do fall under their own application by virtue of their generalization (Johnstone, 1989, p. 248). Though White's analysis of self-refuting propositions might be acceptable given this amendment,[3] his analysis of the self-refuting nature of relativism seems suspect. While White claims that Plato's arguments in the *Theaetetus* do not succeed as self-refutation arguments as stated, he thinks that a recasting of those arguments can demonstrate the self-refutation of relativism.

> From the thesis that *all* propositions are true (and not false) for those who believe them, it follows by instantiation that "No proposition is true for anyone" is true (and not false) for x (x being whoever believes it). But since "No proposition is true for anyone" is self-referring, it follows that this proposition is also false (and not true) for x (more strictly, it is true for x that it is false for x). In short, Protagoras' thesis entails a proposition which is true and false *for the same person*. It is therefore self-refuting: it is false, it provides the grounds of its own falsity, and it does this by entailing a proposition which falsifies itself in being self-referring. (White, 1989, p. 90)

While Peter Davson-Galle argues that this apparent self-refutation may be avoided by reformulating the claim of relativism in terms of an object language and a metalanguage (Davson-Galle, 1991), my concerns with White's argument relate to the role of perspectives in self-refutation arguments with regard to relativism. As noted above, a contradiction may be tolerated within relativism if the perspective in which the contradiction appears endorses a paraconsistent conception of logical consequence, and furthermore, a contradiction would not appear to count as self-refutation against relativism if it appears within a perspective that is not relativistic. White's contradiction would follow on the acceptance of the

---

[3] At least one writer thinks that it is not acceptable. Carl Page challenges the extent to which the self-refutation must rely on self-falsification and the self-application it depends upon (Page, 1992), as White claimed, which leads him to formulate a variety of self-refutation based upon epistemologically responsible operators, as noted in an earlier footnote. Since Page adopts the same formal proof style of argument that Mackie uses to show self-refutation on the basis of these epistemologically responsible operators, my criticisms of Mackie on this basis likewise apply to Page.

8.1. NATURE OF SELF-REFUTATION

proposition "No proposition is true for anyone", but this is not something that needs to be accepted from a relativistic perspective according to the doctrine of relativism.[4] To bring out the perspectival nature of the question of self-refutation against relativism, consider the situation first from a nihilistic perspective. Indeed, a nihilistic perspective could not endorse the proposition "No proposition is true for anyone" without falling into self-contradiction and would therefore need to value every proposition as false including the proposition in question in order to be thoroughly nihilistic. Evaluated from another perspective, though, that proposition might appear effectively to be endorsed within the nihilistic perspective, precisely by virtue of its nihilism, but this judgment would be imposed upon the nihilistic perspective from the outside. From within the nihilistic perspective, though, no such judgment is made, since all propositions are valued false. Now consider the situation comparably from a relativistic perspective. While this nihilistic perspective may be a peculiar one, even to a relativist, the relativist perspective acknowledges a number of peculiar perspectives, including absolutist perspectives, without being bound by their peculiarities, except possibly with regard to the judgment of whether a statement is relative or absolute for that perspective.[5] Thus in this case, White seems to be imposing the putatively relativist doctrine that "All propositions are true for those who believe them" onto a nihilistic perspective, and deriving a contradiction from this imposition within that nihilistic perspective that is supposed to count against the relativistic perspective where no such contradiction is generated. Consequently, I claim that White misses his mark by failing to provide a self-refutation specifically against the relativistic perspective according to the principles endorsed solely from within that perspective. Perhaps White is simply not properly following the consequences of self-refutation with regard to the specific claims of relativism, or perhaps White's analysis of self-refuting propositions is inadequate after all.

Mark Okrent proposes what seems to be a definition of self-refutation specifically with regard to relativism: "A relativism is

---

[4] Graham Priest (in personal conversation) comments that this argument seems directed more toward trivialism, the position according to which everything is true, rather than against relativism.

[5] Though of course these judgments themselves may be relativized to perspectives, as in system RL3.

self-refuting if it is impossible to distinguish between the statement of the relativism seeming to be true and it being true" (Okrent, 1984, p. 355). Yet taken as a definition, Okrent's statement may ultimately beg the question insofar as the claim of some form of relativism might be precisely that there is no distinction to be made with regard to seeming true and being true. In such a case, no proof of self-refutation would be required, since it would follow solely from Okrent's definition. So it might be uncharitable to interpret Okrent's statement as a definition.[6] Perhaps his statement is asserting that whenever any instance of relativism cannot make a distinction between a claim seeming to be true and being true, that form of relativism meets the conditions for self-refutation. Unfortunately, he neither specifies any further conditions for self-refutation nor demonstrates how this failure of certain forms of relativism to make certain distinctions meets those conditions. Perhaps Okrent considers both to be obvious, but I prefer to make both the conditions for self-refutation and the arguments explicit. So I do not think that Okrent successfully makes his case under either interpretation of his account of self-refutation with regard to relativism.

The previous review of the literature on self-refutation seems to have failed to provide a workable conception of self-refutation suitable for evaluating relativism, so I will attempt to formulation a conception myself. In general, it seems that self-refutation is a species of a *reductio ad absurdum* argument, where not only must the tenets of the refuted theory provide all the premises for the argument, but also the rules of inference used to reduce the theory to absurdity, and the absurdity in question must be considered absurd according to the refuted theory. If premises or rules of inference not accepted by the theory were employed, then the putative self-refutation argument would beg the question. If the supposed absurdity were perfectly well countenanced within the

---

[6] According to an earlier formulation in the same article, "Relativism is self-refuting only if that in virtue of which propositions are true is dependent upon mind, context, language, etc. in such a way that it is impossible to distinguish between the mere assertion of such dependence and the truth of such dependence" (Okrent, 1984, p. 351). This formulation is stronger than the later statement quoted above, given that it affirms self-refutation "only if" certain conditions are met. This statement does indeed seem to be formulated as a definition, so my interpretive charity would seem to be pressed very hard at this point.

theory, then it would not count as a refutation at all, but would seem rather to be a reinforcement of the theory.

With regard to the possible self-refutation of relativism, there is a slight problem in identifying what premises are to be employed in the argument. While this study has taken considerable pains to make explicit what conditions need to obtain in order for a claim of relativism to be supported, and therefore would seem to have made all such premises clear, self-refutation arguments are typically not employed against general relativism as such, but rather against some specific form of global relativism. Even if such arguments are generalized, there is still the issue of specifying what should count as global relativism. A claim of relativism that is not global, that restricts its applicability to some specified range of statements, is not typically the target of self-refutation arguments, since the self-applicability that seems to enable self-refutation can be avoided by specifically excluding the statement of relativism from the range of its applicability. In section 7.2.1, I noted that the recognition of multiple kinds of relativity would provide an alternate formulation of the claim of global relativism. Whereas given a single kind of relativity, global relativism would seem to claim that every statement is relative in the same way, the recognition of multiple kinds of relativity supports a formulation of global relativism according to which every statement is relative according to some kind of relativity, but not necessarily the same kind of relativity. This difference in formulation led to the articulation of different relative systems, so the evaluation of global relativism cannot simply adopt a single set of premises, but must examine different sets appropriate to the different formulations of global relativism. With regard to the five relative systems proposed in the previous chapter, a claim of global relativism might rely on different premises by explicitly adopting one of those five systems as the logic that best represents that claim; therefore, it would seem that each system must be evaluated for self-refutation separately. Self-refutation might be demonstrated against one relative system, but given the possibility of alternative formulations of global relativism, self-refutation would be demonstrated against global relativism in general only if there were no relative system in which global relativism could be formulated that was not self-refuting.

There seems to be a further issue with regard to the rules of inference accepted by global relativism, since none of the five proposed relative system specifies any proof theory with rules of inference, as already noted. I mentioned earlier that self-refutation would count against relativism only if the rules of inference used to demonstrate self-refutation were endorsed by a claim of relativism, so this issue may seem to preclude any self-refutation argument on the basis of the five proposed relative systems. However, the issue concerning rules of inference merely suggests that the arguments for self-refutation cannot proceed syntactically, but must be based upon the semantics dictated by each relative system within the metalanguage in which those semantics are articulated.

Lastly, there is an issue determining what should count as an absurdity according to global relativism. Indeed, the doctrine itself has seemed absurd to many philosophers, but this clearly cannot count for much within a self-refutation argument, since such absurdity is asserted from within a non-relativistic perspective. The decisive absurdity against relativism would need to be recognized from within a specifically relativistic perspective. If White and Johnstone are correct, the absurdity would need to result from some variety of self-application of the statement of global relativism. One potential absurdity arising from self-application of a logical system of global relativism might be that the system itself must be recognized absolutely to be the logic of relativism. If there were one and only one proposed logic of relativism, this potential absurdity might seem to have some force. Yet since five separate relative systems have been proposed in the previous chapter, it is not clear that this apparent absurdity carries much weight, since the availability of alternative logical systems of global relativism would suggest that the logic of relativism is not absolute after all.

Traditionally, self-refutation arguments concerning global relativism have focused on the global nature of the claim, identifying an absurdity when some statement can be demonstrated not to be relative where the global scope of the relativism in question would extend to that statement. However, as I argued above with regard to White's self-refutation argument, the perspectival nature of global relativism must be respected in order for a self-refutation argument against relativism to succeed. Even global absolutism is not necessarily fatal to global relativism, provided that global absolutism could be restricted to some perspective. If some statement could be shown to be absolute within a relativistic perspective, this situation would indeed seem to be an embarrassment to global relativism. Yet as already noted above, even this situation is not necessarily fatal, so long as there is some other relativistic perspective according to which everything is relative.

Given these considerations, I propose that *global relativism be understood as a perspective that adopts a certain relative logic and locates itself as a particular perspective within that logic, with the further claim that all statements according to its perspective are relative.* I propose further that *self-refutation with regard to such global relativism be understood as a demonstration that no perspective of global relativism can be located within that logic, since there is no perspective within that logical system according to which all statement are relative.* Since there are multiple relative systems that could be adopted, self-refutation with regard to relativism would need to show further that there is no logical system in which a perspective of global relativism could be located.

8.2 Varieties of Charges of Self-Refutation Against Relativism

Since this study is concerned with relativism in general, rather than any particular form of relativism, arguments concluding that specific kinds of relativism are self-refuting cannot properly be addressed within the scope of this study. To evaluate certain charges of self-refutation against epistemological relativism, for example, it would be necessary to discuss the nature of evidence, justification, warrant, and other related topics that contribute to the way in which epistemic relativism is taken to be self-refuting, and a full discussion of these epistemic notions are beyond the scope of this study. Consequently, particular kinds of relativism will be of interest only insofar as they are self-refuting because of the general nature of relativism rather than because of their specific nature. In particular, I will not engage with the interpretive and explanatory issues relating to Plato's supposed self-refutation arguments against Protagoras in the *Theaetetus* any further than the discussion in section 3.2 above, whose aim was merely to demonstrate that the proposed definition of relativism was applicable to this prototypical instance of relativism.[7]

---

[7] For discussions of Protagoras and the self-refutation arguments, see (Castagnoli, 2004), (M.-K. Lee, 2005), (Castagnoli, 2007), and (Zilioli, 2007).

Given the multiplicity of particular self-refutation arguments against relativism, rather than analyze each argument separately, I propose to group these arguments together according to the general pattern of the arguments, which accords better with the formal approach adopted in this study.[8] I suggest that most self-refutation arguments against relativism fall into one or more of the following categories:

1. *Simple Reflexive*: The statement of relativism is self-refuting when simply applied to itself or to some other statement implied by relativism. This pattern of argument appears in (Plato, 1973, pp. 46–47, 171a–c), (Fitch, 1946, p. 67), (Mackie, 1964, p. 200), (Siegel, 1982, p. 49), (Beach, 1984, p. 12), (White, 1989, pp. 90–91), and (Hales, 1997, p. 35).

2. *Iterative*: Relativism results in a vicious regress since it requires that relative statements themselves be relative throughout all iterations of the relativity operators. This pattern of argument appears in (Burnyeat, 1976b, pp. 194–195), (Vallicella, 1984, pp. 462–463), and (Boghossian, 2006, p. 56).

3. *Dilemma*: The statement of relativism is either absolute or relative, and either option is unacceptable. This pattern of argument combines aspects of both the simple reflexive and iterative styles, and appears in (Trigg, 1973, pp. 2–3), (Siegel, 1982, p. 49), (T. Nagel, 1997, p. 15), and (Lockie, 2003, pp. 322, 327–328). Note that in (Castagnoli, 2007, p. 18), Castagnoli makes the point that the dilemma was the classical structure underlying ancient self-refutation arguments.

4. *For-x*: The claim that some statement is true or false for some perspective or even relatively true or false for some perspective must be absolute. This pattern of argument appears in (Passmore, 1961, p. 68), (Burnyeat, 1976b, pp. 192–194), (Putnam, 1981, p. 121), (Pinto, 1995), (Mosteller, 2006, p. 11), and (Boghossian, 2006, pp. 54–57).

5. *Pragmatic*: The act of asserting relativism, or submitting it for debate, or some other pragmatic aspect of relativism has

---

[8] For a similar approach, see (Preston, 1992), though I intend to take a more comprehensive approach to self-refutation arguments against relativism, rather than merely considering "some objections".

consequences that conflict with the doctrine of relativism. This pattern of argument appears in (Passmore, 1961, pp. 67–68), (Siegel, 1968, pp. 230–231), (Burnyeat, 1976a, p. 59), (Lyons, 1976, p. 113), (Tollefsen, 1987, pp. 211–213), (Zellner, 1995, pp. 292–295), (Boghossian, 2006, p. 118), and (Morris, 2008, pp. 213–214).

6. *Undermining*: Relativism undermines the very foundations needed to establish itself as a doctrine. This pattern of argument appears in (Husserl, 1970, pp. 141–142), (Jordan, 1971, pp. 24–25), (Marshall, Peters, & Shepheard, 1981, p. 46), (Siegel, 1984, p. 366), and (Siegel, 1987, p. 4).

7. *Language*: Relativism violates some condition relating to the nature of statements or propositions. This pattern of argument appears in (Husserl, 1970, p. 140), (Mandelbaum, 1982, p. 49), (Newton-Smith, 1982, p. 107), and (Vallicella, 1984, p. 453).

There are likewise a number of standard patterns of response to these arguments, including charging that the argument begs the question (White, 1989, p. 90), claiming that the argument equivocates on key terms (Hesse, 1980, p. 42), suggesting that a distinction between the object language and the metalanguage can dispel the apparent self-refutation (Davson-Galle, 1991), and even challenging the effectiveness of self-refutation arguments in general (Gadamer, 1989, pp. 344–345).[9] However, these specific responses will not be discussed any more than the specific arguments they challenge. The strategy of this study is to use the logic of relativism to evaluate the charges of self-refutation.

Yet Ugo Zilioli argues that logic seems useless to decide the matter between relativism and objectivism (Zilioli, 2007, p. 140), citing Feyerabend to the same effect.[10] However, as I suggested earlier in this section, insofar as the logic of relativism expresses the nature and behavior of relativism in general, logic should be

---

[9] Richard J. Bernstein cites Hans-Georg Gadamer to this effect (Bernstein, 1983, p. 234 n18), while Gadamer also references Plato's *Seventh Letter* at 343c–d.

[10] Zilioli cites the 2nd edition of *Against Method*, chapter 17, paragraph 9, which correlates to (Feyerabend, 1993, p. 169) in the 3rd edition, where Feyerabend makes similar comments at (pp. 192–195).

relevant in some sense to the question of self-refutation. Still, the review of the seven general patterns of self-refutation argument against relativism suggests that a number of these patterns cannot be decided merely by analysis of the logic of relativism, because the arguments rest either on pragmatics or on the metaphysics of language. Consequently, it seems that the last three patterns of self-refutation argument — pragmatic, undermining, and language — will not lend themselves well to an application of the proposed relative logics outlined in the previous chapter. I will have occasion to comment on these grounds for self-refutation later in section 8.4, however.

Of the remaining patterns of self-refutation, some philosophers employing these patterns rest their arguments primarily on grounds that likewise seem to exceed the scope of what the proposed relative logics can address. For example, the iterative argument can seem to be fatal to relativism for various reasons, whether because an infinite iteration of the relativity of a relative sentence exceeds the ability of a relativist to understand the judgment of its truth (Burnyeat, 1976b, pp. 194–195), or because relative truths cannot be established on the basis of other relative truths in an infinite regress (Vallicella, 1984, p. 463), or because the meaning of any given relative fact cannot be interpreted in terms of an infinitely long proposition (Boghossian, 2006, p. 56). With regard to the first three patterns of self-refutation argument, namely simple reflexive, iterative, and dilemma, what can properly be evaluated by means of a logical analysis is whether any of the proposed relative logics can support a thoroughly relativistic perspective, in which every statement is evaluated to be relative, and this question will be explored in the next section.

There is one novel consideration with regard to the logic of relativism that emerges from this review of the varieties of self-refutation argument against relativism, namely the fourth pattern of argument, For-x. According to this pattern, once a language has been augmented to allow it to express statements concerning what statements are true according to particular perspectives, these new statements need to be recognized as absolute, not relative. Yet the relative systems outlined in the previous chapter lack such expressive resources. Consequently, each of the five proposed relative system will need to be extended with operators expressing the valuation of statements according to perspectives, and those extensions will need to be evaluated with regard to whether they can support thoroughly relativistic perspectives. As I will show in the following section, it is this pattern of argument that poses the greatest challenge to the logic of global relativism.

8.3 Self-Refutation with Regard to the Proposed Relative Systems

Suppose then that a relativist were to adopt one of the five proposed relative systems as representing the logic of a claim of global relativism. Is that claim self-refuting? As argued in the last section, this question depends upon whether that system can support a thoroughly relativist perspective, namely one in which for every sentence the relativity operator 'relative' holds true when applied to that sentence. For RL1, this evaluation proceeds fairly easily. RL1 is not self-refuting in this regard, which can be proved as follows:

Theorem 1. *There is an RL1 model in which $v_m(\text{REL}(\alpha)) = 1$ for every α for some m.*

Let $<M, R, v>$ be an RL1 model as follows:
$M = \{m_1, m_2\}$
$R = \{<m_1, m_1>, <m_1, m_2>, <m_2, m_2>\}$
Let $v_{m_1}(s_i)$ assign values arbitrarily for every simple sentence s_i.
Let $v_{m_2}(s_i) = 1$ where $v_{m_1}(s_i) = 0$ and $v_{m_2}(s_i) = 0$ where $v_{m_1}(s_i) = 1$.
According to the theorem, $v_{m_1}(\text{REL}(\alpha)) = 1$ for all α.

Proof. The proof proceeds by induction on the level of nesting of the relativity operators, since by the formation rules for RL1, α is either a simple sentence s_i, or a sentence of the form $\text{REL}(\beta)$ or $\text{ABS}(\beta)$.

Base case: $\text{REL}(\alpha)$, where α is one of $s_1, s_2, s_3, \ldots$
According to the definition of v in the model:
If $v_{m_1}(s_i) = 1$, then $v_{m_2}(s_i) = 0$
If $v_{m_1}(s_i) = 0$, then $v_{m_2}(s_i) = 1$
m_1 can access both m_1 and m_2
Therefore, for every basic sentence s_i, there are two perspectives, m_1 and m_2 accessible to m_1 where $v_{m_1}(s_i) \neq v_{m_2}(s_i)$, so

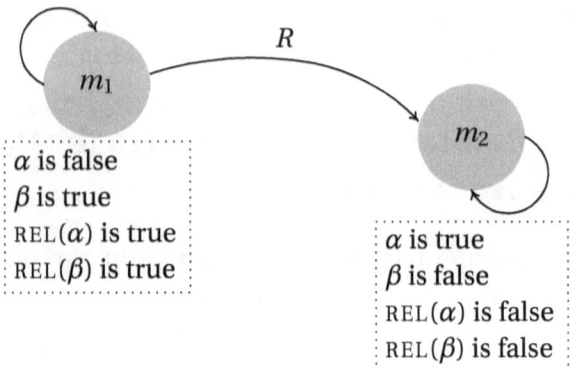

Figure 8.1: Model for Theorem 1

$v_{m_1}(\text{REL}(s_i)) = 1$. This establishes the base case for the first level, where α is a basic sentence with no nested relativity operators.

Inductive step: REL(α), where α is either REL(β) or ABS(β)

Suppose that α is REL(β), with some level of nested relativity operators in β. Then $v_{m_1}(\text{REL}(\beta)) = 1$ for all β, by the inductive hypothesis. Since m_2 can access only itself, in general, $v_{m_2}(\text{REL}(\gamma)) = 0$ for all γ, so $v_{m_2}(\text{REL}(\beta)) = 0$. Therefore, there are two perspectives, m_1 and m_2 accessible to m_1 where $v_{m_1}(\text{REL}(\beta)) \neq v_{m_2}(\text{REL}(\beta))$, so $v_{m_1}(\text{REL}(\text{REL}(\beta))) = 1$.

Suppose now that α is ABS(β). $v_{m_1}(\text{REL}(\beta)) = 1$ for all β, by the inductive hypothesis, so $v_{m_1}(\text{ABS}(\beta)) = 0$. Since m_2 can access only itself, in general, $v_{m_2}(\text{ABS}(\gamma)) = 1$ for all γ, so $v_{m_2}(\text{ABS}(\beta)) = 1$. Therefore, there are two perspectives, m_1 and m_2 accessible to m_1 where $v_{m_1}(\text{ABS}(\beta)) \neq v_{m_2}(\text{ABS}(\beta))$, so $v_{m_1}(\text{REL}(\text{ABS}(\beta))) = 1$.

So if $v_{m_1}(\text{REL}(\beta)) = 1$, where β contains some level of nesting of relativity operators, then $v_{m_1}(\text{REL}(\text{REL}(\beta))) = 1$ and $v_{m_1}(\text{REL}(\text{ABS}(\beta))) = 1$ proving the inductive step.

Therefore, according to the model, $v_{m_1}(\text{REL}(\alpha)) = 1$ for all α.

□

So RL1 is not self-refuting, since there is a model in which there is a thoroughly relativistic perspective, namely m_1 in the proof. However, since RL1 is a special case of each of RL2 through RL5, as noted in the previous chapter, models structurally equivalent

8.3. SELF-REFUTATION AND THE RELATIVE SYSTEMS

to this RL1 model can also be used to demonstrate that these other relative systems are also not self-refuting. So the following theorems can be proved using the same essential model and the same technique as in Theorem 1.

Theorem 2. *There is an RL2 model in which $v_p(\text{REL}(\alpha)) = 1$ for every α for some compound perspective p.*

Theorem 3. *There is an RL3 model in which $v_{m,m'}(\text{REL}(\alpha)) = 1$ for every α for some evaluating perspective m and some evaluated perspective m'.*

Theorem 4. *There is an RL4 model in which $v_{p,p'}(\text{REL}(\alpha)) = 1$ for every α for some evaluating context p and some evaluated context p'.*

Theorem 5. *There is an RL5 model in which $v_m(\text{REL}(\alpha)) = 1$ for every α for some m.*

While the RL1 model from Theorem 1 will suffice as a general basis for the proofs of these theorems, more complex models reflecting the advanced relativistic features of each system can be devised to prove these theorems as well. The strategy for devising such models can be generalized from the RL1 model used in the proof, as follows. First, allow v to assign values to simple sentences such that two perspectives directly contradict each other. Second, allow the designated relativistic perspective full access to all perspectives, including itself, but give the remaining non-relativistic perspectives reflexive access only. Consequently, non-relativistic perspectives will hold all sentences to be absolute, which will therefore allow all sentences in the relativistic perspective to be relative at any level of nesting of the relativity operators.[11]

---

[11] I should note that this strategy is not completely satisfactory with regard to RL2 and RL4, which model several kinds of relativity. The problem is that in order for a designated relativistic perspective in these systems to value every statement to be thoroughly relative, it would seem that all the non-relativistic perspectives must be identical. The evaluation of statements according to compound perspectives across the various accessibility relations seems to undermine the attempt to make one perspective relativistic with all other perspectives absolute. At some level of nesting of the relativity operators, it seems that the valuation of the REL() operator becomes false for all perspectives unless all absolute perspectives have identical sub-theories. I have noticed this situation in attempting to devise models for RL2 and RL4, though I have not formulated a proof. There may

Since not just one but all of the proposed relative systems support thoroughly relativistic perspectives, these proofs serve to refute three of the objections to relativism considered in the last section for all of these systems: simple reflexive, iterative, and dilemma. Against the simple reflexive objection, if one of the sentences in the system is a statement of the thesis of relativism, there is some perspective according to which that sentence is relative. Against the iterative objection, there is some perspective according to which every sentence is relative, regardless of the level of iteration or nesting of the relativity operators. Against the dilemma objection, if the simple reflexive objection fails, then no dilemma presents itself, since there is no problem holding the statement of relativism to be relative.

However, it would be premature to conclude that relativism in general is therefore not self-refuting, since there is another pattern of self-refutation argument that can be addressed by an analysis of these logical systems, namely the For-x objection. The argument of this objection is that if the language of each system is extended to allow it to express the valuations of sentences according to particular perspectives, sentences concerning what is true or false for a perspective turn out to be absolute for all perspectives. None of the five proposed relative systems has a language sufficiently powerful to express the valuation of sentences according to perspective. So the languages of each of these systems will need to be extended in order to evaluate this objection.

Accordingly, let the language of RL1 be extended to include an unlimited number of names a_1, a_2, a_3, ..., and a corresponding

---

be a relation between the number of kinds of relativity, the number of elements in the relativizing domains, and the level of nesting at which statements start to become absolute, though I have not established such a relation yet. While the formal requirements for relativity do not require a one-to-one relation between the relativizing domain and the range of relativized sub-theories, I have expressed some suspicions concerning relativistic claims in which many perspectives share the same sub-theory. Although this situation does not affect the argument of this chapter, it may prove to be significant for someone who might make a claim of global relativism. Since there would indeed appear to be multiple kinds of relativity that could and perhaps should be modeled together in a global system, the way that these multiple relativities seem to undermine global claims of relativity at certain levels of nesting may prove problematic. In such a case, the relativistic claim would need to argue either that the relativizing domain could be redefined to reduce the degree of agreement between perspectives, or that there is nothing suspicious about large numbers of perspectives sharing the same theory.

8.3. SELF-REFUTATION AND THE RELATIVE SYSTEMS

number of operators $\text{FOR}_x()$ where x is one of the names, such as $\text{FOR}_{a_1}()$. The rules for well-formed sentences are extended to include the following:

- If α is a sentence, then so is $\text{FOR}_x(\alpha)$ for all operators $\text{FOR}_x()$.

The model structure for RL1 will likewise need to be extended to $< M, I, R, v >$ where I is an index function mapping each name a_n either to some member of the relativizing domain M or to the empty set (if M does not contain the empty set) in the event that the name does not refer to anything in the relativizing domain. The semantics of the $\text{FOR}_x()$ operators will be as follows:

- $v_m(\text{FOR}_x(\alpha)) = 1$ iff

    (a) I maps x to some element m' in the relativizing domain,

    (b) m' is accessible to m according to R, and

    (c) $v_{m'}(\alpha) = 1$;

    and $= 0$ otherwise.

Clause (a) ensures that some perspective is successfully referenced in the $\text{FOR}_x()$ operator. Call clause (a) the *reference condition*. Clause (b) is needed since if one entire perspective is not accessible to another in the valuation of the relativity operators, then it does not seem proper to allow the second perspective to be able to discuss the values of sentences in the first perspective. Call clause (b) the *accessibility condition*. Clause (c) simply transmits the valuations of true sentences through the accessibility relation. Call clause (c) the *valuation condition*.

Call this extended system RL1+F. Given this language extension, the For-x objection claims the following:

$$v_m(\text{ABS}(\text{FOR}_x(\alpha))) = 1 \text{ for all } \alpha, \text{ all } m, \text{ and all } x$$

I think this claim is not justified for all sentences. I think that RL1+F models can easily be devised according to which all true sentences to which the $\text{FOR}_x()$ operator is applied will be relative. The strategy is similar to the general strategy for finding thoroughly relativistic models mentioned earlier. Designate one perspective to be relativistic. Let a different, non-relativistic perspective value each sentence such that it and the relativistic perspective

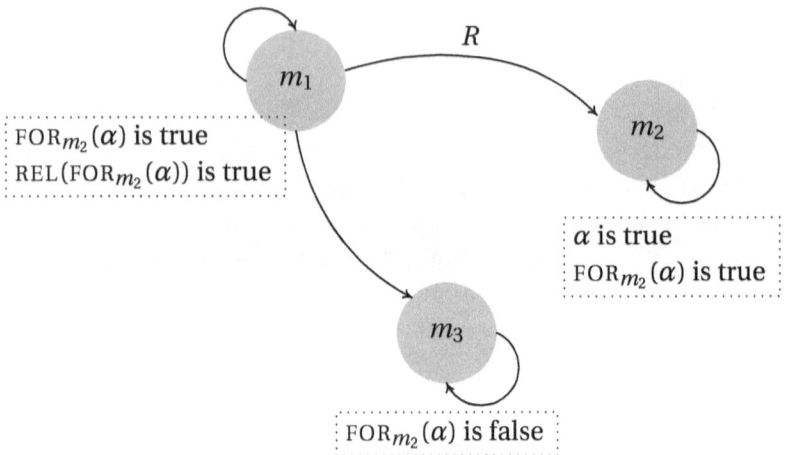

Figure 8.2: Failure of For-x objection for true sentences in RL1+F

contradict each other. Let a different non-relativistic perspective value each sentence arbitrarily. Arrange the accessibility relations such that the relativistic perspective can access all perspectives, including itself, but the non-relativistic perspectives can access only themselves. Consequently, since the accessibility condition fails in each non-relativistic perspective with regard to the $\text{FOR}_x()$ operator with regard to other perspectives, the $\text{FOR}_x()$ operator can be valued true in one perspective but false in another, allowing the relativistic perspective to hold the $\text{FOR}_x()$ operator to be relative. This strategy is illustrated in Figure 8.2, where m_1 is the designated relativistic perspective.

Yet with regard to false sentences in RL1+F, the situation is quite different. Here the valuation condition of the semantics for the $\text{FOR}_x()$ operator fails for all false sentences, so it turns out that the application of the $\text{FOR}_x()$ operator to false sentences becomes absolute. This can be proved as follows:

Theorem 6. *In every model of RL1+F, $v_m(\text{REL}(\text{FOR}_x(\alpha))) = 0$ for every m, where I maps x to m' and $v_{m'}(\alpha) = 0$.*

Proof. Consider an arbitrary RL1+F model. Consider an arbitrary sentence α and an arbitrary $m' \in M$ where $v_{m'}(\alpha) = 0$. Let I map a' to m'.

8.3. SELF-REFUTATION AND THE RELATIVE SYSTEMS 255

Since the valuation condition (c) of the semantics for the FOR$_x$() operator in RL1+F fails, given that $v_{m'}(\alpha) = 0$ by hypothesis, $v_m(\text{FOR}_{a'}(\alpha)) = 0$ for every m. Therefore for every m there are no m'' and m''' where $v_{m''}(\text{FOR}_{a'}(\alpha)) \neq v_{m'''}(\text{FOR}_{a'}(\alpha))$. So $v_m(\text{REL}(\text{FOR}_{a'}(\alpha))) = 0$ for every m.

□

So the For-x objection succeeds against system RL1+F. Yet whereas the refutations of the other objections to relativism did not require the additional relativistic features of RL2 through RL5, it seems that these features may be required to evaluate the For-x objection. Perhaps one of these systems will have sufficient relativistic resources to refute the For-x objection. Consequently, those systems must likewise be extended with suitable FOR$_x$() operators, as follows:

I will discuss RL5 later, since it poses special problems with regard to this objection. Let the languages of RL2 through RL4 be extended as in RL1+F. Let the semantics for the FOR$_x$() operators in these systems be as follows:

- **RL2+F:** $v_{m_1, m_2, \ldots, m_n}(\text{FOR}_x(\alpha)) = 1$ iff

    (a) I maps x to some compound perspective $<m'_1, m'_2, \ldots, m'_n>$ where each m'_i is an element from the corresponding relativizing domain M_i,

    (b) m'_i is accessible to m_i according to R_i for every i, and

    (c) $v_{m'_1, m'_2, \ldots, m'_n} = 1$; and = 0 otherwise.

- **RL3+F:** $v_{m_1, m_2}(\text{FOR}_x(\alpha)) = 1$ iff

    (a) I maps x to some element m'_2 in the relativizing domain,

    (b) m'_2 is accessible to m_2 according to R_{m_1}, and

    (c) $v_{m_1, m'_2}(\alpha) = 1$; and = 0 otherwise.

- **RL4+F:** $v_{p_1, p_2}(\text{FOR}_x(\alpha)) = 1$ iff

    (a) I maps x to some compound perspective p'_2,

    (b) for every position i, where $m_i \in p_2$ and $m'_i \in p'_2$, m'_i is accessible to m_i according to R_{i, p_1}, and

    (c) $v_{p_1, p'_2}(\text{FOR}_x(\alpha)) = 1$; and = 0 otherwise.

The semantics for the $\text{FOR}_x()$ operators in each extended system contain three clauses similar to the conditions for the $\text{FOR}_x()$ operator in RL1+F, namely a reference condition, an accessibility condition, and a valuation condition, as appropriate to the particular system. Since each system also contains a valuation condition that does not differ significantly from the valuation condition of RL1+F, and since Theorem 6 depends solely upon the valuation condition of RL1+F, the same general proof for self-refutation against RL1+F in Theorem 6 will also apply with regard to RL2+F through RL4+F, demonstrating that thoroughly relativistic perspectives cannot be modeled in these systems, given the absoluteness of the application of the $\text{FOR}_x()$ operator to false sentences. Specifically, the following theorems can be proved:

Theorem 7. *In every model of RL2+F, $v_{m_1,m_2,\ldots,m_n}(\text{REL}(\text{FOR}_x(\alpha))) = 0$ for every compound perspective $< m_1, m_2, \ldots, m_n >$, where I maps x to a compound perspective $< m'_1, m'_2, \ldots, m'_n >$, and $v_{m'_1,m'_2,\ldots,m'_n}(\alpha) = 0$.*

Theorem 8. *In every model of RL3+F, $v_{m,m'}(\text{REL}(\text{FOR}_x(\alpha))) = 0$ for every m and m', where I maps x to m'', and $v_{m,m''}(\alpha) = 0$.*

Theorem 9. *In every model of RL4+F, $v_{p,p'}(\text{REL}(\text{FOR}_x(\alpha))) = 0$ for every p and p', where I maps x to p'', and $v_{p,p''}(\alpha) = 0$.*

So whereas the accessibility condition of the semantics for the $\text{FOR}_x()$ operators can be used to generate models that avoid the For-x objection for true sentences, the valuation condition of those semantics enables the For-x objection to succeed against false sentences. Furthermore, it would seem that the reference condition could likewise be used to prove the For-x objection against any model in these systems, if there are names in the language that are not mapped to any perspective in the system. The failure of the reference condition would force the $\text{FOR}_x()$ operators for unmapped names to be valued false for every perspective in the system, thereby forcing those $\text{FOR}_x()$ operators to be absolute. Yet since the use of valuation condition for false sentences is sufficient to prove the For-x objection for RL1+F through RL4+F, I will not pursue any proofs on the basis of a failure of the reference condition. Therefore it would seem that the $\text{FOR}_x()$ operator may indeed be fatal to global relativism, as Passmore, Burnyeat and others have thought. The novel result here is that it is not the truths in

8.3. SELF-REFUTATION AND THE RELATIVE SYSTEMS

a perspective that cause problems for global relativism, but rather the falsehoods. The additional relativistic features of multiple relativities and relativized accessibility relations were insufficient to counter this charge of self-refutation.[12]

Perhaps, though, it may be thought that the addition of the $\text{FOR}_x()$ operator begs the question against relativism, on the grounds of interpretive charity. If the proposed relative systems turn out to be self-refuting only with the addition of the $\text{FOR}_x()$ operator, then perhaps the $\text{FOR}_x()$ operator is not properly part of the claim of relativism and therefore cannot be used to show that the relative systems are self-refuting. While I think it is important to consider the counter-charge of begging the question against relativism, I do not think this particular counter-charge succeeds. I would argue that it is precisely because of the claims of relativism that anyone would need to speak of something being true for a perspective. An absolutist would have no reason to introduce a $\text{FOR}_x()$ operator, because it would introduce a vacuous contrast, since everything true is true for every perspective under absolutism, and likewise for what is false. Consequently, not only does the introduction of the $\text{FOR}_x()$ operator not beg the question against relativism, it seems to be an important part of the claim of relativism, since the relativist perspective in which the doctrine of relativism is enunciated must be able to talk about the valuations of sentences according to different perspectives in order to articulate how the relativity operators work. If the original formulations of RL1 through RL5 resisted the charge of self-refutation, it seems they did so only by suppressing certain features of relativism whose consequences needed to be evaluated. It is the extensions of RL1 through RL5 including the $\text{FOR}_x()$ operator that should properly be proposed as candidate logics of relativism. Unfortunately, the complications introduced in the normal systems RL2, RL3, and RL4 seem to have been insufficient to resist the charge of self-refutation.

However, I have delayed discussing system RL5 and its exten-

---

[12] This does not demonstrate that it was futile to have formulated those systems. Even if they do not play a significant role in the evaluation of self-refutation with regard to relativism, they may have independent value, if someone is interested either in multiple kinds of relativity or in assessor contextualism. In any case, they clearly form part of the logic of relativism, which is the subject of this study.

sion including a FOR$_x$() operator. The problem with this system is that there are at least two possible ways to formulate the semantics of the FOR$_x$() operator in RL5+F. According to the first option, since RL5 is similar to RL1 insofar as it lacks multiple relativities and relativized accessibility relations, the semantics for the FOR$_x$() operator in RL5+F could be the same as in RL1+F. If the semantics are formulated in this way, there would still be a way in which a thoroughly relativistic perspective could appear within RL5+F. Since non-normal perspectives value the REL() operator arbitrarily, then let there be a non-normal perspective that always values REL(FOR$_x(\alpha)$) = 1 for every α. Then this non-normal perspective would be a thoroughly relativistic perspective that could refute the For-x objection.

This alternative might seem to be a fairly unartful dodge to escape the self-refutation charge, but I think there is a more serious objection to be made against it. While this alternative would appear to provide the logical model needed to counter the charge of self-refutation, there is an argumentative problem with this strategy. The five relative systems have been proposed as systems that a relativist might endorse as representing the logic of global relativism. As such, each system articulates the behavior of the relativity operators within perspectives, one of which is understood to be a relativistic perspective. The problem is that if the thoroughly relativistic perspective were identified with a non-normal perspective in which every sentence is arbitrarily taken to be relative, then the putatively relativistic perspective would seem to belie the very relativistic principles that it is articulating.[13] Non-normal perspectives are anarchistic in their treatment of the relativity operators, so if global relativism can only be articulated from within a non-normal perspective, then global relativism would seem not to be relativism at all but anarchy or even blatant irrationality, as some have thought. This would seem to be a straightforward kind of self-refutation, whereby the claim of relativism ultimately undermines itself. Consequently, the global relativist cannot properly claim that the thoroughly relativistic perspective is a non-normal one. It must be a normal perspective in which the behavior of the relativity operators is exactly as relativism says it should be.

---

[13] Indeed validity in a non-normal system, which I have not considered in the formulation of the proposed relative systems in the previous chapter, is typically defined in terms of normal perspectives.

8.3. SELF-REFUTATION AND THE RELATIVE SYSTEMS

According to the second option, though, the presence of non-normal perspectives in RL5+F demands different treatment with regard to the semantics of the $FOR_x()$ operator from the treatment according to RL1+F. This differential treatment should follow analogously to the treatment of the relativity operators. Let the semantics for the $FOR_x()$ operator in RL5+F be as follows:

- **RL5+F:** If $m \in N$, then $v_m(FOR_x(\alpha)) = 1$ iff

    (a) I maps x to some element m' in the relativizing domain,

    (b) m' is accessible to m according to R, and

    (c) $v_{m'}(\alpha) = 1$;

    and $= 0$ otherwise.

    If $m \notin N$, then $v_m(FOR_x(\alpha))$ is assigned arbitrarily.

If m is a normal perspective, then it adopts the semantics for the $FOR_x()$ operator as in RL1+F, but if it is a non-normal perspective, then it assigns values to the operator arbitrarily, as it does for the relativity operators. Under this alternative, the For-x objection fails in RL5+F, which can be proved as follows:

Theorem 10. *There is an RL5+F model in which $v_m(REL(\alpha)) = 1$ for every α for some normal perspective m.*

Let $< M, N, I, R, v >$ be an RL5+F model as follows:
$M = \{m_1, m_2\}$
$N = \{m_1\}$
$I = \{< a_1, m_1 >, < a_2, m_2 >, < a_3, \emptyset >, ...\}$
$R = \{< m_1, m_1 >, < m_1, m_2 >, < m_2, m_2 >\}$
Let $v_{m_1}(s_i)$ assign variables arbitrarily for every simple sentence s_i.
Let $v_{m_2}(s_i) = 1$ where $v_{m_1}(s_i) = 0$, and $v_{m_2}(s_i) = 0$ where $v_{m_1}(s_i) = 1$.

The normal perspective m_1 will value the $REL()$, $ABS()$, and $FOR_x()$ operators according to the semantics for normal perspectives in RL5+F, but the semantics for non-normal perspectives allow m_2 to value those operators arbitrarily. Let the valuation for m_2 be as follows:

Let $v_{m_2}(REL(\alpha)) = 1$ where $v_{m_1}(REL(\alpha)) = 0$, and $v_{m_2}(REL(\alpha)) = 0$ where $v_{m_1}(REL(\alpha)) = 1$.

260   CHAPTER 8. RELATIVISM AND SELF-REFUTATION

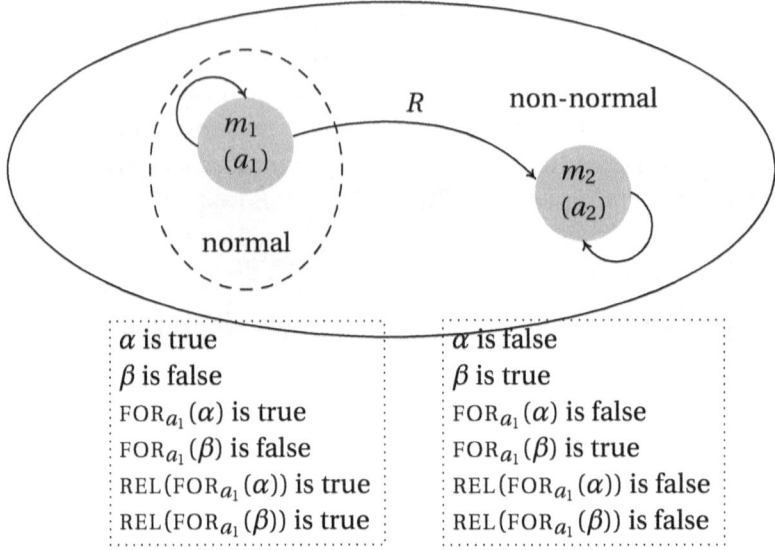

Figure 8.3: Model for Theorem 10

Let $v_{m_2}(\text{ABS}(\alpha)) = 1$ where $v_{m_1}(\text{ABS}(\alpha)) = 0$, and $v_{m_2}(\text{ABS}(\alpha)) = 0$ where $v_{m_1}(\text{ABS}(\alpha)) = 1$.

Let $v_{m_2}(\text{FOR}_x(\alpha)) = 1$ where $v_{m_1}(\text{FOR}_x(\alpha)) = 0$, and $v_{m_2}(\text{FOR}_x(\alpha)) = 0$ where $v_{m_1}(\text{FOR}_x(\alpha)) = 1$.[14]

Consequently, the valuation of every sentence is contradictory between the two perspectives, even for the relativity and $\text{FOR}_x()$ operators.

Then $v_{m_1}(\text{REL}(\alpha)) = 1$ for every α in the normal perspective m_1.

Proof. According to the definition of v for simple sentences s,

$v_{m_1}(s) \neq v_{m_2}(s)$.

According to the definition of v for the non-normal perspective m_2 with regard to the $\text{REL}()$, $\text{ABS}()$, and $\text{FOR}_x()$ operators,

$v_{m_1}(\text{REL}(\beta)) \neq v_{m_2}(\text{REL}(\beta))$
$v_{m_1}(\text{ABS}(\beta)) \neq v_{m_2}(\text{ABS}(\beta))$
$v_{m_1}(\text{FOR}_x(\beta)) \neq v_{m_2}(\text{FOR}_x(\beta))$
for every β.

So whether α is a simple sentence or an application of the

---

[14] Note that these valuation conditions for m_2 are well-defined, since the valuation of the $\text{REL}()$, $\text{ABS}()$, and $\text{FOR}_x()$ operators for m_1 are stipulated to occur according to the semantics for normal perspectives prior to the valuation of these operators for m_2.

8.3. SELF-REFUTATION AND THE RELATIVE SYSTEMS   261

REL(), ABS(), and FOR_x() operators, there are two perspectives, m_1 and m_2 accessible to m_1 where $v_{m_1}(\alpha) \neq v_{m_2}(\alpha)$, so $v_{m_1}(\text{REL}(\alpha)) = 1$ for every α.

□

Note that since the valuation of the non-normal perspective is always contradictory to the normal perspective, this model can overcome the For-x objection based not only on failure of the valuation condition, but also on the failure of the reference condition. If there is some x that does not name any perspective in the model, the normal perspective will value the corresponding FOR_x() operator false for every sentence, but the non-normal perspective will always value the FOR_x() operator true in accordance with the model, thereby allowing the normal perspective to value that FOR_x() operator to be relative, even on failure of reference.

This second alternative likewise might seem to be a dodge, an *ad hoc* maneuver that is completely unmotivated except as a way to escape the self-refutation charge. To the contrary, I would argue that this alternative is precisely what global relativism requires. For something to be relative, there must be a disagreement between perspectives. Under global relativism, this disagreement should extend also to the nature of relativism and to the behavior of the relativity operators. Given such a disagreement, some perspectives cannot be expected to assign values to the relativity operators according to the semantic rules dictated by relativism. Consequently, from a normal relativistic perspective, those deviant perspectives would seem to assign values to the relativity operators arbitrarily as non-normal perspectives, though there may be perfectly comprehensible rules for these valuations from within their own perspectives.[15] In this way, the use of a non-normal system would seem to be required by global relativism. Systems RL1 through RL4 might be suitable for more restricted forms of relativism, and therefore the formulations of these systems was not completely pointless, but RL5 seems conceptually more consonant with the radical nature of global relativism. If non-normal perspectives can be justified in their deviant valuations of the relativity operators in this way, then the same justification can extend to the valuation of the

---

[15] Perhaps Steven D. Hales, with his alternative account of the behavior of the relativity operators as duals, would count as inhabiting such a non-normal perspective, as well as Joseph Margolis with his anti-realist conception of relativism.

FOR$_x$() operator to counter the For-x objection. The deviance in the semantics of these operators within non-normal perspectives merely represents the disagreement that relativism requires as a claim of radical difference between perspectives applied reflexively to its own logic. The non-normal semantics simply provide a fairly elegant way to incorporate situations into a logical system where that logic does not apply.[16]

This point may be pushed further by exploring an additional line of objection. What about statements concerning whether relativism is self-refuting? If there is some relative system that allows global relativism not to be self-refuting, then it may seem that relativism is absolutely not self-refuting, and thereby self-refuting after all. However, since there are four other systems in which a claim of global relativism would be self-refuting, there seems to be some grounds for claiming that relativism is only relatively self-refuting, relative to the system in which it is modeled. Yet what about statements concerning whether relativism is self-refuting according to system RL5+F? It would seem that these statements cannot themselves be relative to a particular logical system.[17]

To address this latter objection, the question of expressibility must first be addressed. Just as the expressibility of the FOR$_x$() operator in the languages of the proposed relative systems affected the proper evaluation of the self-refutation charge against the claims of global relativism, so will the expressibility of whether a particular system is self-refuting or not. If sentences concerning self-refutation are evaluated merely as propositional parameters with no internal logical structure, the valuation of such sentences would be treated arbitrarily in the various relative systems without

---

[16] Similarly, with regard to non-normal logics of the modality of possibility, such logics might be understood to incorporate situations where possibly the behavior of possibility and necessity differs from the system being articulated, in other words, that the nature of possibility is possibly different.

[17] A comparable objection might be raised with regard to the contradictory nature of the two relativity operators. Should not sentences expressing that contradictory nature be absolute across all perspectives? The response is that they should not, because such sentences require the expression of biconditional and negation operators, but the semantics for such operators were allowed to vary across perspectives. The argument concerning non-normal perspectives that follows will apply likewise in this case. While I have adopted a particular normal perspective in outlining the semantics for the relativity operators in this study, non-normal perspectives cannot be expected to agree with my perspective.

8.3. SELF-REFUTATION AND THE RELATIVE SYSTEMS

correlating such sentences to the conditions under which a system is self-refuting. So the languages of the proposed relative systems must be extended to include terms, operators, and predicates sufficient to express whether a particular system is self-refuting or not, and the semantics of those systems must be specified. Suppose this to be done. In RL1 through RL4 as well as in the normal perspectives in RL5, the semantics for these new terms and operators can be assumed to be uniform across perspectives. However, for non-normal perspectives in RL5, those semantics would be expected to be different, for precisely the same reasons that the relativity operators and the $\text{FOR}_x()$ operator had different semantics, namely that global relativism posits a disagreement even on the behavior of these terms and operators, and this disagreement is represented within non-normal perspectives. Consequently, there may be non-normal perspectives within an RL5 model that consider RL5 to be self-refuting even though that system is not self-refuting with regard to thoroughly relativistic normal perspectives in that same model, thus justifying the claim that RL5 is only relatively non-self-refuting within an extension of RL5.

It might seem incoherent or at least bizarre that a perspective within a system would hold a position on that system contrary to that system's metatheory, but this supposed incoherence seems not to take the perspectival nature of these systems seriously. Within any of the proposed relative systems, there may be perspectives that are thoroughly absolutist. From the absolutist perspective, that perspective is not part of a relative system at all, but standing proudly and absolutely alone. Yet that perspective's judgment on itself does not preclude it from being included as a sub-theory within a relative system.[18] Likewise, a non-normal perspective holding RL5 to be self-refuting would not consider itself to be part of RL5 at all, but would consider itself to be standing proudly and deviantly separate from such self-refuting nonsense. Yet this deviant attitude, deviant from a normal, thoroughly relativistic RL5 perspective, does not preclude it from being included within an RL5 system. What would seem to be incoherent is a perspective that held RL5 to be self-refuting, while locating itself within an RL5 system, just as it would seem incoherent if a perspective claimed itself to be thoroughly relativistic in a system that

---

[18] For a comparable point, see (van Haaften, 1996).

could not support such a perspective, which is the effective nature of self-refutation with regard to these relative systems as I argued in section 8.2. Yet whatever semantics are outlined for the extension of the system for the terms and operators allowing the expressibility of self-refutation in the language, these semantics would fall under the same kinds of arguments I have outlined above showing that RL5 is not self-refuting even with the addition of the $\text{FOR}_x()$ operator. So if semantics for a language expressing self-refutation could be devised to extend these relative systems, the deviance of non-normal perspectives in an extension of RL5 should enable the construction of a model according to which a sentence claiming that this very system is not self-refuting could be valued by a normal perspective to be both true and relative.

8.4 Language, Pragmatics, and Incoherence

It may seem that the formal arguments presented above simply ignore the most interesting and most important self-refutation arguments against relativism, namely those based upon the nature of language, pragmatics, and incoherence. Indeed, the question of incoherence seemed to force itself to the surface at the end of the last section. Though I noted earlier that these supposedly more interesting and important self-refutation arguments do not lend themselves well to an analysis based on the proposed relative systems, in this section I will comment briefly on these kinds of arguments. My aim here is not to provide a complete response to these various specific arguments, which would require a much longer study to provide a fully adequate response, since these arguments in many cases rely on substantive doctrines that exceed the primarily formal approach taken in this study. Rather I will examine the general strategies of these arguments and attempt to determine how well the strategies could succeed, given the nature of relativism in general as outlined in this study, and where those strategies are found lacking, I will suggest how such strategies might be strengthened, if possible.

According to one variety of self-refutation argument summarized in section 8.2, relativism violates some key condition of the nature of language, typically relating to the nature of propositions

8.4. LANGUAGE, PRAGMATICS, AND INCOHERENCE 265

or to their truth conditions.[19] However, insofar as these arguments rely on substantive theories of the nature of language, relativism holds that these theories can be relativized, with the result that the claim of relativism would indeed appear to be self-refuting in perspectives that held certain theories of languages, but not necessarily in other perspectives with different linguistic theories. It would indeed be a problem if an explicitly relativistic perspective held a theory of language that did not support relativism, but it is not always clear what theory of language relativists hold.

A stronger and more decisive self-refutation argument on the basis of linguistic concerns would be that there could be no theory of language that can support relativism. Of course, such an argument would need to rely on auxiliary premises accepted by relativism in order to count as a self-refutation argument. Yet even if these premises were provided, it is not clear whether this kind of argument would ultimately succeed, considering that language itself includes certain apparently relative features like indexicality and other forms of context-sensitivity that need to be explained and that seem perfectly congenial to the doctrine of relativism. Whatever theories of language that are available now are still in the process of development and refinement, and it may be premature to speculate on which comprehensive theory of language will be justified at some projected ideal end of inquiry and whether that theory denies the possibility of relativism.[20]

Perhaps this pattern of argument could be strengthened by concentrating not on the nature of language in particular, but on communication in general. Rather than arguing that the nature of language precludes the truth of relativism, it might be argued that given the doctrine of relativism, no communication would be possible between different members of a relativizing domain, such as cultures. Rather than assuming a certain theory of communication, then showing that this theory does not support relativism, perhaps it would be better to show that relativism does not support any communication if it were true, which many relativists seem

---

[19] For example, see (Husserl, 1970, p. 140), (Mandelbaum, 1982, p. 49), (Newton-Smith, 1982, p. 107), and (Vallicella, 1984, p. 453).

[20] The situation may be worse given the evolving nature of language itself. Compare with Barry Stroud's comments on language with regard to transcendental arguments: "it won't be enough to deal simply with all of language *as it is now*" (Stroud, 1968, pp. 251–252).

to illustrate by means of their troubled attempts to communicate their positions. This kind of argument seems tempting with regard to semantic incommensurability as it appears in Kuhn and Feyerabend, whereby perspectives seem to be talking past each other,[21] but I have argued above in chapter 6 that the kind of incommensurability required by relativism in general is not specifically semantic but structural, relying on the possibility of transforming one theory into another, irrespective of the preservation of meaning. In any case, it is not clear that comprehensive theories of communication might not ultimately be congenial to relativism, as with theories of language. Further, even if this proposed argument succeeded, the conclusion would be merely that communication between cultures could not succeed, for example, not that relativism was false. Attempts to communicate between cultures might not succeed in transmitting intended information, but that would not show that the attempts to communicate were completely useless, as will be suggested below with regard to pragmatics.

Another variety of self-refutation argument claims that relativism undermines the foundations needed to establish itself as a doctrine, foundations that are not merely linguistic in nature. Many of these arguments are directed against specific forms of relativism. For example, Husserl argues that anthropologism as a form of relativism according to different species is undermined by the recognition that "the constitution of a species is a fact" (1970, p. 141) which cannot be used relativistically to establish the truth of relativism. James Jordan argues that according to Protagorean relativism, "There being *anything at all* to affirm or deny is held to depend on affirming or believing that there is, but this is plainly impossible, for such an affirmation or belief would require the very thing which it is supposed to conjure up" (1971, p. 24). Other such arguments claim that epistemic relativism challenges the very grounds on which its own truth is established, namely by challenging the nature of truth and justification.[22]

On this latter point, Harold Zellner responds that arguments in favor of relativism need not undermine themselves in this way, if

---

[21] Putnam offers such an argument in (Putnam, 1981, pp. 114–115), but see a response in (Sankey, 1991) that distinguishes between translatability and understanding.

[22] See for example (Marshall et al., 1981, p. 46), (Siegel, 1984, p. 366), and (Siegel, 1987, p. 4).

8.4. LANGUAGE, PRAGMATICS, AND INCOHERENCE 267

those arguments are considered to be *ad hominem* in nature (1995, p. 289).[23] Whereas it may seem that the relativist is adopting principles in the argument for relativism that relativism itself denies, those principles are temporarily adopted solely for the purposes of the argument to convince an opponent who does adopt those principles. Consequently, it seems that the relativist's argument for relativism on the basis of non-relativistic principles is itself a kind of *reductio ad absurdum* self-refutation argument against non-relativism, where the non-relativist's own principles are used against the non-relativist.[24]

Yet this response does not seem to help with regard to the criticisms of Husserl and Jordan, which seem to require the elements of the logic of relativism to be understood absolutely in order to establish the doctrine of relativism and its logic. Husserl argues in effect that the existence of the relativizing domain must be understood to be absolute in order for the logic of relativism to be formulated. Jordan argues in effect that the existence of sentences must be understood to be absolute in order for those sentences to be able to be evaluated according to the logic. These seem to be very strong objections indeed. The formulation of the logic of rela-

---

[23] While Zellner defends relativism against two charges of self-refutation, he levels a different charge that he acknowledges may not strictly qualify as self-defeat: "It is difficult to see how relativistic reasoning can justify *any* beliefs, given that there will always be opposing points of view from which a counter argument can be made, and that if relativism is true there will be no non-relativistic reasons for preferring the one point of view to the other" (Zellner, 1995, p. 294). However, as illustrated in the five proposed relative logics, relativistic reasoning in general is not used to justify any beliefs other than judgments concerning which statements hold relatively or absolutely. The justification of other beliefs does not depend upon specifically relativistic reasoning. Zellner makes the point that a relativist cannot rationally rely upon merely culture-bound methods for generating beliefs, since "it would seem that rational people *discount* purely culture-bound reasons for acquiring beliefs" (p. 294). A feminist epistemologist like Sandra Harding would certainly disagree with this latter statement, as noted in section 5.1. Additionally, in that chapter I argued that relativism can arise in cases where there are in fact shared standards for theory evaluation, which would seem to provide the kind of objectivity and rationality that Zellner finds lacking in relativism. While Zellner's point focuses on methods for forming predictions, insofar as those methods are adopted against the background of overall theories subject to standards of theory evaluation, the same point would hold with regard to prediction-forming methods.

[24] Michael Stack makes this point in general with regard to self-refutation arguments against positions that challenge traditional doctrines (Stack, 1983).

tivism requires certain elements that themselves cannot be relative without undermining the logic itself.

However, as I suggested in the previous section, the logic of relativism can be understood as the full expression of the relativist's own perspective that locates itself and its rivals within a single system. For such a logic to be established, it would seem to be required that the relativist's perspective accept that there is a certain relativizing domain according to which sentences are evaluated relatively. It is not required that every other perspective likewise acknowledge the existence of the relativizing domain and of sentences to be valued. As noted earlier, the logic of a different perspective within a relative system may appear very different from its own perspective. In perspectives in which every sentence was absolute, the relativity operators would be superfluous, thereby eliminating the need to establish a relativizing domain at all. Furthermore, in non-normal perspectives where the relativity operators behave differently, the theories associated with those perspectives might not accept the existence of sentences at all. The point about such non-normal perspectives is that however logic and reasoning may work within those perspectives, that logic and reasoning is radically different from normal perspectives. Yet from normal perspectives, those non-normal perspectives can still appear within the system of relative logic according to which the existence of sentences must be accepted. Consequently, while the features according to which relativism is presented must be accepted within a relativistic perspective, relativism acknowledges that other perspectives can deny those very features. Again, only if the relativistic perspective denied those features would relativism undermine itself.[25]

Of course, specific forms of relativism might make claims that do undermine themselves in the ways suggested here. However, those specific forms of relativism may be self-refuting not because of the formal relativistic features of the claims, which I have argued in the last section are not self-refuting, but because of certain substantive claims made in the application of relativism to a particular domain of discourse. The problem with such claims, then, would lie with the substantive claims and not with their general relativis-

---

[25] Thomas Bennigson makes comparable points (Bennigson, 1999, pp. 216–218).

tic form.

Another important variety of self-refutation argument claims that relativism seems to undermine itself, not according to the doctrines of relativism as such, but according to the pragmatics in asserting or defending relativism, which seem to embody or to entail something absolute. However, pragmatics is a notoriously slippery topic. Whereas it might be thought that the point of asserting or defending involves something absolute, such assertion or defense may be directed toward a different intention altogether.

Such self-refutation arguments often take the form of a dilemma, whereby neither the absolute assertion of relativism nor the relative assertion of relativism is a viable option for relativism. Clearly if relativism were asserted absolutely, then global relativism would seem thereby to fail. The problem with the relative assertion of relativism is typically claimed to be that if the assertion were merely relative, merely applicable to the relativist, then there would be no reason for a non-relativist to be concerned about it. If that were the case, then there would seem to be no reason for the relativist to assert relativism.[26] Even if merely asserting relativism were not self-defeating, the further argument is that when the relativist presents the thesis of relativism for debate and defends the thesis, this act refutes the doctrine of relativism, because the act of defending a thesis must depend upon factors that are not relative in order for the defense to succeed.[27]

Yet the pragmatic nature of these arguments would seem to make them conditional in nature, namely that if the aim of asserting or defending relativism were to convince an opponent, then the act is self-refuting. However, the pragmatics of the situation may be quite different than how they may appear to an opponent of relativism.[28] For example, Jack Meiland suggests that a relativist may not be attempting to persuade an opponent at all, but "may simply be presenting his position in a logically ordered manner" (Meiland, 1980, p. 125).[29] Likewise, a relativist may simply be test-

---

[26] For example, see (Passmore, 1961, pp. 67–68) and (Boghossian, 2006, p. 118).

[27] See (Siegel, 1968, pp. 230–231), (Burnyeat, 1976a, p. 59), (Tollefsen, 1987, pp. 211–213), (Lockie, 2003, p. 334), and (Morris, 2008, pp. 213–214).

[28] Henry Johnstone makes that point that one cannot know how a sentence is used "simply by inspecting the sentence" (Johnstone, 1964, p. 476). Likewise, it is not always clear how an act is to be understood merely by witnessing it.

[29] See also the editorial introduction to (Krausz & Meiland, 1982, p. 32) on this

ing his opponent to see whether he is likewise a relativist, or ultimately may merely be exhorting his opponent to be a relativist as well, or there may some other purpose for what an opponent would mistakenly understand to be a defense of a relativistic thesis.

However, the point of the objection is that if there is some other purpose than asserting and defending the thesis of relativism in such a way that the thesis applies to a non-relativist, then the non-relativist need not take the assertion or defense of relativism seriously. Indeed, Socrates himself considers the defense of Protagorean relativism to be absurd only assuming that Protagoras was being serious when he articulated the doctrine and was not simply just playing around (Plato, 1973, p. 32, 161e–162a).[30] So the issue is not whether there can be some other account of the pragmatics of a putative assertion or defense of the thesis of relativism, but whether there can be an account of the pragmatics that both avoids pragmatic self-refutation and is binding on opponents in some way.

Meiland in fact offers two alternatives that seem to meet this requirement. First, he suggests that the relativist and non-relativist may have some shared presuppositions, and that it is on the basis of these shared presuppositions that an argument for relativism can proceed (Meiland, 1980, p. 125). Other perspectives may not share those presuppositions, so relativity can be maintained, and self-refutation can be avoided. Further, the non-relativist would need to take the argument based on those presuppositions seriously, since those presuppositions are ones that he shares.

Second, Meiland suggests that even if there are no such shared presuppositions between the relativist and non-relativist, the relativist may be seeking to argue for relativism on the grounds of the non-relativist's own presuppositions, which the relativist does not happen to share (Meiland, 1980, p. 125). This is precisely the same kind of *ad hominem* argument that was presented earlier with regard to the question of whether relativism undermines the

---

point, likely written by Meiland.

[30] Of course neither Protagoras nor his friend Theodorus actually defend the doctrine of relativism in the *Theaetetus*. In fact, the only defense of relativism in that work comes from Socrates himself, which is why Socrates' ultimate argument against Protagoras is based on the thesis of objective equity, as explained above in section 3.2.

8.4. LANGUAGE, PRAGMATICS, AND INCOHERENCE 271

grounds for its own support. This pattern of argument on the part of the relativist is not pragmatically self-refuting, since the relativist only temporarily adopts the perspective of the opponent to show that this perspective likewise supports relativism. Again, since the presuppositions belong to the opponent, the opponent must take these arguments seriously.

There seems to be another alternative, besides the two that Meiland suggests, not based on the assumption that the opponent is in a different perspective than the relativist, but rather in the same perspective. Not all forms of relativism, even all forms of epistemic relativism, hold that beliefs are infallible. The formal requirements for relativity hold that a theory must be indexed to elements of the relativizing domain according to a non-arbitrary relation, namely that given some element in the relativizing domain, the theory that holds for that perspective is likewise given. However, there is nothing in this requirement or any other requirement for relativism outlined in this study that specifies that rational agents in a given perspective must know which theory is indexed to that perspective. Specific forms of relativism such as certain interpretations of Protagorean relativism might make such claims, but generic relativism does not. Accordingly, if a relativist asserts or defends relativism with regard to a given opponent, the relativist may understand that opponent to be part of the same relevant perspective as the relativist himself, and that relativism is true for the opponent, even if the opponent does not know it. Even if the relativizing domain consists of cultures wherein the culture to which the relativist belongs clearly rejects relativism by its own testimony and tradition, the relativist may be arguing that relativism is in fact true for the culture, and that the culture should hold a relativistic theory even though it in fact does not.[31]

Of course, the relativist may be mistaken with regard to what perspective the opponent occupies, but such mistakes seem to be part of a general pattern of fallibilism according to which one must argue on the grounds of some assumptions, which may be mistaken. The point here is that the assumptions in question contribute to a particular account of the pragmatics of an instance of assertion or defense of relativism, and that this account may avoid the charge of pragmatic self-refutation by including the op-

---

[31] A comparable point is made in (Zellner, 1995, p. 291).

ponent within the same perspective such that arguments for relativism have some force against the opponent, even though a relativist may recognize that those argument may not have the same force against opponents in different perspectives. If those assumptions happen to be mistaken, this mistake does not involve the relativist in any pragmatic self-refutation.

The key point I would therefore make here is that the question of pragmatic self-refutation in general cannot be decided in advance of the consideration of specific instances of an assertion or defense of relativism, in which the specific parties to the conversation are known and the intentions of those parties are made clear.

The problem of incoherence seems to have loomed in the background of all these discussions, since relativism is either itself taken to be a flatly incoherent doctrine, or to lead to incoherent consequences. Yet it is not clear what such incoherence is supposed to represent. A doctrine may be taken to be incoherent precisely because it is logically or pragmatically self-refuting, for example, but not all claims of incoherence with regard to relativism appeal specifically to self-refutation. Rather it seems to be conceptual incoherence with which relativism is charged, namely that relativism relies on a certain set of concepts that do not all fit together. While it is not perfectly clear what needs to be demonstrated in a claim of incoherence, I think there are two points of caution concerning the use of such arguments with regard to relativism, relating to conceptual schemes and perspectives.

Since conceptual incoherence depends upon a certain set of concepts and the way they are supposed to fit together, it is important to ensure that the pertinent set of concepts is correctly identified in a particular case, else the argument would appear to miss the point of the doctrine that is allegedly incoherent. This point is especially important with regard to forms of relativism that rely on differences in conceptual schemes, since if the incoherence argument rests upon a set of concepts that merely figure as one perspective in an instance of conceptual relativism, the argument would seem to fail if that set of concepts does not represent the perspective of the conceptual relativist.[32] A thoroughly relativistic

---

[32] For example, David Lyons argues that "The threat of incoherence arises for the relativist because he seems to endorse logically incompatible judgments as

8.4. LANGUAGE, PRAGMATICS, AND INCOHERENCE 273

position could accept that relativism would appear to be incoherent according to some perspectives, provided that those perspectives were not considered to be relativistic perspectives. Yet it is not entirely clear what set of concepts must figure into a specifically relativistic perspective. Besides the relativity terms and the proposed $\text{FOR}_x()$ operator, the logic of relativism requires the concepts of theories, relativizing domains, and accessibility relations, where those relations may themselves be relativized as in RL3 and RL4. Yet the question of the coherence of these concepts seems merely to reiterate the question of self-refutation addressed in the previous section, namely the question of whether there can be a thoroughly relativistic perspective within a given relative logic on the basis of those concepts.

Of course incoherence arguments are typically not raised against relativism in general, which has been the focus of this study, but against specific forms of relativism such as Protagorean or epistemological relativism, where the additional concepts of belief, knowledge and justification have been thought to be incoherent with specifically relativistic concepts. Yet the caution I would raise in this case is the same as just noted, namely that the proper set of concepts should be identified to ensure that the incoherence argument is really directed against relativism. If a given claim of relativism seems to use certain epistemic concepts, for example, and the use of those concepts leads to conceptual incoherence, then interpretive charity would suggest that perhaps those incoherent concepts are not really part of the claim. Perhaps different concepts are used, though the same names are used for those concepts as the incoherent ones. An incoherence argument would need to show that no set of epistemic concepts could be used to support epistemological relativism, and it is not immediately clear how any such argument could proceed or succeed.

A related caution that I have already noted concerns the perspectival nature of relativism. Since relativism can support differ-

---

simultaneously true" (Lyons, 1976, p. 113). If endorsement means that relativists themselves make those judgments, then it is not clear that Lyons is correctly representing the relativist position. The relativist certainly *acknowledges* the relativized truth of those judgments, but does not necessarily *endorse* them from the relativist's own perspective. Yet it may be that Lyons makes no distinction between these concepts, thus pointing to a conceptual difference between his perspective and a relativist perspective.

ent sets of concepts, it is important that the set of concepts identified in the incoherence argument specifically belong to a relativistic perspective, else the argument would seem to show only that relativism is incoherent according to some perspectives, not that relativism is absolutely incoherent or specifically incoherent from a relativistic perspective. The problem is then that if an incoherence argument is offered against relativism, how to show that the argument demonstrates the incoherence of relativism, not merely that the person offering the argument belongs to a non-relativistic perspective from which relativism naturally appears incoherent. In fact, the incoherence of relativism according to some perspectives might be seen partially to support the claim of relativism, since I have argued that relativism requires incommensurability between relativized sub-theories, and a successful argument of incoherence from one perspective would strongly suggest incommensurability between that perspective and a relativistic perspective, assuming that relativism is not likewise incoherent according to its own relativistic perspective. The question then is how to ensure that incoherence is demonstrated specifically with regard to the relativistic perspective?[33]

Perhaps it would be best not to focus on identifying the specific set of concepts employed by the relativist perspective at all, since such an argument would likely prompt the response that the wrong set of concepts have been identified. Rather, a stronger argument would be to show that no set of concepts could coherently support relativism, which would by default include any proposed conceptual scheme that a relativist might adopt. However, this kind of argument would be very hard to demonstrate, not only consider-

---

[33] For example, Donald Davidson argues that the very idea of a conceptual scheme is unintelligible and therefore presumably incoherent as well (Davidson, 1973). However, as noted earlier with regard to the relativism of Whorf in section 6.2, it is not clear that Davidson is properly and charitably interpreting the notion of a conceptual schemes with regard to his intended targets, so it is not clear that Davidson meets the two cautions that I have offered here, as illustrated both by his hasty equation of Whorf's notion of calibration to translatability, and by his dubious imputation of a dualism of scheme and content to Whorf. Davidson clearly brings a certain set of concepts to bear in his argument, notably his peculiar conception of philosophical charity. Does the use of this set of concepts really count against conceptual relativism, or does it merely show that Davidson himself occupies a particular perspective within an instance of conceptual relativism? I suspect the latter.

ing the difficulty in formulating such an argument, but also considering that the argument itself would need to rely on some set of concepts in order to be articulated, likewise prompting the relativistic response that such an argument only demonstrates that the person offering the argument is in a different perspective from the relativist, employing a different set of concepts.

For this reason, it would appear that a transcendental argument would be more effective, namely to show that the conditions for the possibility of relativism are incompatible with relativism itself and the concepts it espouses. However, this seems to be precisely what many of the self-refutation arguments in this chapter were supposed to be accomplishing, and I have argued that there are reasons to be suspicious about the success of such arguments. Nor is it clear what kind of argument could successfully demonstrate the incoherence of relativism that does not take the form of one of the self-refutation arguments discussed in this chapter. Some novel approach would need to be devised.

Finally, before I close this discussion of self-refutation, I want to consider the possibility that relativism might well and truly be shown to be self-refuting in some absolutely damaging way in the future. It seems to be assumed that if such self-refutation could be demonstrated, then relativism can simply be ignored as a pernicious doctrine that has unnecessarily consumed so much time and effort throughout the history of philosophy. I want to suggest in closing that this conclusion may be too hasty, and that even if relativism is indeed self-refuting, there may still be a point in presenting and defending the doctrine.

John Visvader has described what he calls uroboric philosophies, based on the image of a serpent swallowing its own tail (Visvader, 1978). Such philosophies involve the use of self-referential paradoxes often resulting in the erasure of their own doctrines, a pattern found not only in certain Asian philosophies, but also in the skeptical arguments of Sextus Empiricus and in Wittgenstein. The point that Visvader makes is that that these philosophies represent a kind of therapeutic device, and point to a transformation of the doctrine into something else, something that perhaps could not have been achieved directly, but only through the medium of the uroboric philosophy.

Therefore, if relativism turns out to be self-refuting in some way that I have not considered or a way that I have misunderstood in this study, there may still be some benefit from its articulation, some further philosophical position that can best be understood and appreciated only by traversing relativism as a prolegomena. For example, Joseph Margolis has argued that the truth about relativism lies in the flux of things. I have argued in section 3.5 that this conception of relativism should not be considered to be an instance of relativism according to the definition offered in this study. Yet it may be that if relativism as understood according to that definition turns out to be self-refuting, it may be instrumental to appreciating the flux of all things. Perhaps Heraclitus could apprehend the flux directly, but others of us may need to start first by relativizing all things, then progressing to the flux as relativism collapses under self-refutation.

However, these uroboric considerations would be required only if relativism could be shown to be self-refuting. A major result of this study is that there is a relative system according to which thoroughly relativistic perspectives can be supported, even with the addition of a $\text{FOR}_x()$ operator, and that relativism is therefore not logically self-refuting. While I have not argued that pragmatic and other similar self-refutation arguments absolutely fail, I have suggested that these arguments need to be strengthened in order to accomplish their stated purposes, and that they need to be strengthened precisely by taking relativism and its perspectival nature more seriously.

Chapter 9

Conclusion

This study has proposed a definition of relativism as radical indexed pluralism and has motivated that definition by a consideration of how relativism differs from other, structurally similar notions, such as conventionalism and contextualism. The proposed definition yielded three theses that any instance of relativism should demonstrate: the formal requirements for relativity, the thesis of objective equity, and the thesis of incommensurability. Each of these theses was explored in some detail to determine what these theses require to be shown.

On the basis of this understanding of relativism, five formal systems were proposed as potential candidates for the logic according to which global relativism might be articulated, containing such relativistic features as multiple kinds of relativity and relativized accessibility relations between perspectives. One of these systems, based on a non-normal modal logic, was shown to resist certain key objections to relativism according to which relativism was self-refuting. This non-normal relative system seemed to be precisely the kind of system required by a radical claim of global relativism. The result of this study is that the identification of one relative system that resists charges of self-refutation suggests that relativism is a coherent notion even in its global form.

The charge of self-refutation has dogged relativism from its early history, and it seems to be a very peculiar sort of charge. Not only does a charge of self-refutation aim to prove that relativism is false, but it also seems to humiliate relativists by demonstrating their stupidity at adopting a doctrine that undermines itself so decisively. How could relativists be so foolish? More importantly, perhaps, a self-refutation charge does not aim simply to show that relativism fails to obtain in the world, but that it could not possibly obtain in the world, since the doctrine itself is not coherent. Consequently, self-refutation seems to aim for a quick refutation on formal grounds according to the structure of relativism itself, rather than on the grounds of a detailed demonstration that the concrete claims of relativism are not in fact justified.

Despite the proliferation of self-refutation claims against it, relativism has not been relegated to the graveyard of philosophical doctrines. This study has challenged some of the key structural self-refutation arguments by demonstrating that there is at least one formal system that supports a model in which there is a thoroughly relativistic perspective. Yet I doubt that this study will have stifled the preference for self-refutation arguments against relativism. More likely, the arguments in this study will merely stimulate a fresh wave of attempts to bury relativism by the shortest route possible, namely by devising some clever self-refutation or incoherence argument.

However, I would suggest here that the strategy of self-refutation and incoherence arguments against relativism should be abandoned. Not only does it seem to me that such arguments have failed to dissipate the fascination with relativism that seems at least as strong as the fascination with self-refutation arguments against it, but it also seems to me that there is a better way to address the question of relativism. I suggest that any opponent of relativism should take relativism more seriously and should aim to show that particular claims of relativism are simply not justified. One strategy would be to look at the substantive claims made by a given relativistic position and to demonstrate that those substantive claims are not justified or are falsified by some factual consideration. If a claim of epistemological relativism relies on certain claims about the nature of knowledge or of justification, for example, this strategy would aim to show that knowledge or justification is not in fact the way that the epistemological relativist claims it to be. Fortunately, many opponents of relativism do in fact adopt this strategy, whether successfully or otherwise.

Yet more importantly for the formal nature of this study, and perhaps more interestingly, another strategy would be to show that a putative claim of relativism does not in fact qualify as relativism at all, but collapses to some other kind of doctrine. This strategy requires a detailed understanding of the nature of relativism, which this study has aimed to provide. Three specific theses were examined to determine what must be shown by a claim of relativism. If any one of these theses fails to be demonstrated by a given claim, then that claim would not qualify as relativism. This strategy would seek to show that a claim has wrongly classified its position as relativism, rather than seeking to demonstrate that the claim refutes itself. In this way, this strategy is more charitable than the strategy of devising self-refutation arguments by taking the putatively relativistic claims more seriously.

The formal requirements for relativity articulated the conditions under which the general formula "x is relative to y" would apply in any given case. Failure of the formal requirements for relativity could suggest that an instance of putative relativism was actually an instance of pluralism, conventionalism, or even possibly indexicality.

The thesis of objective equity is designed to support the relativistic treatment of an instance of irreconcilable disagreement, according to which all of the parties to the disagreement are in some way equally justified. This study has analyzed this thesis in terms of shared standards for theory appraisal, whereby either failure to share standards or equal evaluation under shared standards would constitute objective equity between rival positions. Failure of the thesis of objective equity could suggest that an instance of putative relativism was actually an instance of absolutism or possibly reductionism in certain cases.

The thesis of incommensurability is designed to show that the rival positions are radically opposed to each other, rather than merely representing contextual variants. This study has analyzed this thesis in terms of a transformation of rival theories into each other across shared dimensions. Failure of the thesis of incommensurability could suggest that an instance of putative relativism was actually an instance of relativity in general or contextualism.

In each case, the failure of one of these theses results in the collapse of a case of putative relativism into some other doctrine, and if that other doctrine is objectionable in some way, then a detailed study of that doctrine should reveal what is so objectionable about it. This study has suggested that the thesis of incommensurability is the most objectionable feature of relativism, distinguishing relativism from less objectionable forms of relativity in general, such as contextualism or the scientifically respectable special theory of relativity. It therefore seems to me that a focus on the possible commensurability between rival relativized theories would be the most interesting and most fruitful approach to evaluating specific claims of relativism. I have characterized commensurability earlier in this study as providing a path between rival theories, ultimately a transformational path across certain dimensions. An articulation of these dimensions and the way that they facilitate a transformation of one theory into another would serve not only to challenge a claim of relativism with regard to some topic, such as ethics, but it seems to me that it would also reveal deep features of that topic that other approaches may not easily uncover. The approach of taking relativism seriously with regard to these topics could thereby provide methodological advantages far beyond the mere refutation of relativism.

Of course, relativism may yet be true with regard to some topic, though this study has not endorsed any variety of relativism. While the argument in chapter 8 ultimately constituted a defense of relativism in general against the charge of self-refutation, this defense does not demonstrate the truth of relativism, but only the structural coherence of the notion of relativism. Whether relativism is true or false with regard to some topic can only be shown by careful consideration of the specific relativistic claims with regard to that topic. What this study has aimed to provide is a deeper understanding of the nature of relativism and its structural requirements. My hope is that it will contribute to more fruitful discussions of relativism and will help reduce the tedious confusions that surround this complex topic.

References

Annas, J., & Barnes, J. (1985). *The Modes of Scepticism*. Cambridge: Cambridge University Press.
Aristotle. (1984). *The Complete Works of Aristotle* (Vol. 2). Princeton: Princeton University Press.
Baghramian, M. (2004). *Relativism*. New York: Routledge.
Balaban, O. (1999). *Plato and Protagoras: Truth and Relativism in Ancient Greek Philosophy*. Lanham, MD: Lexington Books.
Barnes, J. (1979). *The Presocratic Philosophers* (Vol. 2). London: Routledge & Kegan Paul.
Beach, E. (1984). The Paradox of Cognitive Relativism Revisited: A Reply to Jack Meiland. *Metaphilosophy, 15*, 1–15.
Beatch, B. R. (1996). The Radical Nature of Margolis' Relativism. *Journal of Philosophical Research, 21*, 81–93.
Bedau, H. A. (1957). Review of *Language, Thought, and Reality: Selected Writings of Benjamin Lee Whorf*. *Philosophy of Science, 24*(3), 289–293.
Ben-Menahem, Y. (2006). *Conventionalism*. Cambridge: Cambridge University Press.
Bennigson, T. (1999). Is Relativism Really Self-Refuting? *Philosophical Studies, 94*, 211–236.
Bernstein, R. J. (1983). *Beyond Objectivism and Relativism: Science, Hermeneutics, and Praxis*. Philadelphia: University of Pennsylvania Press.
Bevir, M. (1994). Objectivity in History. *History and Theory, 33*(3), 328–344.
Blackburn, S. (2005). *Truth: A Guide for the Perplexed*. London: Allen Lane.
Blake, C. (1955). Can History Be Objective? *Mind, 64*(253), 61–78.
Boghossian, P. A. (2006). *Fear of Knowledge: Against Relativism and Constructivism*. Oxford: Oxford University Press.

Bonney, W. L. (1966). Operational Self-Refutation. *The Philosophical Quarterly, 16*(65), 348–351.

Brendel, E., & Jäger, C. (2004). Contextualist Approaches to Epistemology: Problems and Prospects. *Erkenntnis, 61*(2–3), 143–172.

Brent, J. (1998). *Charles Sanders Peirce: A Life.* Bloomington, Indiana: Indiana University Press.

Burnyeat, M. F. (1976a). Protagoras and Self-Refutation in Later Greek Philosophy. *The Philosophical Review, 85*(1), 44–69.

Burnyeat, M. F. (1976b). Protagoras and Self-Refutation in Plato's Theaetetus. *The Philosophical Review, 85*(2), 172–195.

Burnyeat, M. F. (1990). *The Theaetetus of Plato.* Indianapolis: Hackett Publishing Company.

Castagnoli, L. (2004). Protagoras Refuted: How Clever is Socrates' "Most Clever" Argument at Theaetetus 171a–c? *Topoi, 23,* 3–32.

Castagnoli, L. (2007). 'Everything is True', 'Everything is False': Self-refutation Arguments from Democritus to Augustine. *Antiquorum Philosophia, 1,* 11–74.

Causey, R. L. (1972). Attribute-Identities in Microreductions. *The Journal of Philosophy, 69*(14), 407–422.

Cooke, B. (2002). Critical Pluralism Unmasked. *British Journal of Aesthetics, 42*(3), 296–309.

Cunningham, F. (1973). *Objectivity in Social Science.* Toronto: University of Toronto Press.

Daston, L. (1992). Objectivity and the Escape from Perspective. *Social Studies of Science, 22*(4), 597–618.

Daston, L., & Galison, P. (1992). The Image of Objectivity. *Representations, 40,* 81–128.

Daston, L., & Galison, P. (2007). *Objectivity.* New York: Zone Books.

Davidson, D. (1973). On the Very Idea of a Conceptual Scheme. *Proceedings and Addresses of the American Philosophical Association, 47,* 5–20.

Davson-Galle, P. (1991). Self-Refuting Propositions and Relativism. *Metaphilosophy, 22*(1–2), 175–178.

Davson-Galle, P. (1998). *The Possibility of Relative Truth.* Brookfield, VT: Ashgate.

Devine, P. E. (1984). Relativism. *Monist, 67*(3), 405–418.

Egan, A., Hawthorne, J., & Weatherson, B. (2005). Epistemic Modals in Context. In G. Preyer & G. Peter (Eds.), *Contextu-*

alism in Philosophy: Knowledge, Meaning, and Truth (pp. 131–168). Oxford: Oxford University Press.

Einstein, A. (1954). *Relativity: The Special and the General Theory* (15th ed.). Strand: Methuen and Company, Ltd.

Euclid. (1956). *The Thirteen Books of Euclid's Elements* (T. L. Heath, Trans. 2nd ed. Vol. 3). New York: Dover Publications, Inc.

Feyerabend, P. (1981). *Realism, Rationalism and Scientific Method: Philosophical Papers, Volume 1*. Cambridge: Cambridge University Press.

Feyerabend, P. (1987). *Farewell to Reason*. London: Verso.

Feyerabend, P. (1993). *Against Method* (3rd ed.). London: Verso.

Field, H. (1982). Realism and Relativism. *The Journal of Philosophy, 79*(10), 553–567.

Fitch, F. B. (1946). Self-Reference in Philosophy. *Mind, 55*(217), 64–73.

Ford, A. (1994). Protagoras' Head: Interpreting Philosophic Fragments in Theaetetus. *The American Journal of Philology, 115*(2), 199–218.

Gadamer, H.-G. (1989). *Truth and Method* (J. Weinsheimer & D. G. Marshall, Trans. 2nd revised ed.). New York: Crossroad.

García-Carpintero, M., & Kölbel, M. (Eds.). (2008). *Relative Truth*. Oxford: Oxford University Press.

Goodman, N. (1972). The Way the World Is. In *Problems and Projects* (pp. 24–32). Indianapolis: The Bobbs-Merrill Company.

Goodman, N. (1978). *Ways of Worldmaking*. Indianapolis: Hackett Publishing Company.

Goodman, N. (1980). On Starmaking. *Synthese, 45*, 211–215.

Goodman, N. (1983). Realism, Relativism, and Reality. *New Literary History, 14*(2), 269–272.

Griffin, J. (1977). Are There Incommensurable Values? *Philosophy and Public Affairs, 7*(1), 39–59.

Griffin, J. (1997). Incommensurability: What's the Problem? In R. Chang (Ed.), *Incommensurability, Incomparability, and Practical Reason* (pp. 35–51). Cambridge, MA: Harvard University Press.

Haack, S. (1996). Reflections on Relativism: from Momentous Tautology to Seductive Contradiction. In J. E. Tomberlin (Ed.), *Philosophical Perspectives* (Vol. 10, pp. 297–315). Oxford: Blackwell.

Hales, S. D. (1997). A Consistent Relativism. *Mind, 106*(421), 33–52.

Hales, S. D. (2004). Intuition, Revelation, and Relativism. *International Journal of Philosophical Studies, 12*(3), 271–295.

Hales, S. D. (2006). *Relativism and the Foundations of Philosophy.* Cambridge, MA: The MIT Press.

Hales, S. D., & Welshon, R. (2000). *Nietzsche's Perspectivism.* Urbana: University of Illinois Press.

Harding, S. G. (1993). Rethinking Standpoint Epistemology: What Is Strong Objectivity? In L. Alcoff (Ed.), *Feminist Epistemologies.* New York: Routledge.

Harding, S. G. (1995). Strong Objectivity: A Response to the New Objectivity Question. *Synthese, 104*(3), 331–349.

Harman, G. (1975). Moral Relativism Defended. *The Philosophical Review, 84*(1), 3–22.

Harman, G., & Thomson, J. J. (1996). *Moral Relativism and Moral Objectivity.* Oxford: Blackwell.

Harré, R., & Krausz, M. (1996). *Varieties of Relativism.* Oxford: Blackwell.

Harrison, G. (1976). Relativism and Tolerance. *Ethics, 86*(2), 122–135.

Heck, R. G. (2006). MacFarlane on Relative Truth. *Philosophical Issues, 16*(1), 88–100.

Hesse, M. (1980). *Revolutions and Reconstructions in the Philosophy of Science.* Brighton: Harvester Press.

Husserl, E. (1970). *Logical Investigations* (J. N. Findlay, Trans., Vol. I). London: Routledge & Kegan Paul.

Johnstone, H. W., Jr. (1964). Self-Refutation and Validity. *Monist, 48,* 467-485.

Johnstone, H. W., Jr. (1989). Self-Application in Philosophical Argumentation. *Metaphilosophy, 20,* 247–261.

Jordan, J. N. (1971). Protagoras and Relativism: Criticisms Bad and Good. *Southwestern Journal of Philosophy, 2,* 7–29.

Kaplan, D. (1978). On the Logic of Demonstratives. *Journal of Philosophical Logic, 8,* 81–98.

Kemeny, J. G., & Oppenheim, P. (1956). On Reduction. *Philosophical Studies, 7,* 6–19.

Kölbel, M. (1999). Saving Relativism from Its Saviour. *Crítica: Revista Hispanoamericana de Filosofía, 31*(91), 91–103.

Kölbel, M. (2002). *Truth Without Objectivity.* London: Routledge.

Kölbel, M. (2003). Faultless Disagreement. *Proceedings of the*

Aristotelian Society, 104(1), 53–73.

Kölbel, M. (2004). Indexical Relativism versus Genuine Relativism. *International Journal of Philosophical Studies, 12*(3), 297–313.

Krausz, M. (1984). Relativism and Foundationalism: Some Distinctions and Strategies. *Monist, 67*(3), 395–404.

Krausz, M., & Meiland, J. W. (Eds.). (1982). *Relativism: Cognitive and Moral.* Notre Dame, IN: University of Notre Dame Press.

Kripke, S. A. (1965). Semantical Analysis of Modal Logic II. Non-Normal Modal Propositional Calculi. In J. W. Addison, L. Henkin & A. Tarski (Eds.), *The Theory of Models* (pp. 206–220). Amsterdam: North-Holland Publishing Company.

Kuhn, T. S. (1977). *The Essential Tension.* Chicago: The University of Chicago Press.

Kuhn, T. S. (1996). *The Structure of Scientific Revolutions* (3rd ed.). Chicago: The University of Chicago Press.

Kuhn, T. S. (2000). *The Road Since Structure.* Chicago: The University of Chicago Press.

Laudan, L., & Leplin, J. (1991). Empirical Equivalence and Underdetermination. *The Journal of Philosophy, 88*(9), 449–472.

Lee, E. N. (1973). "Hoist with His Own Petard": Ironic and Comic Elements in Plato's Critique of Protagoras (*Tht.* 161–171). In E. N. Lee, A. P. D. Mourelatos & R. Rorty (Eds.), *Exegesis and Argument: Studies in Greek Philosophy Presented to Gregory Vlastos* (pp. 225–261). Assen, The Netherlands: Van Gorcum & Comp. B.V.

Lee, M.-K. (2005). *Epistemology After Protagoras: Responses to Relativism in Plato, Aristotle, and Democritus.* Oxford: Oxford University Press.

Levy, N. (2002). *Moral Relativism: A Short Introduction.* Oxford: Oneworld Publications.

Lewis, D. K. (2002). *Convention: A Philosophical Study* (Reissue ed.). Oxford: Blackwell Publishing.

Lockie, R. (2003). Relativism and Reflexivity. *International Journal of Philosophical Studies, 11*(3), 319–339.

Lokhorst, G.-J. C. (1998). The Logic of Logical Relativism. *Logique et Analyse, 41*(161-162-163), 57–65.

Ludlow, P. (2005). Contextualism and the New Linguistic Turn in Epistemology. In G. Preyer & G. Peter (Eds.), *Contextualism in Philosophy: Knowledge, Meaning, and Truth* (pp. 11–50). Oxford: Oxford University Press.

Lynch, M. (1998). *Truth in Context: An Essay on Pluralism and Objectivity*. Cambridge, MA: The MIT Press.

Lyons, D. (1976). Ethical Relativism and the Problem of Incoherence. *Ethics, 86*(2), 107–121.

Lyotard, J.-F. (1984). *The Postmodern Condition: A Report on Knowledge* (G. Bennington & B. Massumi, Trans.). Manchester: Manchester University Press.

Lyotard, J.-F. (1988). *The Differend: Phrases in Dispute* (G. V. D. Abbeele, Trans.). Minneapolis: University of Minnesota Press.

MacFarlane, J. (2003). Future Contingents and Relative Truth. *Philosophical Quarterly, 53*(212), 321–336.

MacFarlane, J. (2005). Making Sense of Relative Truth. *Proceedings of the Aristotelian Society, 105*, 321–339.

MacFarlane, J. (2009). Nonindexical Contextualism. *Synthese, 166*(2), 231–250.

MacIntyre, A. (1985). Relativism, Power and Philosophy. *Proceedings and Addresses of the American Philosophical Association, 59*(1), 5–22.

Mackie, J. L. (1964). Self-Refutation—A Formal Analysis. *The Philosophical Quarterly, 14*(56), 193–203.

Mandelbaum, M. (1982). Subjective, Objective, and Conceptual Relativisms. In J. W. Meiland & M. Krausz (Eds.), *Relativism: Cognitive and Moral* (pp. 34–61). Notre Dame: University of Notre Dame Press.

Margolis, J. (1976). Robust Relativism. *The Journal of Aesthetics and Art Criticism, 35*(1), 37–46.

Margolis, J. (1982). The Reasonableness of Relativism. *Philosophy and Phenomenological Research, 43*(1), 91–97.

Margolis, J. (1983). The Nature and Strategies of Relativism. *Mind, 92*(368), 548–567.

Margolis, J. (1984). Historicism, Universalism, and the Threat of Relativism. *Monist, 67*(3), 308–326.

Margolis, J. (1991). *The Truth About Relativism*. Oxford: Blackwell.

Margolis, J. (1995). Plain Talk about Interpretation on a Relativistic Model. *The Journal of Aesthetics and Art Criticism, 53*(1), 1–7.

Margolis, J. (1996). Relativism vs. Pluralism and Objectivism. *Journal of Philosophical Research, 21*, 95–106.

Margolis, J. (2006). Pluralism, Relativism, and Historicism. In J. R. Shook & J. Margolis (Eds.), *A Companion to Pragmatism*. Malden MA: Blackwell Publishing.

Marshall, J., Peters, M., & Shepheard, M. (1981). Self Refutation Arguments Against Young's Epistemology. *Educational Philosophy and Theory, 13*(2), 43–50.

Meiland, J. W. (1974). Kuhn, Scheffler, and Objectivity in Science. *Philosophy of Science, 41*(2), 179–187.

Meiland, J. W. (1979). Is Protagorean Relativism Self-Refuting? *Grazer Philosophische Studien, 9*, 51–68.

Meiland, J. W. (1980). On The Paradox Of Cognitive Relativism. *Metaphilosophy, 11*, 115–126.

Morris, J. (2008). Pragmatic Reflexivity in Self-defeating and Self-justifying Expressions. *Argumentation, 22*(2), 205–216.

Mosteller, T. (2006). *Relativism in Contemporary American Philosophy*. London: Continuum.

Mosteller, T. (2008). *Relativism: A Guide for the Perplexed*. London: Continuum.

Nagel, E. (1961). *The Structure of Science*. London: Routledge & Kegan Paul.

Nagel, T. (1986). *The View From Nowhere*. Oxford: Oxford University Press.

Nagel, T. (1997). *The Last Word*. Oxford: Oxford University Press.

Newton-Smith, W. (1982). Relativism and the Possibility of Interpretation. In M. Hollis & S. Lukes (Eds.), *Rationality and Relativism*. Cambridge, MA: The MIT Press.

Nietzsche, F. (1994). *On the Genealogy of Morality* (C. Diethe, Trans.). Cambridge: Cambridge University Press.

Norris, C. (1997). *Against Relativism: Philosophy of Science, Deconstruction, and Critical Theory* Oxford: Blackwell.

Novick, P. (1988). *That Noble Dream: The "Objectivity Question" and the American Historical Profession*. Cambridge: Cambridge University Press.

Nozick, R. (2001). *Invariances: The Structure of the Objective World*. Cambridge, MA: Harvard University Press.

Okrent, M. B. (1984). Relativism, Context, and Truth. *Monist, 67*, 341–358.

Oppenheim, P., & Putnam, H. (1956). Unity of Science as a Working Hypothesis. In H. Feigl, M. Scriven & G. Maxwell (Eds.), *Minnesota Studies in the Philosophy of Science* (Vol. II). Minneapolis: University of Minnesota Press.

Page, C. (1992). On Being False by Self-Refutation. *Metaphilosophy, 23*(4), 410–426.

Passmore, J. A. (1958). The Objectivity of History. *Philosophy, 33*(125), 97–111.

Passmore, J. A. (1961). *Philosophical Reasoning*. London: Duckworth.

Perry, J. (1979). The Problem of the Essential Indexical. *Noûs, 13*(1), 3–21.

Phillips, P. J. J. (2007). *Challenge of Relativism: Its Nature and Limits*. London: Continuum.

Pinto, R. C. (1995). Inconsistency, Rationality and Relativism. *Informal Logic, 17*(2), 279–288.

Plato. (1973). *Theaetetus* (J. McDowell, Trans.). Oxford: Oxford University Press.

Popkin, R. H. (2003). *The History of Scepticism: From Savonarola to Bayle*. Oxford: Oxford University Press.

Preston, J. (1992). On Some Objections to Relativism. *Ratio, 5*(1), 57–73.

Preyer, G., & Peter, G. (Eds.). (2005). *Contextualism in Philosophy: Knowledge, Meaning, and Truth*. Oxford: Oxford University Press.

Priest, G. (2006a). *Doubt Truth to Be a Liar*. Oxford: Oxford University Press.

Priest, G. (2006b). *In Contradiction* (2nd ed.). Oxford: Oxford University Press.

Priest, G. (2008). *Introduction to Non-Classical Logic: From If to Is* (2nd ed.). Cambridge: Cambridge University Press.

Putnam, H. (1981). *Reason, Truth and History*. Cambridge: Cambridge University Press.

Quine, W. V. O. (1964). Ontological Reduction and the World of Numbers. *The Journal of Philosophy, 61*(7), 209–216.

Quine, W. V. O. (1969). Ontological Relativity. In *Ontological Relativity and Other Essays* (pp. 26–68). New York: Columbia University Press.

Quine, W. V. O. (1975). On Empirically Equivalent Systems of the World. *Erkenntnis, 9*(3), 313–328.

Quine, W. V. O. (1984). Relativism and Absolutism. *Monist, 67*(3), 293–296.

Quine, W. V. O. (1986). *Philosophy of Logic* (2nd ed.). Cambridge, MA: Harvard University Press.

Quine, W. V. O. (1992). *Pursuit of Truth* (Revised ed.). Cambridge, MA: Harvard University Press.

Quine, W. V. O., & Ullian, J. S. (1978). *The Web of Belief*. New York: McGraw-Hill.

Raz, J. (1986). Value Incommensurability. *Proceedings of the Aristotelian Society, 86*, 117–134.

Reale, G. (1997). *Toward a New Interpretation of Plato* (J. R. Catan & R. Davies, Trans.). Washington, DC: Catholic University of America Press.

Rescher, N. (1993). *Pluralism: Against the Demand for Consensus*. Oxford: Oxford University Press.

Rescher, N. (1997). *Objectivity: The Obligations of Impersonal Reason*. Notre Dame: University of Notre Dame Press.

Ressler, M. (2012). Thoroughly Relativistic Perspectives. *Notre Dame Journal of Formal Logic, 53*(1), 89–112.

Robischon, T. (1958). What is Objective Relativism? *The Journal of Philosophy, 55*(26), 1117–1132.

Rorty, R. (1980). *Philosophy and the Mirror of Nature*. Princeton: Princeton University Press.

Rorty, R. (1982). *Consequences of Pragmatism*. Minneapolis: University of Minnesota Press.

Rorty, R. (1989). Solidarity or Objectivity? In M. Krausz (Ed.), *Relativism: Interpretation and Confrontation* (pp. 35–50). Notre Dame: University of Notre Dame Press.

Sankey, H. (1991). Incommensurability, Translation and Understanding. *The Philosophical Quarterly, 41*(165), 414–426.

Sapir, E. (1963a). The Grammarian and His Language. In D. G. Mandelbaum (Ed.), *Selected Writings of Edward Sapir in Language Culture and Personality* (pp. 150–159). Berkeley, CA: University of California Press.

Sapir, E. (1963b). The Status of Linguistics as a Science. In D. G. Mandelbaum (Ed.), *Selected Writings of Edward Sapir in Language Culture and Personality* (pp. 160–166). Berkeley: University of California Press.

Schaffer, J. (2005). What Shifts? Thresholds, Standards, or Alternatives? In G. Preyer & G. Peter (Eds.), *Contextualism in Philosophy: Knowledge, Meaning, and Truth* (pp. 115–130). Oxford: Oxford University Press.

Shapere, D. (1982). The Concept of Observation in Science and Philosophy. *Philosophy of Science, 49*(4), 485–525.

Shapere, D. (1984). *Reason and the Search for Knowledge*. Dordrecht: D. Reidel Publishing Company.

Shogenji, T. (1997). The Consistency of Global Relativism. *Mind, 106*(424), 745–747.

Siegel, H. (1968). Relativism, Truth, and Incoherence. *Synthese, 68*(2), 225–259.

Siegel, H. (1982). Relativism Refuted. *Educational Philosophy and Theory, 14*(2), 47–50.

Siegel, H. (1984). Goodmanian Relativism. *Monist, 67*(3), 359–375.

Siegel, H. (1987). *Relativism Refuted: A Critique of Contemporary Epistemological Relativism*. Dordrecht: Reidel.

Stack, M. (1983). Self-Refuting Arguments. *Metaphilosophy, 14*(3-4), 327–335.

Stanley, J. (2005). *Knowledge and Practical Interests*. Oxford: Oxford University Press.

Stevenson, C. L. (1962). Relativism and Non-Relativism in the Theory of Value. *Proceedings and Addresses of the American Philosophical Association, 35*, 25–44.

Stroud, B. (1968). Transcendental Arguments. *The Journal of Philosophy, 65*(9), 241–256.

Tollefsen, O. (1987). The Equivocation Defense of Cognitive Relativism. In S. J. Bartlett & P. Suber (Eds.), *Self-Reference: Reflections on Reflexivity* (pp. 209–217). Dordrecht: Martinus Nijhoff Publishers.

Trigg, R. (1973). *Reason and Commitment*. Cambridge: Cambridge University Press.

Unger, P. (1984). *Philosophical Relativity*. Oxford: Basil Blackwell.

Vallicella, W. F. (1984). Relativism, Truth and the Symmetry Thesis. *Monist, 67*(3), 452–466.

van Haaften, W. (1996). Relativism and Absolutism: How Can Both Be Right? *Metaphilosophy, 27*(3), 324–326.

Visvader, J. (1978). The Use of Paradox in Uroboric Philosophies. *Philosophy East and West, 28*(4), 455–467.

Vlastos, G. (1956). Introduction. In G. Vlastos (Ed.), *Plato's Protagoras*. New York: Liberal Arts Press.

Waterlow, S. (1977). Protagoras and Inconsistency. *Archiv für Geschichte der Philosophie, 57*(1), 19–36.

Weckert, J. (1984). Is Relativism Self-Refuting? *Educational Philosophy and Theory, 16*, 29–42.

White, F. C. (1982). Knowledge and Relativism I. *Educational Philosophy and Theory, 14*(1), 1–13.

White, F. C. (1989). Self-Refuting Propositions and Relativism.

Metaphilosophy, 20, 84–92.

Whorf, B. L. (1956). *Language, Thought and Reality.* Cambridge, MA: Technology Press of Massachusetts Institute of Technology.

Williams, B. (1981). The Truth in Relativism. In *Relativism: Cognitive and Moral* (pp. 175–188). Notre Dame: University of Notre Dame Press.

Williamson, T. (2005). Knowledge, Context, and the Agent's Point of View. In G. Preyer & G. Peter (Eds.), *Contextualism in Philosophy: Knowledge, Meaning, and Truth* (pp. 91–114). Oxford: Oxford University Press.

Wong, D. B. (1989). Three Kinds of Incommensurability. In M. Krausz (Ed.), *Relativism: Interpretation and Confrontation* (pp. 140–158). Notre Dame: University of Notre Dame Press.

Woodger, J. H. (1952). *Biology and Language.* Cambridge: Cambridge University Press.

Wright, C. (1986). *Realism, Meaning, and Truth.* Oxford: Blackwell.

Wright, C. (2008). Relativism about Truth Itself: Haphazard Thoughts about the Very Idea. In M. García-Carpintero & M. Kölbel (Eds.), *Relative Truth* (pp. 157–185). Oxford: Oxford University Press.

Zellner, H. (1995). Is Relativism Self-Defeating? *Journal of Philosophical Research, 20,* 287–295.

Zilioli, U. (2007). *Protagoras and the Challenge of Relativism: Plato's Subtlest Enemy.* Burlington, VT: Ashgate.